Polycentric Governance and the Good Society

POLYCENTRICITY: STUDIES IN INSTITUTIONAL DIVERSITY AND VOLUNTARY GOVERNANCE

Series Editors: Lenore T. Ealy and Paul Dragos Aligica

This interdisciplinary series explores the varieties of social institutions, processes, and patterns of governance that emerge through individuals' coordination, cooperation, and competition in governance systems based on freedom of choice, freedom of exchange, and freedom of association. Under conditions of relative freedom of association, human diversity leads to institutional diversity and polycentric structures. In contrast to monocentric, unitary, and hierarchical command and control systems, polycentric social systems comprise many decision centers interacting freely under an overarching set of common rules. First introduced by Michael Polanyi as a descriptive and normative feature of free societies and further elaborated by Nobel Prize in Economics recipient Elinor Ostrom and public choice political economy co-founder Vincent Ostrom, the notion of polycentricity has proven to offer a powerful analytical framework for expanding our understanding of the operation of governance regimes, constitutional federalism, law, public administration, private ordering, civics and citizenship, subsidiarity, nonprofit organization, cultural pluralism, civil society, and entrepreneurship. Studies in this series will refine the conceptual framework of polycentricity and its governance theory implications, while expanding their application in the study of what Alexis de Tocqueville called the art and science of association. These studies should be of interest to scholars, policymakers, executives, social entrepreneurs, and citizens working to devise ways of living together harmoniously in civil societies.

Polycentric Governance and the Good Society: A Normative and Philosophical Investigation edited by David Thunder and Pablo Paniagua

Social Movements and Liberal Political Economy by Mikayla Novak

The Uses of Diversity: Essays in Polycentricity by David Ellerman

Cryptodemocracy: Blockchain Technology and Democratic Governance by Darcy W.E. Allen, Chris Berg, and Aaron Matthew Lane

Polycentric Governance and the Good Society

A Normative and Philosophical Investigation

Edited by David Thunder
and Pablo Paniagua

LEXINGTON BOOKS
Lanham • Boulder • New York • London

Published by Lexington Books
An imprint of The Rowman & Littlefield Publishing Group, Inc.
4501 Forbes Boulevard, Suite 200, Lanham, Maryland 20706
www.rowman.com

86-90 Paul Street, London EC2A 4NE

British Library Cataloguing in Publication Information Available

Library of Congress Cataloging-in-Publication Data Available

ISBN 978-1-66695-168-4 (cloth)
ISBN 978-1-66695-169-1 (electronic)

Contents

Introduction: The Timeliness of Polycentric Theories of Governance 1
Pablo Paniagua and David Thunder

PART I: THE ETHICS OF POLYCENTRIC GOVERNANCE 17

Chapter 1: An Ethical Case for Bottom-Up, Polycentric Governance in a Complex Society 19
David Thunder

Chapter 2: Is an Architectonic Pluralism Possible? 41
Mark Hoipkemier

Chapter 3: Polycentric Justice 63
John Thrasher

PART II: THE FEASIBILITY OF POLYCENTRIC ORDERS 85

Chapter 4: The Problem of Complexity and the Emergence of Polycentric Political Order 87
Dries Daems and Alexander Schaefer

Chapter 5: Whither Stability? Polycentric Democracy and Social Order 115
Pablo Paniagua and Kaveh Pourvand

Chapter 6: Self-Governance Solutions to Social Dilemmas: A Polycentric Approach 137
Vlad Tarko

PART III: PRINCIPLES OF POLYCENTRIC LAW AND STATECRAFT 163

Chapter 7: Panarchy: Non-Territorial Polycentricity 165
Aviezer Tucker

Chapter 8: Polycentricism, the Rule of Law, and the Intelligibility of Human Rights Law 187
Pilar Zambrano

Chapter 9: The Constitution of Liberties: Polycentric Constitutionalism and the Westminster Export Model 201
W. Elliot Bulmer

Index 223

About the Contributors 235

Introduction

The Timeliness of Polycentric Theories of Governance[1]

Pablo Paniagua and David Thunder

Many theorists who investigate how society ought to be governed assume that a highly centralized or monocentric State administration is the most appropriate mechanism for governing social life, and then go on to investigate how such a centralized State should be structured and which principles should animate its governing organs. For example, local governments are treated as mere emanations of "the State" rather than independent political units, or principles of justice are devised for a "State" without taking into consideration the authority and diverging priorities of sub-state governments. In this book, we wish to critically interrogate the assumption that the governance of social life should be conducted in a highly centralized manner. Our critical examination will be conducted at the intersection of politics, philosophy, law, and economics.

Specifically, the goal of this book is twofold: first, to critically examine the role of the monocentric state in either supporting or undermining the health and stability of the social order; and second, to explore the philosophical foundations of alternative polycentric arrangements of governmental power and authority, and how they can help promote a good society. In this collected volume, our authors employ a variety of different philosophical and methodological perspectives as they elaborate approaches to governance and political order that grapple seriously with the complex and multifaceted nature of social life. This is the first serious attempt in the literature to explore in depth what it means, not only from an economic and organizational standpoint but also from a broader ethical, sociological, and anthropological perspective, to live in a polycentric political system and how polycentric orders might contribute to human and societal flourishing.

THE SCOPE OF THE BOOK

Since the age of monarchical absolutism, when King James (1566–1625) described himself as "God's lieutenant on earth," political theorists and actors have expended a great deal of energy spelling out the need for a central government to establish a fully integrated public order and oversee social, political, and economic life across a national territory. While these centralizing tendencies have not gone unchallenged, polycentric and dispersed forms of governance remain underrated and understudied by mainstream political theorists, philosophers, and PPE (Philosophy, Politics, and Economics) scholars alike.

This collection of essays aims to place the idea of polycentric governance under the analytic microscope, not merely as an explanatory tool for making sense of particular social practices, nor simply as a potential strategy for solving local coordination problems, such as the provision of policing and water, but as a normative ideal for social life conceived more broadly. When we speak of polycentric governance, we have in mind a plurality of units of governance enjoying substantial mutual autonomy yet sharing some common interests, submitting to shared rules and decision procedures, and responding adaptively to each other's decisions. The diverse units of a polycentric governance arrangement may be guided by a similar logic or rationale, e.g., the logic of market exchange or utility maximization; or alternatively, they may be guided by heterogeneous logics or rationales, e.g., the logic of economic production, religious fidelity, public administration, or artistic creativity.

In this book, we are not interested exclusively in offering a morally detached description of a set of social phenomena and their operations; rather, we wish to examine the advantages of polycentricity as a method or philosophy of governance, when compared to more monocentric approaches. Polycentric approaches to governance may be distinguished from their more monocentric or centralizing counterparts inasmuch as they maintain that effective or successful social governance requires (i) a plurality of organs of governance, (ii) enjoying substantial levels of mutual autonomy, (iii) capable of interacting with each other and submitting to shared rules and decision procedures, in productive and functional ways, (iv) without being controlled by a uniquely sovereign or supreme super-coordinator.[2] A centralizing approach could accept (i) and (iii)—a plurality of governmental organs capable of interacting with each other productively under shared rules and decision procedures—but would reject (iv), instead viewing the subordination of the prerogatives of local governments to a sovereign super-coordinator as inevitable or essential for public order.

Of course, we are not the first to discuss the theory and practice of polycentric governance and coordination. Governmental and institutional polycentricity have been ably investigated by political economists like Vincent and Elinor Ostrom, political and economic historians like James Scott, theorists of federalism such as Daniel Elazar, and political theorists such as Chandran Kukathas and Gerald Gaus. The latter, in particular, has led the way in investigating how a stable political order could emerge from a plural and diverse society. Without wishing to detract from the value of these contributions, we contend that the practice of polycentric governance and its ethical and institutional foundations remain under-theorized. For example, a variety of political economists have discussed the efficiency gains of polycentric governance and the inefficiency of hyper-centralization, but we see few explicit and systematic defenses of polycentricity that are anchored in a general discussion of human and societal flourishing, broadly construed.

What makes this volume distinctive is that it seeks to explore the implications of a polycentrically governed social order not only for economic cooperation and efficiency, but also for fundamental human aspirations, such as friendship, community life, political stability, and rational self-government. We have yet to see the emergence of a compelling institutional and normative theory of polycentric governance as an effective framework for a flourishing, welfare-enhancing society—or if such a theory does exist, it has not garnered the attention it deserves. Our goal in this edited volume is to lay some of the philosophical and institutional-theoretical groundwork for such a theory.

Perhaps more than any well-defined doctrine about social life, what unites the authors of this volume is a suspicion of overly systematizing and homogenizing conceptions of social and economic order, and a rejection of the notion that society could be sculpted into a perfectly integrated whole, such as a tightly harmonized constitutional system. Scholars friendly to polycentricity and decentralization are disinclined to read systematicity, homogeneity, and full harmonization into situations that are, on their face, riddled with heterogeneity and complexity, such as the teeming life of a city or the political life of a nation. In other words, polycentrists—two notable examples being Elinor Ostrom and James Scott—are philosophically and methodologically disposed to resist the temptation to purchase explanatory elegance at the cost of social reality. A flattened, two-dimensional social order may be easier to decipher. However, it is a fictitious projection that artificially flattens out the structural, ideological, cultural, and institutional heterogeneity of modern societies and consequently underestimates the challenges of effective governance.

We are optimistic that a serious examination of the benefits of polycentric governance for human society will show that polycentricity is not just a valuable tool of public administration, but an indispensable conceptual framework and normative guide for a human society capable of servicing its members' needs and responding to their reasonable hopes and expectations as human persons. Hence, this book could be read as an attempt to lay out, in a rough and preliminary fashion, the foundational principles of a normative and philosophical theory of polycentric law and politics, with the potential to reinvigorate scholarly debates about governance and civil order in complex and diverse societies.

POLYCENTRIC THINKING IN PHILOSOPHY AND THE SOCIAL SCIENCES

The pushback against overly homogenizing and centralizing approaches to governance and social order is already well underway. One of the most influential schools of polycentric thinking is what has become known as the Bloomington School of Political Economy, spearheaded by studies of polycentric governance led by Elinor and Vincent Ostrom, starting in the 1960s (e.g., V. Ostrom, Tiebout, and Warren 1961). One representative example of their blending of theoretical and empirical investigation is their study of the comparative merits of decentralized versus centralized policing systems (E. Ostrom, Parks, and Whitaker 1973).

Since then, much of the work on polycentric systems of social coordination has followed in the Ostroms' footsteps, investigating methods through which the provision of public goods and services and the solution of a variety of problems of social and economic coordination may be achieved by multiple organs of governance with substantial levels of mutual autonomy, cooperating on a more or less voluntary basis (e.g., Schneider 1989, McGinnis 1999, Pennington 2008, Paniagua 2022, Paniagua 2020, Aligica and Tarko 2013, Aligica 2014). These sorts of studies seek to interrogate the practical benefits of polycentric governance for the production and provision of public goods, such as security, public health, roads, and water infrastructure, and to disprove widely held assumptions concerning the preferability of monocentric models of public administration.

We have also seen important discussions of polycentric governance in studies of federal and confederal political systems (Buchanan 1996, Elazar 1987, Kriesi and Trechsel 2008, V. Ostrom 1991) and governance beyond the State (Stringham 2015, Ellickson 2009, Auerbach 1984, Risse 2013, Scott 2014), not to mention a wave of literature in recent decades on political and legal pluralism (Delmas-Marty 2009, Griffiths 1986, Teubner 2012b, Cerny 2010, Hirst 2013, Tully 1995, Muñiz-Fraticelli 2014, Levy 2015), which shows the futility of attempts by modern thinkers to integrate social order under a single, uniform system of law or governance. Nevertheless, one comes away from this impressive bank of research wondering why polycentricity, especially in a world in which the old, centralized models are losing their grip on social reality, is not on the tip of the tongue of every serious political scientist, lawyer, political philosopher, and social theorist.

How might we explain the relatively low visibility of polycentric governance in contemporary social science and philosophy? Two possible explanations come to mind. First, even if the concept is relevant to many aspects of social, political, and economic life and has able and sophisticated defenders, it remains countercultural in the Kuhnian sense of not fitting squarely into the centralizing paradigms of modern social science, whether internationalism, which divides the world up into States as collective rational actors; statism, which views the State as the supreme source of order in the national sphere; or certain versions of legal positivism, which essentially assume the existence of a single system of law in any given territory (two prominent exponents of this view are Hans Kelsen 2002/1934 and H.L.A. Hart 1994/1961).

Highly centralized and State-centric paradigms of social governance and law are undoubtedly propagated and reinforced by State-controlled educational curricula and media, not to mention highly stylized images of more chaotic eras of feudal oppression, anarchy, and religious warfare (based on questionable historical generalizations), intended to serve as a stern warning against the pitfalls of decentralizing political and social authority. As Nobel Prize winner Elinor Ostrom lamented in 2005, "Leviathan is alive and well in our policy textbooks. The state is viewed as a substitute for the shortcomings of individual behavior and the presumed failure of community" (Ostrom 2000, 5). One could argue that some of the major works in political philosophy (e.g., Rawls 1971), political science (e.g., Downs 1957), and political economy (e.g., Samuelson 1948) published since World War II have significantly boosted the salience and prestige of State-centric visions of social order, relegating competing paradigms to the margins of academia.

A second possible explanation for the low visibility of polycentricity in modern social science and philosophy is that those who have broken with centralizing conventions to seriously investigate the potential explanatory and normative payoffs of attending to polycentric structures of social governance tend to be scattered across methodologically and topically heterogeneous fields of research, many of which pay limited attention to each other's findings and insights, and few of which pretend to offer anything like a "grand" unifying theory of politics or society.

The relative specialization and insulation of many domains of polycentric research, such as the institutional dynamics of federal polities (e.g., Bednar 2008), the proliferation of constitutional orders that govern diverse spheres of society (Teubner 2012), or the complex, multilayered political economy of metropolitan areas (Ostrom 1972), leads to an incomplete grasp of polycentrism's larger significance for the social sciences and weakens scholars' capacity to develop an account of polycentric governance capable of speaking across disciplinary boundaries. Hence, if we wish to expand its analytical usefulness and theoretical visibility, it seems wise to adopt a broader, more integrated PPE (Philosophy, Politics, and Economy) perspective on polycentric governance. This is what we have done in this book.

SCHOLARLY CONTRIBUTION

During recent decades, the challenges of hyper-centralized political and financial power, illiberal technocracy, political polarization, and civic fragmentation have threatened the very foundations of liberal democracies. The liberal ideal of the Open Society, as F. A. Hayek (Hayek 1978) understood it, namely a tolerant, free-market society of strangers governed by impersonal rules, has come to be severely questioned from within, especially when some sectors of society see their quality of life decline in what they take to be a free-market economy. Indeed, as we can see from the steady polarization of Western politics and growing distrust in public institutions, the Open Society is a precarious achievement, whose future is far from guaranteed. This gives rise to a fundamental, yet highly neglected, question, namely, how can we realize the Hayekian ideal of the Open Society in a manner that is resilient to the challenges of centralized power, burgeoning technocracy, political polarization, and civic fragmentation?

Specialized and applied studies of polycentric governance can effectively exemplify and illustrate the power of polycentric approaches to social order and coordination. Three prominent examples of works of this sort are three edited volumes published over the past twenty-five years: *Polycentricity and Local Public Economies: Readings from the Workshop in Political Theory and Policy Analysis* (1999), edited by Michael D. McGinnis; *Governing Complexity: Analyzing and Applying Polycentricity* (2019), edited by Thiel, Blomquist, and Garrick; and *Polycentricity in the European Union* (2019), edited by van Zeben and Bobić. Each of these three volumes examines the concept of polycentric governance and order through the lens of applied problems such as water management, municipal governance, and inter-institutional governance within the European Union. Even though these contributions are extremely valuable in their applied fields of inquiry, their level of specialization prevents them from offering a broader, more ambitious vision of the role of polycentric governance in the good society and its contribution to human flourishing. We address this gap in the literature by taking up these larger questions in a way that aims to be accessible to students and scholars from a cross-disciplinary audience. In this way, we hope to push the idea of polycentric governance further into the mainstream of contemporary academic discourse and promote serious consideration of polycentric solutions to a wide range of coordination problems confronting communities across the world.

This collection of essays is the first to carry forward the political economy tradition of polycentric governance and the Open Society, not exclusively on its own terms, but also under the broader umbrella of moral, political, and social philosophy. Building on works like *The Open Society and Its Complexities* (Gerald Gaus 2021) and a diverse body of work at the intersection of philosophy, politics, law, and economics, the arguments advanced in this volume suggest that under the right conditions, polycentric governance can be the institutional cornerstone of a resilient Open Society. The book offers normative arguments to show the ethical attractiveness of polycentric governance in a world marked by moral, cultural, and political diversity, disagreement, and conflict. But it also marshals PPE arguments and evidence to show that a resilient Open Society must rely on polycentric systems of governance if it hopes to attain political stability in the face of complexity and disagreement. Such arguments should offer valuable food for thought about the relationship between modern democracy and institutional and cultural pluralism, as well as the limitations of monocentric solutions to the problem of political order.

We aim to illuminate the value of polycentric governance arrangements and their fit with human needs in ways that resonate with the findings of Ostromian institutional economists, yet also examine this topic through the lenses of neighboring disciplines, such as moral philosophy, law, history, and political science. We take a step back from the intricacies of specialized debates within federalism and institutional economics, which often focus narrowly on governmental stability and the efficient satisfaction of economic needs, to ask larger philosophical and normative questions about the theoretical grounding for polycentrism and its general merits as a principle of social organization, when compared with more monocentric approaches. While there have been a number of individual works offering a broad philosophical treatment of polycentrically structured social orders (e.g., Müller 2019, Thunder 2018, Aligica 2019), to the best of our knowledge, there have been no edited collections, like this one, presenting a variety of approaches to the justification, design, and implementation of polycentric social orders with a broad philosophical and normative focus beyond the fields of political economy and public choice theory.

An academic world immersed in centralizing paradigms of social order, in particular those that look to the State or global actors to impose order from the top down, is gradually waking up to the fact that centralizing and homogenizing paradigms of social governance, such as Statism and internationalism, are unsatisfactory both as explanatory and action-guiding principles. The dream of a centrally planned and controlled society nourished by August Comte and other European Enlightenment thinkers is fading into the distant past as we wake up to the reality of social complexity and its far-reaching implications for effective social governance. In this context, a broad and multidisciplinary investigation of the types of institutional arrangements that can rise to the challenges of governance and accommodate diverse ways of life under conditions of social complexity is long overdue.

A strong case can be made that polycentric governance arrangements, far from being a recipe for anarchy or social disorder, are actually more responsive to the challenges of governing a complex and multifaceted social order than their centralizing counterparts, and they may more reliably respond to a plurality of human needs and aspirations on the ground. Rather than following the conventional path of suppressing complexity and diversity for the sake of reaching agreement on justice and political stability, we see complexity and diversity as assets that should be leveraged to make the Open Society a more prosperous, resilient, and flourishing place to live.

We hope that *Polycentric Governance and the Good Society* will become a valuable reference work for academics and students looking for a probing, cross-disciplinary discussion of the ethos and institutions of liberal democracy under conditions of social pluralism, in particular the challenge of creating and preserving stable political institutions in a morally, politically, and culturally diverse Open Society. A book of this nature should appeal to students, academics, and researchers interested in the problem of order and governance under conditions of advanced social complexity in fields such as political science, moral and political philosophy, political economy, public administration, and legal and constitutional theory. This book should be of special interest to the PPE community of scholars interested in the justification, emergence, and preservation of a resilient Open Society.

Last but not least, we believe this book will hold interest for non-academic citizens who want to deepen their understanding of the challenges confronting free, democratic, and open societies in a world of deep moral and cultural pluralism. At a moment when the old idea of a State-centric society is under threat from the globalization of markets and politics, the rise of moral and cultural fragmentation, and the crisis of the welfare state, a volume developing alternatives to monocentric paradigms of order should appeal not only to specialized academic scholars, but also to a lay public interested in learning more about novel approaches to governance that break with traditional Statist paradigms of civil order.

OVERVIEW OF THE CHAPTERS

In this collection, we investigate the politics, philosophy, and economics of polycentrism not merely as an empirical description of a particular type of social arrangement, but as a normative and philosophical position on how society ought to be governed or might be most successfully governed. To think polycentrically about social order is to view social life as a plurality rather than a singularity: to acknowledge and attempt to do justice to the plurality of communities, narratives, and normative orders that interact dynamically in any extended social space. Echoing Isaiah Berlin's famous allegory, to think polycentrically about social order is to recognize that modern societies should not be conceived as a "compact coral reef," but as a complex ecosystem inhabited by an irreducible plurality of lifestyles and values, which cannot be fully embodied within a single human life or a single community. There is much at stake in vindicating this pluralist vision, given that personal and societal flourishing have suffered enormous harms from the suppression of diversity through unitary conceptions of justice, top-down conceptions of economic planning, or hyper-centralized forms of public administration.

This volume comprises nine contributions, reflecting on the logic and merits of polycentric governance from ethical, organizational, sociological, political, economic, historical, and legal-constitutional perspectives. The book is divided into three main sections: i) the ethics of polycentric governance, ii) the feasibility of polycentric orders, and iii) the principles of polycentric law and statecraft. In Part I, the ethics of polycentric governance, we have three contributions by David Thunder, Mark Hoipkemier, and John Thrasher, respectively.

In Chapter 1, "An Ethical Case for Bottom-Up, Polycentric Governance in a Complex Society," David Thunder seeks to complement and further illuminate existing defenses of social and institutional pluralism by more explicitly grounding the case for polycentric governance in the social and institutional infrastructure of flourishing communities. Building off the central value of the "freedom to flourish" and its social preconditions, Thunder lays out three guiding principles for a polycentric regime: individual and corporate voluntarism, proximity of rulers to ruled, and the bottom-up constitution of power. The aim of good governance and sound social coordination, on the approach defended by Thunder, should not be to monopolize the functions of social governance, but to cooperate with other relevant actors in facilitating the expansion of opportunities for human flourishing while fostering and protecting the integrity of the complex, multidimensional infrastructure of human flourishing.

In Chapter 2, "Is an Architectonic Pluralism Possible?" Mark Hoipkemier makes a bold case that Aristotelian thinking about the common good, contrary to popular belief, actually supports the ideal of a free and pluralistic society. Hoipkemier argues that political pluralists have nothing to fear from embracing the politics of the common good, rightly understood. It is a staple of Aristotelian doctrine, on Hoipkemier's interpretation, that the political community includes and oversees all aspects of human flourishing, while Catholic scholars frequently identify the "common good" as simultaneously including the whole good of the person, and being the proper object of State supervision. But this all-encompassing conception of the common good as something to be promoted by the State seems to license totalitarian meddling in every dimension of supposedly "private" life. In response to this challenge to the philosophy of the common good, Hoipkemier argues that the common good should not be understood in this highly integrated manner. Instead, we should understand the common goal citizens share as the public order among various human goods and projects. In Hoipkemier's view, this order does concern all of life's domains, but it only licenses political scrutiny over locally shared goods insofar as their role in this larger order is in question.

In Chapter 3, "Polycentric Justice," John Thrasher argues for an extension of the concept of polycentricity from institutions and organizations to norms of justice. Thrasher argues that justice as a global standard of legitimacy and a universal evaluative norm is ill-suited to a polycentric system of governance. While polycentric orders need legitimacy in the traditional sense and higher-level regulative norms, both are better achieved through a non-Rawlsian form of contractualism, which is not focused on justifying a universal conception of justice. A polycentric-friendly version of contractualism will justify less substantive procedural norms and institutional rules instead. The insight that polycentric theory leads us to, on Thrasher's view, is that contractual public justification can generate a standard of legitimacy without relying on justice as a basic norm. This chapter offers an original non-Rawlsian interpretation of contractualism, consistent with a diverse and polycentric social order.

In Part II, three essays address the feasibility of polycentric orders. The contributions come from Dries Daems and Alexander Schaefer, Pablo Paniagua and Kaveh Pourvand, and Vlad Tarko, respectively.

In Chapter 4, "The Problem of Complexity and the Emergence of Polycentric Political Order," Alexander Schaefer and Dries Daems examine the conditions under which polycentric political systems will likely emerge. Various normative and empirical aspects of polycentric political governance have garnered much attention, but political scientists have yet to closely examine the process through which polycentric political systems emerge. Schaefer and Daems aim to fill this gap by proposing an explanation of the emergence of the polycentric state. They illustrate their explanation of the emergence of polycentric political order with a comparative case study focusing on Han China's and ancient Rome's governance structures. This chapter is methodologically innovative, using analytic models and historical analysis to understand the formation of polycentric orders.

In Chapter 5, "Whither Stability? Polycentric Democracy and Social Order," Pablo Paniagua and Kaveh Pourvand address a perennial question of political theory, namely how to stabilize a just regime. They view this problem as especially pressing in the context of the highly globalized and diversified social orders of the late twentieth and early twenty-first centuries, and as further accentuated by the emergence of the Weberian state that anchors society under a single, coercive structure of governance, strangely at odds with the fluidity and complexity of modern societies. Paniagua and Pourvand make a case for polycentric democracy as a better solution than the centralized nation-state to the challenge of stability. They argue that polycentric democracies, characterized by plural and overlapping centers of governance, are more robust (anti-fragile) in the face of political diversity, conflict, and instability than their more centralized counterparts, much as a variegated ecology is more robust than a monoculture. This chapter, operating at the intersection of political economy and political theory, offers valuable insights into the resilience and robustness of polycentric political systems.

Our third contribution on the feasibility of polycentric order comes from Vlad Tarko. In Chapter 6, "Self-Governance Solutions to Social Dilemmas: A Polycentric Approach," Tarko argues that effective self-governance is an important tool for solving "social dilemmas," understood as situations in which parties affected by a social problem do not have sufficient incentives to behave in ways that could solve it. Following in the footsteps of Vincent and Elinor Ostrom, Tarko rejects the traditional market-versus-State dichotomy, pointing us to a third approach, in which interested parties can play an active role in creating and developing regulatory and enforcement schemes from the bottom up. This approach is inherently polycentric due to the autonomy it necessarily affords to local actors. Tarko illustrates the power of self-governance as a solution to social dilemmas by explaining how it has been leveraged to solve problems of water governance, and then delves into the theoretical significance of these phenomena in light of debates about self-governance by authors such as Robert Dahl and James Buchanan. Tarko rounds out the chapter by exploring how the concepts of polycentricity and entangled political economy allow us to move from the analysis of small-scale communities to large-scale federal and international organizations.

In Part III, our volume is brought to a close by a set of essays on polycentric law and statecraft.

In Chapter 7, in "Panarchy: Non-Territorial Polycentricity," Aviezer Tucker defends a "panarchist" theory of state formation. The dominant Westphalian model of the state based on a territorial monopoly over the legitimate use of violence fits seventeenth-century technology, developed at a time when geographical distances could not be traversed efficiently, and even information took months to travel the globe. However, these monistic, top-down conceptions of political order are of limited relevance in a politically, culturally, and economically specialized, fragmented, and globalized world. Panarchy, a meta-political theory of non-territorial states founded on explicit social contracts, was first introduced in 1860 by the Belgian scholar Emil DePuydt. He proposed that citizens may sign a social contract with a State and may change their States without moving. Tucker suggests that in today's world, where citizens of nation-states have radically different ideas of the common good, panarchy may allow them to live together peacefully, each self-selecting into his or her own preferred contractual arrangement. This chapter shows how the intellectual tradition of panarchy may enrich and complement other forms of polycentric thinking.

In Chapter 8, "Polycentrism, the Rule of Law, and the Intelligibility of Human Rights Law," Pilar Zambrano inquires whether a polycentric legal system could, potentially, address the challenges that both legal and moral pluralism raise for the intelligibility of law. She describes the fact of legal pluralism and its impact on present-day legal practices, pointing out how bottom-up and top-down sources of law overlap and interact in complex ways not contemplated by top-down, Statist paradigms of law, giving rise to what Francesco Viola calls the "legal space." She argues that the fact of legal pluralism raises serious difficulties for the intelligibility of law, to the extent that society-wide and global laws tend to be ever more deracinated from embodied social practices. Finally, she argues that this problem seems to point us in the direction of a polycentric theoretical approach to the creation and adjudication of law, though this approach is quite underdeveloped in the philosophy of law.

Finally, in Chapter 9, "The Constitution of Liberties: Polycentric Constitutionalism and the 'Westminster Export Model,'" Elliot Bulmer argues that a polycentric political and legal framework may not necessarily require novel (or radically old) constitutional ideas and practices, but could be achieved within prevailing constitutional models. It is recognized that much of modern Western constitutional thought is based on monocentric notions: "the People" is often construed as a singular collective actor, expressing a "national will" and possessing nominal sovereignty, in whose name constitutions are made and remade, and from whom all public powers are derived. However, Bulmer reminds us that monocentric popular sovereignty is not the only foundation for modern constitutionalism. In particular, while the British-derived constitutions that spread around the world in the decolonization era mostly copied the majoritarian governance structures of the "Westminster Model" parliamentary democracy, they also responded to the needs of divided societies by incorporating an array of innovative approaches to the problem of "deep, pervasive and persistent disagreements," including on matters of religion and identity (De Smith 1964). This final chapter shows how certain constitutional theories and practices are already compatible, in significant respects, with polycentric political systems.

This collection of essays aims to illuminate the idea of a polycentric society in a more comprehensive and multidisciplinary fashion than previous works. We hope that this more philosophically ambitious discussion of polycentric order will open fruitful and unexpected avenues of research, revitalizing the study of polycentric order both in the social sciences and the humanities. We are convinced that only by seriously engaging with and leveraging the ideas of polycentric systems of social organization and governance can we hope to build more resilient, tolerant, and prosperous democracies. We leave it up to the reader to judge whether we have succeeded in contributing, albeit modestly, to this important task.

NOTES

1. We would like to thank the participants in the RESPUBLICA research project (2021–2023) for providing constructive feedback on an early draft of several of these chapters. We also wish to extend a special word of thanks to Fundación Ciudadanía y Valores Proeduca Summa S.L. for generously supporting our work.

2. This definition is broadly consistent with that offered in the introduction to the volume *Governing Complexity: Analyzing and Applying Polycentricity* (Thiel, Blomquist, and Garrick 2019).

REFERENCES

Aligica, Paul Dragos. 2014. *Institutional Diversity and Political Economy: The Ostroms and Beyond*. Oxford University Press.

———. 2019. *Public Entrepreneurship, Citizenship, and Self-Governance*. Cambridge: Cambridge University Press.

Aligica, Paul Dragos, and Vlad Tarko. 2013. "Co-Production, Polycentricity, and Value Heterogeneity: The Ostroms' Public Choice Institutionalism Revisited." *American Political Science Review* 107 (04): 726–41.

Auerbach, Jerold S. 1984. *Justice Without Law? Resolving Disputes Without Lawyers*. Oxford: Oxford University Press.

Bednar, Jenna. 2008. *The Robust Federation.Principles of Design*: Cambridge University Press.

Buchanan, James M. 1996. "Federalism and Individual Sovereignty." *Cato Journal* 15 (2–3): 259–68.

Cerny, Philip G. 2010. *Rethinking World Politics: A Theory of Transnational Neopluralism*. Oxford University Press.

De Smith, Stanley Alexander. 1964. *The New Commonwealth and its Constitutions*. London: Stevens & Sons.

Delmas-Marty, Mireille. 2009. *Ordering Pluralism. A Conceptual Framework for Understanding the Transnational Legal World*. Bloomsbury Publishing.

Downs, Anthony. 1957. *An Economic Theory of Democracy*. New York: Harper Press.

Elazar, Daniel J. 1987. *Exploring Federalism*. Tuscaloosa, AL: University of Alabama Press.

Ellickson, Robert C. 2009. *Order Without Law: How Neighbors Settle Disputes*. Harvard University Press.

Gaus, Gerald. 2021. *The Open Society and Its Complexities*. New York: Oxford University Press.

Griffiths, John. 1986. "What Is Legal Pluralism?" *The Journal of Legal Pluralism and Unofficial Law* 18 (24): 1–55.

Hart, H. L. A. 1994. *The Concept of Law*. Oxford: Oxford University Press, 1961.

Hayek, Friedrich A. 1978. Law, Legislation and Liberty. Vols. I–III. Chicago: University of Chicago Press, 1973.

Hirst, Paul. 2013. *From Statism to Pluralism: Democracy, Civil Society and Global Politics*. New York: Routledge.

Kelsen, Hans. 2002. *Introduction to the Problems of Legal Theory*. Oxford: Clarendon Press, 1934.

Kriesi, Hanspeter, and Alexander H. Trechsel. 2008. *The Politics of Switzerland: Continuity and Change in a Consensus Democracy*. Cambridge University Press.

Levy, Jacob T. 2015. *Rationalism, Pluralism, and Freedom*. New York: Oxford University Press.

McGinnis, Michael D. 1999. *Polycentricity and Local Public Economies: Readings from the Workshop in Political Theory and Policy Analysis,* edited by Michael D. McGinnis. Michigan: University of Michigan Press.

Müller, Julian F. 2019. *Political Pluralism, Disagreement and Justice: The Case for Polycentric Democracy*. New York: Routledge.

Muñiz-Fraticelli, Victor M. 2014. *The Structure of Pluralism*. Oxford: Oxford University Press.

Ostrom, Elinor. 1972. "Metropolitan Reform: Propositions Derived from Two Traditions." *Social Science Quarterly*; 3 (3): 474–93.

———. 2000. "Crowding out Citizenship." *Scandinavian Political Studies* 23 (1): 3–16.

Ostrom, Elinor, Roger B. Parks, and Gordon P. Whitaker. 1973. "Do We Really Want to Consolidate Urban Police Forces? A Reappraisal of Some Old Assertions." *Public Administration Review* 33 (5): 423–32.

Ostrom, Vincent. 1991. *The Meaning of American Federalism: Constituting a Self-Governing Society*. San Francisco: ICS Press.
Ostrom, Vincent, Charles M. Tiebout, and Robert Warren. 1961. "The Organization of Government in Metropolitan Areas: A Theoretical Inquiry." *American Political Science Review* 55 (04): 831–42.
Paniagua, Pablo. 2020. "Governing the (Banking) Commons: Polycentric Solutions to Bank Runs." In *The Political Economy and Social Philosophy of Vincent and Elinor Ostrom*, edited by P. Boettke, R. Herzberg, and B. Kogelmann, 115–44. New York: Rowman & Littlefield.
———. 2022. "Elinor Ostrom and Public Health." *Economy and Society* 51 (4).
Pennington, Mark. 2008. "Classical liberalism and ecological rationality: The case for polycentric environmental law." *Environmental Politics* 17 (3): 431–48.
Rawls, John. 1971. *A Theory of Justice*. Oxford: Oxford University Press.
Risse, Matthias, ed. 2013. *Governance Without a State? Policies and Politics in Areas of Limited Statehoods*. New York: Columbia University Press.
Samuelson, Paul. 1948. *Economics*. New York: McGraw-Hill.
Schneider, Mark. 1989. *The Competitive City: The Political Economy of Suburbia*. Pittsburgh: University of Pittsburgh Press.
Scott, James C. 2014. *The Art of Not Being Governed: An Anarchist History of Upland Southeast Asia*. Yale University Press.
Stringham, Edward Peter. 2015. *Private Governance. Creating Order in Economic and Social Life*. Oxford: Oxford University Press.
Teubner, Gunther. 2012a. *Constitutional Fragments: Societal Constitutionalism and Globalization*. New York: Oxford University Press.
———. 2012b. *Constitutional Fragments: Societal Constitutionalism and Globalization*. Oxford: Oxford University Press.
Thiel, Andreas, William A. Blomquist, and Dustin E. Garrick. 2019. *Governing Complexity: Analyzing and Applying Polycentricity*, edited by William A. Blomquist, Dustin E. Garrick, Andreas Thiel. Cambridge University Press.
Thunder, David. 2018. "From Polis to Metropolis: On the Limits of Classical Approaches to Governance in a Fragmented Social Landscape." In *Disciplines of the City*, edited by Julia Urabayen. New York: Nova Science Publishers.
Tully, James. 1995. *Strange Multiplicity: Constitutionalism in an Age of Diversity*. Cambridge University Press.

PART I

The Ethics of Polycentric Governance

Chapter 1

An Ethical Case for Bottom-Up, Polycentric Governance in a Complex Society[1]

David Thunder

Since the early twentieth century, we have seen numerous critiques by political philosophers, jurists, historians, and political economists of the Enlightenment ambition to introduce order into the social fabric through the centralized administrative State. Whereas monistic thinkers writing in the shadow of Hobbesian and Lockean political theory tend to associate high levels of social, institutional, and governmental diversity and fragmentation with instability and disorder, this new crop of pluralist thinkers came to view complex and multidimensional social orders not only as a potential source of conflict, but as an essential feature of a well-functioning society and even as an asset for tackling an infinite variety of social problems not susceptible to one-size-fits-all solutions. The aim of this chapter is to complement and further illuminate existing defenses of social and institutional pluralism by more explicitly building a case for polycentric governance based on the requisites of human flourishing in a complex society. The aim of good governance and sound social coordination, on the approach I defend, is not to monopolize the functions of social governance, but to cooperate with other relevant actors in facilitating the expansion of opportunities for human flourishing, while fostering and protecting the integrity of the complex social infrastructure of flourishing.

Thomas Hobbes's *Leviathan* marked a watershed moment in Western political thought. Most medieval and some early modern political theories had sought to uncover a principle of unity consistent with a multilayered, complex, and differentiated social landscape (e.g., Gierke 2014 and Althusius

1995). Much of the political philosophy that comes after Hobbes, by contrast, tends to view the task of the political philosopher as that of bypassing the prevailing social infrastructure, with a view to formulating principles and institutional mechanisms capable of unifying a vast number of individuals together under the terms of a *unique* social contract, or a *unique* shared system of government. An enormous amount of effort was devoted to overcoming the fragmented loyalties associated with feudalism, and installing in their place a single overriding loyalty to the political project of the modern State. This integrating project was invigorated by the urgency of developing a type of political belonging that was not splintered by religious warfare.

Given the great harms inflicted by the wars of religion, one can readily understand why political philosophers undertook to develop a political theory capable of legitimating a highly integrated, large-scale civil order apt to secure the conditions of peace and cooperation across large and diverse populations. Monistically inclined, State-centric theorists generally viewed social and institutional complexity as a wild beast to be tamed and domesticated by the State (e.g., Schmitt 2007; Weber 1964; Kelsen 2002; and Rawls 1971). However, over the course of the twentieth century, especially in its latter decades, a growing number of political theorists, jurists, and social scientists came to have second thoughts about this integrating project.

A new crop of thinkers across a variety of fields, including law, history, political philosophy, institutional economics, and public choice theory, began to make the case that Statist political theory and social science had grossly oversimplified the nature of political order and governance, by (i) exaggerating the power of the State to confer order on a diverse social landscape, and (ii) underestimating forms of order and governance that were not derived from the institutions of the State, but were already latent in the fabric of a complex society.[2]

This essay could be seen as a contribution to this broad re-valorization of social and institutional complexity. I propose to tap into a broadly neo-Aristotelian account of human flourishing along similar lines to Alasdair MacIntyre's (1981), to illuminate the benefits of social complexity and differentiation for humans' well-being, and infer from this account some fundamental principles of sound social coordination and good governance. My argument on behalf of social complexity goes further than that of most other authors insofar as it shows, in an explicit way, how a highly differentiated social landscape configured by a plurality of independent normative orders provides an *indispensable social infrastructure* for free and flourishing human life, and how this ethical interpretation of complexity might shape our approach to social coordination and good governance.[3]

The argument will unfold in six steps: I begin by very briefly reviewing four well-established strategies pursued by political and legal philosophers, political economists, and historians for defending the necessity and/or value of social complexity, and suggesting that the fourth of these strategies, a *strictly ethical* defense of complexity, remains relatively underdeveloped in the literature. I then begin to set the foundations for my approach to complexity by explaining what I take to be a touchstone value for a good society: the "freedom to flourish." Third, I suggest that the freedom to flourish cannot be realized outside the context of a social group guided by a shared set of ends, norms, customs, and narratives, or what I call a "normative order." Fourth, I argue that given the complex and multidimensional character of the human good, a plurality of independent associations, each guided by its own distinctive and autonomous normative order, is a necessary precondition for people to enjoy adequate opportunities for personal growth and flourishing. Fifth, I adduce some reasons for pessimism concerning the capacity of a State equipped with wide-ranging sovereign power to offer reasonable accommodation to a plurality of distinct normative orders within its territorial jurisdiction. Finally, I round out the argument by suggesting that three important values for a social arrangement friendly to the freedom to flourish are voluntarism, proximity of rulers to the ruled, and the bottom-up constitution of power.

1. PREVAILING ARGUMENTS FOR THE VALUE AND/OR NECESSITY OF SOCIAL AND INSTITUTIONAL COMPLEXITY

There are many sophisticated discussions in the social science literature concerning the nature of complex phenomena, complex systems, and complex social arrangements (see, for example, Gaus 2021; Hayek 1967; Mitchell 2011; and Paniagua 2023). For present purposes, I shall understand a complex society as one that exhibits the following features: (i) it is a collection of individual persons and groups of persons engaged in purposeful activities (ii) that interact with each other and respond to each other dynamically over time (iii) in ways that (intentionally or unintentionally) produce both local and large-scale societal outcomes and patterns, such as wealth production and distribution, social norms and attitudes, war and peace, and institutional and linguistic development, where (iv) distinct groups of individuals are guided and shaped in their group activities by their own distinctive normative orders (purposes, projects, values, customs, and rules) and (v) these diverse normative orders are sufficiently heterogeneous that they cannot all be simultaneously embodied within a single human life or within a simple, austere, or homogeneous social structure.[4]

Political and moral philosophers have viewed social and institutional complexity as either valuable or necessary from a number of different perspectives. To begin with, social complexity may be viewed as something to be accepted as an *unavoidable outcome* of personal freedom. In a large and diverse society, if you permit people to act on their preferences and life plans, they will inevitably pursue divergent ends, and generate a wide range of diversely structured and governed associations. The resulting social arrangement must be managed rather than suppressed, on this view, either as a pragmatic concession to human nature, or out of deference to the value of personal freedom. Either way, the acceptance of complexity is usually tempered by some normative constraints, whether procedure-oriented principles of justice, such as freedom of contract, private property rights, and non-aggression (Nozick 1974 and Kukathas 2003), or alternatively by a more demanding, outcome-oriented conception of distributive justice (Rawls 1993 and Christiano 2008).

A second way to view the value of social complexity is as a necessary precondition for diverse identities, projects, and ways of life to thrive and enjoy some degree of social recognition. Only in a society with a certain minimum amount of cultural and institutional differentiation is it possible for people to pursue projects and forms of life they can identify with or find meaning in. This argument is consistent with William Galston's eloquent defense of freedom of association, which couches the value of living a meaningful life in the language of "expressive liberty" (Galston 2002). Another well-known version of the argument for accommodating diverse ways of life based on their importance for people's sense of meaning and purpose is made by Will Kymlicka and James Tully (Kymlicka 1995 and Tully 1995) in relation to the rights of indigenous peoples to have access to a social, political, and legal framework within which they can coherently orient their lives, even if that means carving out exemptions to the normal rules and conventions established by a territorial government or a liberal constitutional State. Analogous arguments have been made by the English pluralists in defense of the integrity of non-State associations, such as churches and guilds (see Cole 2015; Laski 2008; and Figgis 2013).

A third way to view social complexity is as an asset for more efficiently solving problems of social coordination and meeting citizens' grassroots needs in a large and diverse society. The Ostromian school of political economy, otherwise known as the "Bloomington school," is perhaps the most well-known representative of this approach. Elinor and Vincent Ostrom and their colleagues took the lead in investigating the value of institutional decentralization, diversity, and competition, as ways for different social groups to evolve tailored solutions, often on a trial-and-error basis, to well-defined common problems, such as the provision of non-excludable common goods ("common pool resources") like policing and water, and the protection of natural resources from excessive exploitation or pollution (see especially E. Ostrom 2015). Similar conclusions about the pragmatic value of social and institutional complexity and the limits of centralized, technocratic governance as problem-solving tools were reached by institutional historian James Scott (1999) and journalist-activist Jane Jacobs (1992).

These three arguments in favor of accepting or endorsing complex and differentiated social structures all have their merits, but they also lack a crucial lens for grasping and further articulating the value of social complexity, namely, the ways in which a complex and differentiated social order is necessary in order to service the *rounded human flourishing* of its participants. This is an ethical and anthropological argument that is broader than coordination problems like urban and agrarian planning, the management of shared resources like water, or the effective coordination of a policing system. The failure to engage with ethics in a fundamental and rigorous way leaves most normative defenses of social and institutional complexity incomplete: while they may justify complexity either as a necessary consequence of freedom, or based on some *specific dimension* of flourishing, such as cultural identity, political self-determination, economic efficiency, or informed decision-making, they do not do so based on a broad account of human flourishing and its requirements. This chapter, while it cannot hope to offer a fully developed or comprehensive ethical account of the value of social and institutional complexity, is intended to offer a preliminary sketch of what such an account might look like. My hope is that such a sketch might facilitate a richer and broader cross-disciplinary conversation on the value of social and institutional complexity and its implications for the governmental structures of political and economic institutions.

2. THE FREEDOM TO FLOURISH

One of the principal burdens of this chapter is to show that a certain sort of social complexity is critical to the enterprise of living a flourishing or worthwhile human life, and it can only be preserved by a method of governance and cooperation that is, in important respects, voluntarist, localist, and bottom-up in spirit and in operation. In order to reach an accurate assessment of complex social structures and their governmental exigencies, we must begin by understanding what makes for a functional and attractive social order. My argument will assume that any functional and attractive social order must be consistent with the freedom to flourish. Let me explain what I mean by the freedom to flourish:

Since human beings can only realize worthwhile lives in and through their own free choices, freedom is a necessary ingredient of human flourishing.[5] The value of freedom in a human life is hard to make sense of unless it enables the freedom-bearer to achieve some aspect of flourishing. Freedom cut off from the possibility of human flourishing is simply not worth having, not inherently desirable or choice-worthy. While one could stipulate a purely formal definition of freedom as self-determination in accordance with an agent's goals, whatever they happen to be, this by itself would not make a human life worth living, nor could it be a central value or normative pillar of a functional or thriving society. That is because the value of freedom only becomes intelligible as a *value worth pursuing and protecting* when its bearer has the possibility of choosing worthwhile human ends. For example, a person enjoying perfect liberty to make his or her own choices independently from external threats or interference could find herself stranded alone on a desert island, with no way to channel that freedom toward a way of life she has reason to value, involving basic human goods such as love, friendship, the pursuit of complex projects, the enjoyment of beauty, and so forth. Or as Jeremy Waldron has persuasively argued, the homeless man who has the legal freedom to purchase or rent a home, if deprived of real opportunities to better his lot, is unlikely to put much stock on his freedom from interference or domination (Waldron 1991).

Bearing these considerations in mind, in the context of the present argument, we may stipulate that freedom is *the capacity of individuals and groups to direct their lives toward personal and communal flourishing in ways that are responsive to their own rationally informed and uncoerced choices and sense of meaning and purpose.*[6] I call this conception of freedom the *freedom to flourish*, to highlight the fact that individual and collective freedom is conceived as a genuine personal and social value only insofar as it involves realistic opportunities to realize flourishing human lives. According to this account, which is largely consistent with Joseph Raz's view (Raz 1986), an agent only enjoys a valuable or choice-worthy form of freedom—the sort of freedom we have reason to promote and protect—when he or she has the possibility of choosing objectively valuable human ends, i.e., ends that help to contribute to, or constitute, a flourishing human life; while the optimal use of freedom is that which issues in the enjoyment of such ends.[7]

Freedom is promoted by multiplying opportunities for flourishing. However, this does not license a centralized State to engage in ambitious forms of social engineering, for two reasons: first, because *any* social intervention must be consistent with the reasonable autonomy of citizens, and must aim at securing the consent of relevant stakeholders, both through individual assent and through the assent of representatives of associations; and second, because once we admit the importance of social, cultural, and institutional pluralism for human flourishing (an argument I make in section 4), this precludes any government from imposing a single, homogeneous normative order unilaterally over the whole social fabric. Paradoxical as it may at first appear, the best way to expand opportunities for genuine human flourishing is through a form of *political restraint* that respects and protects the agency and choices of individual and corporate actors as much as possible, within the bounds of widely shared norms of civil and lawful conduct.

Since freedom is worthless if separated from human flourishing, an argument in defense of human freedom must rely on some conception of human flourishing, however modest. The conception of human flourishing my argument relies on is characterized by the following four features: (i) first, deliberation and choice are critical constitutive ingredients of a flourishing human life; (ii) second, the pursuit and achievement of human flourishing is inherently an *embodied, developmental, and socially embedded* enterprise; (iii) third, the content of human flourishing is extraordinarily complex or multifaceted; (iv) and fourth, in spite of this complexity, there is no reason to rule out the possibility of adjudicating the comparative merits of diverse human ends, or identifying universal requirements of a flourishing human life. Let us unpack these features one by one:

(i) Rational Deliberation and Choice as Critical Ingredients of a Flourishing Life

Rational deliberation and choice are not just instruments for achieving a flourishing human life, but they are *constitutive elements* of a flourishing human life, in the sense that the very act of deliberating and choosing, and becoming better at deliberating and choosing, is part of what it means to thrive as a human being. Even if one enjoyed certain physical, intellectual, spiritual, and emotional dimensions of flourishing, one's life would be profoundly impoverished to the extent that one acted entirely at the mercy of fate, or other people's choices, rather than living a life at least partly informed by one's own choices about how to act and live.

Rationality should not be confused with a hubristic conception of the power of reason, or a denial that life is an adventure full of mystery and surprises. However, as rational agents, we are answerable for our choices, and if we take our own lives seriously, then we will live responsibly, cultivating an awareness of the available choice set, and reflecting upon what is at stake in how we choose to live.[8] To forsake rational deliberation about the requirements of a good human life is to live recklessly, unmoored from rationally informed judgment, and risk collapsing into unthinking conformism, incivility, and callous indifference to the needs of others.

(ii) The Embodied, Developmental, and Social Character of Flourishing

The notion of "good" or "human flourishing" I will rely upon in this chapter is rooted in an anthropology of embodied dependence, much along the lines of what Alasdair MacIntyre (1999) lays out in *Dependent Rational Animals*. Human beings are embodied and dependent creatures, with a natural lifespan, and a potential for physical, intellectual, moral, emotional, and spiritual development. Just as a competent medical doctor can identify the difference between the normal, healthy development of a human organism, and its pathological development, in a similar way, a psychologist can identify the difference between someone who is able to function and adapt to their social environment in more or less healthy ways, without relapsing into childhood neuroses or destructive addictions. Similarly, a responsible parent can tell the difference between a child who is becoming a generous, kind, compassionate, and prudent person, and a child who is becoming steadily more selfish, narcissistic, cruel, or reckless. In each of these cases, there is a potential in the human being to mature and grow along some dimension of human flourishing, whether physiological, emotional, or intellectual, and that potential may be either squandered or successfully enlarged and developed.[9]

Besides being embodied and developmental, the pursuit and realization of the human good is necessarily *socially embedded*: that is to say, social groups provide an inescapable context for our efforts to realize our full human potential. Living an asocial life, we may be either "gods" or "beasts," as Aristotle put it (*Politics*, 1.2.1253a28-30), but we are not living a fully human life, a life in which distinctively human capacities, such as the capacity for deliberation, play, and friendship, are given a chance to develop. Human beings thrive by learning to become better at making choices about how to live and respond to the world around them; and this is achieved by learning to participate more competently and responsibly in the life of human communities.[10]

(iii) The Complexity of Human Flourishing

In general, human beings and human communities cannot reach their full potential by developing exclusively along a single dimension of flourishing: Individual human beings require a *complex package of goods* in order to flourish as human beings, including physical and mental health; emotional bonding with lovers, family, and friends; the sincere and diligent pursuit of truth; the enjoyment of art and leisure; and the advancement of some socially or professionally fruitful project. Human communities typically seek to flourish along many different dimensions, including the possession of sufficient material resources to cover the community's vital needs; peace and friendship among their members; success at advancing associational ends; the development of structures and habits of good governance; and equitable distribution of the community's material resources and knowledge.

There is another important sense in which human flourishing is immensely complex: there are many different ways individual human beings may reasonably interpret and realize their own flourishing, which may vary according to their peculiar circumstances, capacities, virtues, resources, choices, and sense of calling. This is most obvious in the case of the individual: there are many different legitimate ways to live a flourishing human life, and no single, narrow path can be prescribed for everyone. Even if we accept that certain dispositions of character are necessary to live a good human life—for example, justice, courage, prudence, and temperance—different individuals, on account of their personal aspirations, latent talents, personal history, or sense of calling and purpose, may require different conditions in order to realize their own personal potential. *Mutatis mutandis*, similar considerations apply to human communities, whose flourishing inevitably depends on their unique history, resources, composition, sense of collective purpose, and of course, the continuing choices of their members in regard to the life of the community in question.

(iv) Universal Requirements of Human Flourishing

Now, admitting the complex and pluri-dimensional character of the human good in no way requires us to renounce the possibility of making valid comparative judgments between human ends, or identifying general requirements of a flourishing human life. For the complexity of the human good is not tantamount to moral relativism: it is constrained by the embodied and psychic nature of the human being, and by the indispensability of certain goods for a worthwhile and functional human life. If pluralism were *absolute or unconstrained*, we could not say that one form of life was superior to another, or that some choices and lifestyles are abhorrent or ignoble. But the type of pluralism I am endorsing here need not rule out comparative judgments, and it is constrained by certain goods without which, I take it that any human life would be significantly impaired or impoverished.

What might such essential goods be? There are certain basic human capabilities, as Amartya Sen (1999) and Martha Nussbaum (2011) have argued, without which *any* human life would be significantly impoverished. On this list we could include the capacity to breathe, receive nourishment, and maintain one's bodily integrity; the capacity to move relatively freely from place to place; the capacity to live in a safe home; the capacity to develop lasting human friendships; the capacity to love and be loved; the capacity to enjoy a sense of inner peace; the capacity to think clearly about one's choices and projects; the capacity to exercise a significant measure of rational mastery over one's life; the capacity to cooperate with one's peers in shared projects with worthwhile ends; and the capacity to enjoy recreational and restful activities.[11]

3. ASSOCIATIONS AND NORMATIVE ORDERS AS GUIDING FRAMEWORKS FOR HUMAN FLOURISHING

If we wish to understand the contribution of social complexity and differentiation to human flourishing, we must pay close attention to the structure and functions of social groups and how they condition the quality and intelligibility of the lives of their participants. In other words, we need to develop a *social ontology of flourishing*: an account of the complex social structures, relationships, and norms through which human beings may realize rounded and flourishing lives.

Outside of human society, distinctively human capacities, such as the capacity for rational deliberation, love, and friendship, are not given a chance to develop. Thus, effective or functional participation in the life of social groups is a necessity, not a luxury, for human beings. In order to participate competently or rationally in the life of a social group, one needs to adapt one's attitudes and behavior to the goods and purposes around which the group is organized, the goods and purposes that render the group's activities and projects intelligible.

This process of adaptation is made possible by participation in social practices guided by shared expectations and rules that are either declared or manifested in the life of the group. These shared expectations and rules may be thought of as a set of *public signals* or signposts—not just rules, but customs, shared narratives, and role models as well—that give a sense of meaning and purpose to associational life and transmit to group members a pattern of behavior, attitudes, intentions, and dispositions that is appropriate, desirable, obligatory, inappropriate, undesirable, or prohibited. A cluster of interrelated and more or less coherent signals of this sort, salient within a particular social group, is what I shall call a "normative order." A normative order is the indispensable cultural and institutional infrastructure without which orderly and intelligent participation in the life of *any* human community—whether a society of saints or a band of thieves—would be impossible.[12]

Normative orders, be they institutional structures, customs, collective narratives, or social norms, feed the moral imagination and shape the suite of opportunities, practical possibilities, and eligible strategies that confront the members of a social group. Nonetheless, they need not be understood as deterministic or inherently opposed to personal freedom. It ultimately falls to each new individual, and each new generation, to make what they will of their institutional and cultural inheritance. As Barden and Murphy (2010, 21–22) point out, customs gain their authority precisely from being affirmed, time and again, by the choices of individuals to treat a certain pattern of behavior as normative, desirable, or reasonable—and the same could surely be said of institutional norms.

4. WHY INSTITUTIONAL AND NORMATIVE DIVERSITY IS NECESSARY FOR HUMAN FLOURISHING

Given that not all communities and social groups pursue identical goals, we can reasonably assume that rational cooperation in a large and complex social space, e.g., the population of a national territory, will require a plurality of normative orders (including rules, customs, and methods of governance), corresponding to a plurality of goods and purposes. To live a complete or well-rounded human life, one must normally participate in *more than one* association, precisely because each human association is capable of advancing a particular, limited dimension of human flourishing, not human flourishing in its totality. The goods served by a monastic settlement are not the same as the goods served by a university, and the goods of a university are not the same as the goods of a city, technical school, church, athletic club, trade association, philanthropic society, volunteering community, dance club, and so forth.

Of special importance for my argument, the differences between these diverse normative orders cannot be somehow neatly reconciled within a single, perfectly coherent normative order. The range of goods pursued across different associations cannot be adequately pursued without the institutional and cultural infrastructure of plural, and sometimes conflicting, normative orders—diverse community narratives, diverse missions, diverse social norms and expectations, diverse ideals of character and human excellence. That is to say, the human good is too complex and multidimensional to be tracked exclusively by the normative order of a single community or association. That would overestimate the cognitive capacities of rulers and underestimate the degree to which different associations pursue incommensurable purposes. I do not believe there has ever been a historical moment in which a uniform, society-wide scheme of law or normativity has been able to perfectly harmonize with the reasonable missions, values, and prerogatives of all human associations regulated by it. There is a certain level of interpretive contestability and rationally irresolvable "stalemate" latent in any wide-ranging coordination scheme in a large, diverse society.[13] For these reasons, a single, overarching normative scheme *cannot systematically displace, absorb, or reconcile* local normative orders without doing serious damage to their distinctive goods and purposes.

This does not mean that associations governed by diverse normative orders cannot communicate or coordinate joint activities, nor does it mean that diverse normative orders must be tolerated unconditionally, without reference to wider norms and purposes. Nor does it mean that rule of law is impossible, or that we are destined to be endlessly at war with our neighbors. It does mean, however, that the standard modern conception of rule of law, enforced by a single, irresistible, dominating actor, needs to be replaced by a more restrained and polycentric conception of rule of law as emergent and socially contested (even if certain minimum standards are agreed), under the joint supervision of a plurality of social stakeholders, judicial systems, and enforcement agencies.

5. THE COLONIZING TENDENCIES OF THE SOVEREIGN STATE

It is impossible in the context of the present chapter to show, in a definitive way, that the sovereign State is inconsistent with the complex social ecology of human flourishing.[14] Nevertheless, I will offer some important reasons to be pessimistic about the capacity of a State that conceives itself as sovereign over the social order, to accommodate a plurality of independent normative orders servicing distinct dimensions of the human good. The normative order of the modern State, particularly in its more consolidated or centralized forms, has three features that lead it to colonize rival normative orders in such a way as to undermine their integrity: First, it is a normative order deeply influenced by the rather top-down, mono-centric social ontology of certain influential strands of modern liberalism, according to which individuals are viewed primarily as independent rights-bearers and citizens of a *State-based association*, and only secondarily as individuals with allegiances to non-State groups; second, it claims for itself a supreme or unrivaled form of authority over the social sphere, which enjoys substantial social recognition (legislators, judges, and state officials typically view non-state associations as fully integrated within the normative order of the State, and only valid insofar as they conform fully to that normative order); and third, it exercises its supreme authority not merely with moral persuasion or market incentives, but with the support of *non-voluntary taxes* on income and resources, and *coercive sanctions* for non-compliance with its decisions.

Due to the complexity and heterogeneity of the social order, many fiscal and regulatory interventions of the sovereign State, however well-intentioned, are liable to damage non-State associations' capacity to promote the goods they seek to pursue, in at least four ways:[15] First, the rules imposed by the sovereign State may interfere with the rules, norms, and customs an association recognizes as germane to its mission. Second, the rules imposed by the sovereign State may have a chilling effect on the birth of new associations, many of which may fail to institute their preferred normative orders simply because they anticipate that the normative order they wish to institute will very likely be suppressed, inhibited, or overridden by that of the State. Third, the taxing powers of the State enable it to coercively siphon a substantial quantity of material resources and income away from citizens and groups toward its own favored projects, leaving many associations with a heavily reduced capacity to raise funds among their members, with a view to financing their own distinctive projects. Fourth, the coercive taxing powers of the State provide it with a powerful tool to impose its own normative order unilaterally, by introducing regulatory preconditions for the public financing of projects. In this instance, the rules of the State are not "imposed," strictly speaking, but insofar as compliance carries a large payoff funded by tax contributions and/or public debt, and insofar as the State may easily outbid many other financiers, associations have a very powerful incentive to adopt the regulations of the State.[16]

It should be noted here that I am not suggesting that *any* attempt by an independently constituted authority to limit social pluralism or regulate associational life is to be ruled out a priori. A society free from regulation would involve a large amount of oppression and injustice both within and across associations. Rather, my point is that the logic of *sovereign rule*, widely associated with the modern State, puts small- and medium-sized associations at an enormous disadvantage, both ideologically and institutionally, vis-à-vis the sovereign regulator. Modern doctrines of political sovereignty (which crucially conceive the State as possessing a form of authority over the social landscape that is general-purpose, supreme, exclusionary, and coercive) provide an ideological pretext for heavy-handed interventions by the State in the life of associations that exist within its territory, rather than encouraging the sort of caution and deference that is frequently exercised toward foreign authorities.

6. THE ETHICS OF COOPERATION: A VOLUNTARIST AND BOTTOM-UP APPROACH

So far, I have argued that social and institutional complexity of a certain sort—namely, the co-presence of a plurality of associations guided by diverse normative orders not replaceable by a single "uber" order—is a necessary feature of a society that affords its members meaningful opportunities to live free and flourishing lives. In addition, I have argued that the modern State, insofar as it exerts a general-purpose and supreme regulatory authority over the social order at large, is likely to progressively erode social complexity by colonizing rival normative orders with its own. But if we are to construct a civil order that is friendlier than the sovereign State to the social ecology of flourishing, then we need to start by going back to basics: *what sorts of values and principles should inform a cooperative scheme consistent with the freedom to flourish and its complex social infrastructure?* In the remainder of this chapter, I outline three fundamental values that might guide social cooperation and governance while accommodating the type of social and institutional complexity that could support flourishing persons and communities: (i) individual and corporate voluntarism; (ii) a preference for proximity of rulers to ruled; and (iii) bottom-up delegation and control of power and authority.

(i) Individual and Corporate Voluntarism

Freedom goes to the core of who we are as human beings, and it sets us apart from non-human animals, which act emotionally and instinctually, but not in accordance with reflexive, rationally informed deliberation and choices. One crucial aspect of healthy relationships is that they are conducted in such a manner that each party conserves their freedom to flourish at all times. That implies that the relationship is initiated, modified, and developed over time in ways that respect the free will and fundamental interests of each party, to the extent that this is practicable. A relationship marked by intimidation, domination, manipulation, or coercion by one party over another, or a relationship in which one party consistently derives the benefits of the relationship at the expense of the other, is ethically degrading inasmuch as it does not honor the freedom to flourish.

If we are committed to honoring the freedom to flourish, this has implications for how we view the requirements of healthy interpersonal relations: first, interpersonal dealings must be conducted on a maximally voluntarist basis; second, intergroup dealings must be conducted on a maximally voluntarist basis. The importance of voluntarism in interpersonal dealings is both intuitively obvious and widely treated by liberal and republican theorists alike (see, for example, Rawls 1993; Buchanan and Tullock 1999; and Pettit 2012). One of its important implications is that individuals should be free to *exit* associations that are not to their pleasing. Given the fundamental role of interpersonal freedom in a flourishing life, the right of exit, along with legal protection from injuries to life and limb and tangible threats to the life and safety of third parties, mark clear limits to freedom of association.[17]

The importance of voluntarism in *inter-group* dealings, on the other hand, seems to be less well understood. The individual necessarily finds meaning and purpose in the context of group life. Representatives of groups are authorized to represent and serve their members' identity, interests, and needs. That function can only be performed adequately if inter-group dealings respect the consent of groups and their representatives. Where mutuality and consent in inter-group dealings are jettisoned, or the public standing and claims of a group in its corporate capacity are treated with disdain, representatives or trustees of groups lose any effective power to advocate for or defend the vital interests of the group and its membership. A group's representatives may be respected internally, within the group, but if they are disregarded or ignored outside the group, the group loses its capacity to defend its interests in relation to the wider society.

Voluntarism should not be understood as a value to be unconditionally maximized, but a value to be cultivated and protected, in conjunction with other important social norms, such as rule of law, bodily integrity, and freedom of contract. Voluntarism in interpersonal and inter-group dealings is not an absolute value—clearly, there are circumstances in which the will of individuals and groups should be controlled or limited; and there are respects in which social life inevitably conditions individual and corporate freedom, whether we like it or not. Nevertheless, there is a big difference between a society that aims to cultivate voluntarism, and one that is either indifferent to, or hostile to, such an ideal.

(ii) A Preference for Proximity of Rulers to Ruled

In order to facilitate social cooperation, certain individuals and groups of persons are invested with governmental and rule-making authority. The institutionalization of governmental and rule-making functions may occur in the coordination of more or less specialized domains of human activity, say a chess club, gym, university, school, business, or agricultural cooperative; or it may occur in the coordination of broader domains of activity, such as the regulation of taxes and public finances for a city or region. Either way, anyone involved in the design or reform of governing institutions ought to be guided by a preference for the proximity of rulers and ruling institutions to the groups and activities over which they hold sway. Stated somewhat differently, governance should, to the extent practicable, be conducted on a human scale, *close up* to the activities and persons being governed.

The preference for proximity, which expresses one important aspect of the principle of subsidiarity,[18] may be expressed more precisely by the following principles of institutional design and policymaking: first, *epistemic and cultural* proximity: either rulers themselves or their trusted advisors and administrators should, where practicable, be sufficiently familiar with the domain of life they are governing, and sufficiently familiar with the language, priorities, culture, and needs of stakeholders, that they can make *well-informed decisions* and tend to the association's normative order without subsuming it violently under an alien order. Second, *affective* proximity: rulers should, whenever possible, have something *personally at stake* in the adequacy of their decisions and the success of the activity they are governing. For example, the leader of a small business, because of his affective bond with the project and his colleagues, cares about making decisions that lead his business to thrive, not fail.

Third, *spatial* proximity: rulers should ideally either reside in or frequent social and geographic spaces in which the activities they govern unfold. This enables their stakeholders to interact with them without excessive difficulty, hold them accountable, share information with them, and gradually build up bonds of trust and goodwill with them. Epistemic, affective, and spatial proximity of rulers and ruling institutions to the activities and persons they are ruling over entails an additional principle of institutional design, namely, the principle of *limited scale of units of governance*: the size of independent governmental units should, whenever possible, be small enough to permit frequent social interaction and familiarity between rulers and those subject to their rule.[19]

(iii) Bottom-Up Delegation and Control of Power and Authority

In order for a complex, geographically extended political community to be governed in ways that are adequately adapted to the evolving and heterogeneous needs of its plural constituents and stakeholders, it must have an articulated, multilayered structure that incorporates a mix of local and general units of governance, some territorial and others non-territorial in character. The challenge posed by governance under conditions of social complexity is to delegate governance functions upward to inter-associational bodies without giving up on the advantages of ruler proximity discussed in the previous section. There is no way to guarantee ruler proximity in all important social decisions. However, if we aim to make the delegation and control of power and authority occur, to the extent practicable, from the bottom up rather than from the top down, we may be able to mitigate some of the harms of remote governance and preserve an important role for local organs of governance as shapers of social order.

It is reasonable for associations to submit certain dimensions of their life to external regulation. But how should this delegation of power be controlled? The natural presumption, once we grant the importance of associational integrity and autonomy, is that matters that predominantly touch the life of the group should be handled by its own internal decision-making and governmental procedures. One of the decisions that is likely to have a very substantial impact on the life of the group is the decision to delegate some aspects of its internal governance to an external governmental organ. It seems fair to assume that the persons best placed to decide whether such a decision is appropriate and beneficial for the group is the group itself and its membership, rather than any third party.

Of course, distinguishing between matters that are properly internal to an association, and matters that are not, is not an entirely straightforward task; nor is it an easy task to determine how a group may exert control over powers that have been conditionally transferred to an external government. Similarly, it is not always easy to determine when the preference for bottom-up delegation and control of power is trumped by some other overriding consideration, especially gray areas that do not reach the gravity of flagrant human rights violations or egregious criminality. Nonetheless, I hope these remarks will suffice to communicate in its essentials the preference for bottom-up delegation and control of power and authority, and its normative basis. This bottom-up vision of cooperation is not consistent with the presence of a sovereign actor that can exert its authority unilaterally over the whole social fabric, while it is suggestive of an intensely federated scheme of governance, in which public authority and power are robustly dispersed across a wide plurality of territorial and non-territorial actors.[20]

The main purpose of this chapter has been to make the case, from a strictly ethical standpoint, for the desirability and indeed indispensability of a complex and differentiated social order, to advance some reasons for pessimism concerning the capacity of more or less centralized sovereign States to accommodate such complexity, and to gesture toward some elementary principles of a pluralist, bottom-up ideal of social cooperation more friendly to the complex and differentiated social ecology of human flourishing. This is not the place to lay out an account of civil order that satisfies the requirements of the freedom to flourish. But I hope the ethical and anthropological case I have made for affording a high degree of autonomy to local associations can further illuminate and justify the shared commitment to social and institutional diversity of neo-Aristotelian virtue theorists, English pluralists and their successors, political economists, and constitutional pluralists, as well as providing some useful ethical orientation to those who must rise to the challenge of governing, or theorizing governance, under conditions of social complexity.

NOTES

1. I would like to extend a special thanks to my wife, Olivia Serrano, and numerous colleagues for feedback and conversations that helped me work through the ideas I build on in this chapter, in particular Mark Hoipkemier, Julian Müller, Paul Aligica, Mark Pennington, Michael Zuckert, Kelvin Knight, Maria Cahill, Pilar Zambrano, Elliot Bulmer, Montserrat Herrero, Alfredo Cruz, Juan Pablo Domínguez, and Pablo Paniagua. Last but not least, I am grateful for the financial support of Fundación Ciudadanía y Valores Proeduca Summa S.L

* Research Fellow, Institute for Culture and Society, University of Navarra, Spain.

2. A selection of works from this pluralistically inclined literature will be referenced in section 1, "Prevailing Arguments for the Value and/or Necessity of Social and Institutional Complexity."

3. For a fuller statement of the implications of this re-valorization of complexity for the structure of political and social institutions, see Thunder (2024).

4. This is reminiscent of Berlin's insistence (1990/1969) that the full panoply of human goods and values cannot all be fully reconciled or harmonized within a single way of life.

5. There is no uniquely valid definition of human flourishing. It is a basic concept that may be understood as interchangeable with full human development, or the full unfolding of human potential. I will discuss some of its key ingredients shortly.

6. By "rationally informed" choice, I mean one that is responsive to rational considerations such as the pros and cons, costs and benefits, goods and bads of choosing A or B. A choice completely blind to rationality does not enable an agent's full and rounded development. What counts as a rationally informed versus uninformed choice will often be socially contested, but there are plenty of cases upon which there is broad social agreement.

7. An objectively valuable human end is one that is valuable not merely because the agent opts for it, but because it embodies some mind-independent dimension of human flourishing. That the content of objectively valuable ends may be socially contested does not mean they do not exist or cannot be correctly ascertained by a wise actor.

8. Even if one opts to live spontaneously or one decides to follow the path marked out by the traditions of one's elders, one is implicitly accepting that this is, all things considered, a good or fruitful way to live.

9. Mill (1991/1859) (partly inspired by Alexander von Humboldt) has a view of human flourishing that is similar inasmuch as it entails the full unfolding of human potential.

10. Much more could be said about the socially embedded character of human flourishing. But I defer this discussion to a consideration, in the next section of the

chapter, of normative orders as action-guiding frameworks inscribed into the social order.

11. I believe our moral experiences and discourses presuppose that the human good is, in important respects, not determined exclusively by subjective perceptions, but also discovered and participated in. But I cannot unpack this argument in detail here.

12. The notion of a normative order is relatively open-ended, in the sense that while all normative orders are structured by common purposes, some normative orders may be evil or destructive, and others may only embody a very partial or highly selective dimension of human excellence.

13. For a much more detailed case against "neat," all-encompassing social orders capable of tidying up inter-group conflict with solutions that are fully rationally justified, cf. Levy 2015 and Muñiz-Fraticelli 2014. The inevitability of inter-group conflict has much to do with the fact, pointed out by Isaiah Berlin, that diverse human goods can be in tension with each other or make conflicting moral and political demands.

14. But for one important contribution to this argument, see Scott (1999).

15. Here, I am concerned exclusively with the homogenizing effects of the rule of a sovereign State. The homogenizing effects of modern capitalist economies are significant, but they exceed the remit of my argument.

16. Of course, market forces are highly relevant too. But market actors do not have the advantage of a socially accepted right to collect involuntary taxes and coerce citizens into compliance with their policies.

17. For a more detailed discussion of the right of exit and some of its potential difficulties, see Kukathas 2003, chap. 3, "Freedom of Association and Liberty of Conscience." I do not share Kukathas's broader theory of freedom, which has a strong anti-perfectionist thrust (the "freedom to flourish" does not figure in his theory), but he offers a useful discussion of the right of exit.

18. I am indebted to Maria Cahill for this notion of a "preference for proximity." See Cahill 2021.

19. For one practical application of this principle, see V. Ostrom, Tiebout, and Warren 1961.

20. A detailed discussion of federalism would take me beyond the remit of this essay. But for two useful treatments, see Elazar 1987 and V. Ostrom 1991.

REFERENCES

Althusius, Johannes. 1995. *Politica: An Abridged Translation of Politics Methodically Set Forth and Illustrated with Sacred and Profane Examples*, Translated by S. Carney Frederick. Indianapolis: Liberty Fund, 1614.

Barden, Garrett, and Tim Murphy. 2010. *Law and Justice in Community*. Oxford: Oxford University Press.

Berlin, Isaiah. 1990. *Four Essays on Liberty*. Oxford: Oxford University Press, 1969.

Buchanan, James M., and Gordon Tullock. 1999. *The Calculus of Consent: Logical Foundations of Constitutional Democracy*, edited by Charles K Rowley. Vol. 2: The Selected Works of Gordon Tullock. Indianapolis: Liberty Fund, 1962.

Cahill, Maria. 2021. "Subsidiarity as the Preference for Proximity." *American Journal of Jurisprudence* 66 (1): 129–43.

Christiano, Thomas. 2008. *The Constitution of Equality: Democratic Authority and Its Limits*. Oxford: Oxford University Press.

Cole, G. D. H. 2015. *Social Theory*. Leopold Classic Library, 1920.

Elazar, Daniel J. 1987. *Exploring Federalism*. Tuscaloosa, AL: University of Alabama Press.

Figgis, John N. 2013. *Churches in the Modern State*. HardPress Publishing, 1913.

Galston, William. 2002. *Liberal Pluralism: The Implications of Value Pluralism for Political Theory and Practice.Cambridge University Press*:

Gaus, Gerald. 2021. *The Open Society and Its Complexities*. New York: Oxford University Press.

Gierke, Otto von. 2014. *Political Theories of the Middle Age*, translated by F. W. Maitland. Martino Fine Books, 1881.

Hayek, Friedrich A. von. 1967. "The Theory of Complex Phenomena." In *Studies in Philosophy, Politics and Economics*. London: Routledge & Kegan Paul.

Jacobs, Jane. 1992. *The Death and Life of Great American Cities*. New York: Vintage Books Editions, 1961.

Kelsen, Hans. 2002. *Introduction to the Problems of Legal Theory*, translated by B. L. Paulson and S. L. Paulson. Oxford: Clarendon Press, 1934.

Kukathas, Chandran. 2003. *The Liberal Archipelago: A Theory of Diversity and Freedom*. Oxford: Oxford University Press.

Kymlicka, Will. 1995. *Multicultural Citizenship: A Liberal Theory of Minority Rights*. Oxford: Oxford University Press.

Laski, Harold J. 2008. *The State in Theory and Practice*, edited by A. Pearson Sidney Jr. Transaction Publishers, 1935.

Levy, Jacob T. 2015. *Rationalism, Pluralism, and Freedom*. Oxford: Oxford University Press.

MacIntyre, Alasdair. 1981. *After Virtue: A Study in Moral Theory*. London: Duckworth.

———. 1999. *Dependent Rational Animals: Why Human Beings Need the Virtues*. The Paul Carus Lecture Series. Chicago: Open Court.

Mill, John Stuart. 1991. "On Liberty." In *On Liberty and Other Essays*, edited by John Gray, 5–128. Oxford and New York: Oxford University Press, 1859.

Mitchell, Melanie. 2011. *Complexity: A Guided Tour*. Oxford: Oxford University Press.

Muñiz-Fraticelli, Victor M. 2014. *The Structure of Pluralism*. Oxford: Oxford University Press.

Nozick, Robert. 1974. *Anarchy, State, and Utopia*. New York: Basic Books.

Nussbaum, Martha C. 2011. *Creating Capabilities: The Human Development Approach*.

Ostrom, Elinor. 2015. *Governing the Commons*. Cambridge: Cambridge University Press, 1990.

Ostrom, Vincent. 1991. *The Meaning of American Federalism: Constituting a Self-Governing Society*. San Francisco: ICS Press.

Ostrom, Vincent, Charles M. Tiebout, and Robert Warren. 1961. "The Organization of Government in Metropolitan Areas: A Theoretical Inquiry." *American Political Science Review* 55 (04): 831–42.

Paniagua, Pablo. 2023. "Complexity Defying Macroeconomics." *Cambridge Journal of Economics* 47 (3): 575–92.

Pettit, Philip. 2012. *On the People's Terms: A Republican Theory and Model of Democracy*. Cambridge: Cambridge University Press.

Rawls, John. 1971. *A Theory of Justice*. Oxford: Oxford University Press.

———. 1993. *Political Liberalism*. The John Dewey Essays in Philosophy. New York: Columbia University Press.

Raz, Joseph. 1986. *The Morality of Freedom*. Oxford: Clarendon Press.

Schmitt, Carl. 2007. *The Concept of the Political*, translated by George Schwab. Chicago: University of Chicago Press, 1932.

Scott, James C. 1999. *Seeing Like a State: How Certain Schemes to Improve the Human Condition Have Failed*. New Haven, CT: Yale University Press.

Sen, Amartya. 1999. *Commodities and Capabilities*. Oxford: Oxford University Press.

Thunder, David. 2024. *The Polycentric Republic: A Theory of Civil Order for Free and Diverse Societies*. New York: Routledge. Forthcoming in 2024.

Tully, James. 1995. *Strange Multiplicity: Constitutionalism in an Age of Diversity*. Cambridge: Cambridge University Press.

Waldron, Jeremy. 1991. "Homelessness and the Issue of Freedom." *UCLA Law Review* 39: 295–24.

Weber, Max. 1964. *The Theory of Social and Economic Organization*, translated by A. M. Henderson and Talcott Parsons, edited by Morton Schoolman and David Campbell. New York: Free Press.

Chapter 2

Is an Architectonic Pluralism Possible?

Mark Hoipkemier

Many pluralists would abjure the pursuit of a dominant single political end or goal, the better to secure freedom for individuals and groups to pursue their own goals.[1] But classical proponents of the common good argue that it is precisely such a supreme goal that defines the best regime (and possibly any regime). Although these two camps disagree about whether it is desirable to pursue an architectonic common good in politics, they agree that doing so would be incompatible with political pluralism. It is this point of agreement that I wish to contest, for it rests on a flawed view of the Common Good as monolithic and all-consuming, a view that misunderstands the basic logic of common action. A more supple account of the common good does not oblige us to choose between a politics of plural communities and an architectonic common good. In any case, the effort to eschew an architectonic common good is misplaced, since, as I shall argue, politics inevitably enacts some morally formative vision of life as a whole. If I am right on this point, then the only viable pluralism is a common good pluralism.

Admittedly, the notion of "common good pluralism" has something paradoxical about it. "Common good" suggests that all concerned parties share (and possibly enforce) some single normative vision, while "pluralism" suggests just the opposite. The tension grows more acute if we suppose, as I think we should, that a political common project inescapably shapes the whole range of human affairs. Yet this tension is not an all-or-nothing choice between sharing everything and sharing nothing. Different moral goals are "made common" by different groups. The common good of any community is its flourishing as whatever kind of community it is—family, firm, church, school, polity, etc. The goal of politics is only one common good among others or, more precisely put, *over* others—thanks to its unique role in shaping and coordinating them. The project shared by citizens *qua* citizens always embodies some vision of the good life in broad outline, but their common interests do not plausibly extend to every last detail of personal and associational goods.[2] The challenge is to articulate a balanced conception that relates autonomous, locally shared goods to the world-shaping project of citizens.

This chapter will first explain the meaning of "architectonic" politics and explain why even convinced pluralists should engage constructively with this idea: in a word, because it is unavoidable. I will then critique the dominant interpretation of the common good as "all-encompassing," which is both flawed in its own right and unfaithful to Aquinas and Aristotle. Finally, I will propose an alternative account, drawing on neo-Aristotelian thought, of citizens' common project as a morally thick but non-comprehensive public order. On this view, political order always embodies some overall vision of the human good, but this shared vision will not permeate all domains to the same degree, for it corresponds to legitimate public involvement in each domain. The autonomy and integrity of locally realized common goods are rightly subject to political scrutiny only insofar as their role in this larger order comes into question. The approach that I term *Aristotelian pluralism* arises from the dual affirmation of freedom for groups to pursue their own common projects, and also the overarching directive influence that politics cannot help but exert. The resulting limited-but-architectonic order precludes a regime of total virtue as much as it does a society free from the encroachment of politics and its goals. These moderated aspirations are a reasonable price to pay for an approach to the common good that is morally serious, practicable, and pluralist.

1. AN "ARCHITECTONIC" PLURALISM: WHAT AND WHY

This chapter is concerned with only one of the various concepts of pluralism abroad today. I will focus on "governance pluralism," which affirms the legitimate autonomy and value of polycentric, non-State authorities, as against a monism of the sovereign State.[3] I will not engage directly with the meta-ethical "value pluralism" of Isaiah Berlin, who emphasized the "many different ends that men may seek and still be fully rational, fully men" (Berlin 2013, 11). Thinkers in the Aristotelian tradition have often denied both sorts, grounding State supremacy on a unified, objective order of values. But governance pluralism does not presuppose any position on value pluralism, either pro or con. A better reason for us to entertain the apparent paradox of a common-good polycentrism follows from the inevitably architectonic role of political institutions.

What does it mean to say that politics, or its normative goal of the Common Good, is "architectonic"? Aristotle is the fountainhead of such language, and I will take my cue from his basic usage. At the beginning of the *Nicomachean Ethics*, Aristotle notes that in various domains of life, there is a hierarchy of practices, in which subordinate pursuits are controlled by and oriented to an "architectonic" (*architectonike*) (Aristotle 1985, NE 1094a15) master practice and its goals. The term obviously calls to mind buildings and construction, in which the master builder oversees other workers, but Aristotle's own example is that saddle makers and cavalrymen are subordinate to the army's general and the goal of military victory. He then observes that political science seems to be the most "architectonic" of all, because it rules over all other master practices (Aristotle 1985, NE 1094a30). How so? Politics can permit or outlaw them; it makes use of their results for its own ends; it takes priority in cases of conflict; and so on. Inasmuch as politics sits atop all human pursuits—all the parts of a whole life—Aristotle concludes that the ultimate aim of this most architectonic of practices is the good life overall, and even "the good for man."

To fix terms, I will say that politics has an architectonic aspect to the extent that it exhibits two core features:

a. *Breadth*: it embodies or enacts some relatively complete vision of the good life as a whole, somewhat as an architect designs a whole building.
b. *Dominance*: it directs or orders persons and practices toward this broad end, somewhat as an architect directs other workers.

By design, these definitions contain some vague and troublesome terms, which I will not try to specify at this preliminary stage. What level of detail is implied by "relatively complete"? How much control goes into "directs or orders"? Within the family of architectonic doctrines, there are different possible answers to such questions, which are not equally consistent with polycentrism. I should note that my own answers may depart from Aristotle's, as some scholars read him as favoring an all-encompassing hierarchy overseen by a single agent (Lane 2020), whereas I interpret an architectonic order as a more limited, directive political order in which power and knowledge are fragmented.

One large goal of this chapter is to show the proponents of an architectonic common good why they should embrace an interpretation of their ideal that is consistent with pluralism. "Architectonic" is not equivalent to "all-encompassing": the architect does not build the whole house, even if she controls the overall design and oversees other workers to some degree. She is in charge of the ruling pattern, but it is the craftsmen who work out the details, each in their own sphere. Somewhat as a competent architect cannot *not* have an overall plan, the political order cannot help but embody some society-spanning ideals such as freedom or virtue, but these may entail more or (preferably) less involvement in the towns, workplaces, schools, or families where the principles are lived out.

I should also like to address convinced social and political pluralists, some of whom may believe they are better off prescinding from any notion of architectonic politics. After all, the pluralists' case appears simpler if we set this classical notion aside, instead construing politics in terms of, say, rules for limited areas of human conduct. But suppose it is the case that, as Alasdair MacIntyre puts it, "every political and social order embodies and gives expression to an ordering of different human goods and therefore also . . . to some particular conception of the human good" (MacIntyre 1998, 247). For many proponents of classical views, that politics is architectonic is not a moral desideratum, but an unavoidable fact. The basic idea is that all functioning polities will find themselves, willy-nilly, enacting some "relatively complete" vision of human life and the good society. If this is true, then even the most die-hard pluralist should accept the broad-scope claims of "architectonic politics" for the sake of seeing the world as it really is.

Could it be true that politics is inescapably architectonic? Aristotle arrives at this view in an empirical manner. He first surveys the polities of the Greek-speaking world and finds that what people call "cities" or "States" are only those organized groups that address a full range of human activities: not only mutual defense and rules of just conduct, but also patriotism and living together in "affection," communal practices of marriage and religion, and a shared concern for moral character. He concludes that a really existing city is a community of free citizens that is self-sufficient in respect to living well. On this view, political interest in a "complete" human life is not first a philosophical abstraction or an ethical recommendation; it is what actual cities actually share.

The obvious rejoinder to Aristotle's inductive line of reasoning is that cities or States are not necessarily like that. Have not liberal polities abandoned the all-encompassing search for flourishing in favor of freedom and limited government? Modern debate about the political common good concerns the legitimate scope of law and political action at least as much as their normative content. It seems perfectly plausible—or even obviously right—to say that political communities do and should narrow the scope of their coercive or directive action to less than the whole of human affairs. Yet it is hardly fair to criticize Aristotle's empirically minded argument by appealing to normative ideals rather than data. What matters most is not abstract theory, but the principles that are embodied in actual political institutions and practices. Here are three factors speaking to the relevance of the always-architectonic view:

1. *The size of modern government.* Putatively "limited" States apply more resources to more issue domains than even the most feverishly totalitarian ancient theorist could have imagined: health insurance, welfare, energy, science, transportation, climate, space travel, housing, and so on indefinitely.
2. *Questions of distribution.* Many ordinary political decisions cannot be made without presuming some broad idea of what it is best for humans to do and to be. Who deserves tax breaks or burdens, legal impediments or cultural prestige? The answers to such garden-variety distributive questions always refer, at least implicitly, to the relative value of citizens and the proper goals of their shared project.
3. *The reach of the law.* The law in its many guises has something to say about virtually every domain of human life, from religion to work to leisure, from birth to child rearing to death. Underwriting the legal freedom of citizens in a given domain is itself a form of value judgment.

Michael Ignatieff puts the overall point this way: "for all the apparent relativism of liberal society—our interminable debate about what the good in politics consists in—in practice a shared good is administered in our name by the welfare bureaucracies of the modern State" (Ignatieff 1985, 136). Whatever rank ordering is publicly established *de facto*, whether by custom or overt political action, will imply or presuppose some vision of the good life, in effect where not by design, in broad outline where not in detail. If so, it would be best not to ignore the fact.

I will not even pretend to have convinced those pluralists who are deeply skeptical of the rightful "completeness" of political community. Yet even the classical liberal who denies that political practice *should* be architectonic can admit that many States *are so,* in fact, to a great degree. At least as a tactical matter, then, polycentrists of all stripes could benefit from taking architectonic politics seriously even if they aspire to make the idea less applicable to the real world. The realities to which the always architectonic position refers are very much with us in ordinary political practice, and cannot be easily wished away. But they are not necessarily inimical to pluralism—or so I shall argue.

2. THE PROBLEM OF THE ALL-ENCOMPASSING COMMON GOOD

There are different ways to construe "architectonic" politics, and in this section I will explain and critique today's most prominent interpretation. We may call this the "all-encompassing" or "inclusivist" account of the common good. On this view, which predominates among Roman Catholics, the Common Good without qualifiers names the supreme goal of law and politics, perhaps indeed of all moral action. As the motto of a Catholic business school has it, "All for the common good." In the words of Pope Leo XII, "after God, [the common good] is the first and last law in society . . . " (Pope Leo XIII 1892, sec. 19). This ideal can occupy a place of incontestable supremacy because it maximally subsumes every other rival good or moral standard—the goods of individuals and groups, the goods of economics or culture, and so forth. The full realization of this comprehensive good would entail that every person and every aspect of society (or the globe, even the universe) be completely excellent or flourishing to the fullest extent. As a Catholic magisterial document puts it, the common good in this maximal sense is "the good of all people and of the whole person" (Vatican 2006, 265). There is an eschatological dimension to this lofty goal, but here below it can serve as a regulative ideal buttressing the supremacy and authority of politics and law.

Plainly, the all-encompassing account of the common good is not meant to settle vexed political questions, but rather to provide a shared standard beyond critique, which all reasonable persons can, or indeed already do, affirm. The politics of this common good would be maximally "architectonic," in the sense outlined above, inasmuch as it would pursue an unqualifiedly complete vision of the good life that directs or orients society in the large as well as sub-political groups and individual persons. These enormous aspirations render the all-encompassing account untenable.

2.1 Three Axioms and an Objection

To see why, we must first say a bit more clearly what the all-encompassing common good really requires or implies, beyond majestic supremacy. Consider three relatively uncontroversial (among Aristotelians) axioms concerning the logic of common goods, which I draw from prominent Thomists with no special pluralist leanings:

> *Axiom 1) A good or goal is "common" to various persons insofar as it is an object of their common action/striving/attention. Every common good is the good of some identifiable community and its members (*Utz 1958).[4]

Illustration: "Promoting great art" may be a generally valuable thing, but it will not be a common good except insofar as persons are acting together so as to further or achieve that goal, e.g., by creating an art museum.

*Axiom 2) The common good of a given community is its overall excellence as a specific form of common action, defined by its characteristic shared work and the goals of its members qua members (*De Koninck 1943).[5]

Illustration: The common good for the museum *qua* community is primarily to be an excellent art museum (by promoting and preserving fine art). One would not fault it for failing to solve broad social problems such as prejudice or poverty, which it has neither the ability nor the duty to do.

*Axiom 3) A community enjoys rightful authority over the shared actions and relationships that are constitutive of its common good (*Simon 1962).[6]

Illustration: The art museum rightfully sets its own employee policies and curates its own exhibitions, but it has no say over the home lives of its workers nor the personal projects of its artists.

With these axioms in mind, we can say more precisely what the all-inclusive account of the common good amounts to. Axiom 1 implies that comprehensive human flourishing is the characteristic shared goal of the political community, i.e., of citizens *qua* citizens. Axiom 2 implies that citizens can and should realize this goal by their common action as members of the political community. Axiom 3 implies that the political community has rightful authority, in some sense or other, over all the aspects of human life in their detail.

Pluralists would not be wrong to see little room here for self-governing groups to pursue their own goods in significant independence from political projects. To be fair, the all-encompassing view might be implemented in a very hands-off way, but in principle it implies an expansive scope for citizenship and government, along the lines of ancient Sparta. On this model, every ostensibly private concern—e.g., within a family, a school, or an individual's own life—is at root a political matter that could, if necessary, be rightfully made a focus of citizens' attention (and presumably intervention). And who would willingly sacrifice all private freedoms and actions to the privilege of collective self-rule?

2.2. Two Unsuccessful Refinements: Aggregation and Changing the Subject

Sensitive to the dangers of conceding everything to the State, defenders of the all-encompassing common good have refined the approach in two intriguing but ultimately unsuccessful ways. The first is to redefine the supreme common goal as partially an aggregate of non-political goods, which are not the concern of citizens to realize. This is a crucial step for the all-encompassing account, because citizens *qua* citizens do not and cannot share all the essential goods of a flourishing life as their characteristic shared goals. To act as a parent, or a child, or a friend, is not to act as a citizen. But how could the political common good claim to be unqualifiedly supreme, if it did not include or encompass these relational goods? On this "aggregative" interpretation, the common good includes "the non-social (and even social but non-political) goods of each and every member of the political community" (Murphy 2005, 152). In concrete terms, as Matthew Wright puts it, "the political common good must be in part the 'good of friendship' + 'good of family' + 'good of church' + 'good of civil associations'" (Wright 2019, 80).[7]

This leads to a second modification, which reframes the social setting of the all-embracing common good. Every common good is the good of some identifiable community, but that need not be the coercive, bureaucratic State. Even the friends of the modern State will agree that it is not well-suited to realizing an all-encompassing common good, and that it would likely abuse the power that such a goal would entail. Wright concurs with Jacques Maritain in shifting the locus of the all-encompassing common good toward "the political community." As Maritain puts it, "the political society is the whole. The State is a part—the topmost part. . . . which specializes in the interests of the whole" (Maritain 1951, 10, 12). The State is a legal-governmental entity that registers citizens and passes laws, while the political community is something much broader, which includes all the social or cultural elements of common life falling outside the legitimate sphere of government. This distinction of social subjects also permits a distinction of common goods: a limited, "specifically political" common good that is "interdefined with the responsibilities of state government and law" (Finnis 1998, sec. VI), as opposed to the Common Good in the supreme and all-encompassing sense, which is the full flourishing of the broader body politic and its members. As Wright puts it, "political community *qua* ultimate is not specifically political, and *qua* specifically political is not ultimate" (Wright 2019, 83).

In my judgment, these refinements do make the common good more practically attractive, but at the price of theoretical incoherence. The problem with the second proposal is that the "body politic" does not look like a single social unit, but rather like many complex overlapping communities. By what distinctive name would its members be called, and what would bring them together? If the supreme unity-maker is the State, then the distinctiveness of the body politic as a social entity unto itself, with its own characteristic activities and goals, vanishes. Other less-political rivals (e.g., "French culture," "Judeo-Christian values," etc.) do not seem sufficiently detailed, agreed-upon, and binding to hold together a social order apart from the instrumentalities of law and government. The second refinement, then, attempts to attribute a single, all-embracing common good without identifying some distinct social order of which it is the goal.

The first refinement, aggregation, directly contradicts the basic logic of common goods. For some good to be a *common* good at all, it should be the defining shared goal of some community, whose members have the right and the ability to realize that goal in acting together. But the very point of the aggregative account is that the political common good should be partially defined by goals that *cannot* be realized by citizens as such, but only by friends, family members, business colleagues, etc. "The common good of community X" is meant to serve the life and decisions of that community by delineating the goals that its members can and should achieve together. To define citizens' flourishing by goods they do not share and cannot realize together is to abandon the logical structure of the common good in favor of a vague and impractical moralizing.

2.3 Sketching an Explanation

Before outlining a more promising approach to architectonic politics, I pause to suggest an explanation for this problematic conflation of the whole human good with the political common good. Where might it originate? To my mind, this conflation runs together the distinct visions of the two eponymous giants of the Thomistic-Aristotelian tradition. Aristotle and Aquinas generally agree about the basic logic of the common good, but they differ over *what* the central case of that good is, and *who* shares it as a common goal (see Hoipkemier 2016). Treating their accounts as equivalent leads to the quandaries highlighted above.

Aristotle originated the claim that the political community is the crucial locus of the common good. Yet he did not equate the standard of the common good with human virtue or overall flourishing. Rather, for Aristotle the common good was a matter of political justice, of giving citizens their due as citizens. I have developed this interpretation at greater length elsewhere (Hoipkemier 2018), but here are two suggestive bits of evidence: 1) Aristotle never mentions the term *common good* in his treatment of happiness or the best regime; 2) his mixed regime of polity has a gravely deficient view of human flourishing, yet it is said to be "in the common good" without qualification.

Thomas Aquinas, on the other hand, clearly does regard "the common good" in the central sense as encompassing all human good, but he can plausibly define the term in this way only because he has a different community's good in mind. He is not primarily a theorist of human social order as such, but of divine order. For Aquinas, the paradigmatic common good is the flourishing of the whole cosmos as ruled by God's eternal law and oriented to the divine glory (Verpaalen 1954). This providential order coordinates all things without exception, and it can move individuals "from the inside," as it were, in a way that human institutions cannot. Granting his premises, the requirements and rewards of this cosmic "community" could very plausibly include every last human act, relation, and value. In this widest of all contexts, Aquinas can write without blushing that "when a man wills some particular good, his act of willing is upright only if it refers that good to the common good as its end" (Aquinas 1947 I–II 19.10). He is considerably more circumspect when he turns to human communities and their law: "man is not ordained to the body politic, according to all that he is and has" (Aquinas 1947 I–II 21.4, ad 3).

Whatever one may think of these accounts on the whole, it is clear that both of them accord well with the logic of the common good. Both theories posit a distinct kind of community that plausibly has both the rightful authority and the factual ability to realize its distinctive shared end through common action. The problem arises when one grafts the comprehensive scope of Aquinas's cosmic common good onto Aristotle's political setting. This conflation ascribes a goal to the political community that is clearly beyond its power or its rightful jurisdiction. No human membership could have either the capacity or the right to claim the fullness of human flourishing as its shared task or goal. Even if one considers entire civilizations rather than legally defined polities, one would still hesitate to say that the full flourishing of individuals or groups were an act of persons *qua* members of that society, still less of the society as such.

The lesson to be drawn, in my view, is that only a cosmic or theological community could count as that single form of common action oriented to the human good in its fullness. In this sense, one need not reject the classical idea that human flourishing as a whole is a common good, i.e., is the goal of some identifiable community that can claim unqualified moral supremacy. Conversely, this cosmic standard is *not* the appropriate goal for guiding and appraising the common action of citizens. What should citizens invoke instead, when they deliberate about their common good?

3. TOWARDS AN ARCHITECTONIC ORDER

My critique has exposed serious flaws in the "all-encompassing" vision of the common good, and in attempts to rehabilitate it. If politics is not morally unlimited, then it is limited in some way. Whatever its limited goals turn out to be, they are what citizens should look to when acting together. Having come so far, the pluralist's next step might be to restrict the moral remit of politics to, say, underwriting the law of freedom, or protecting natural rights, or to some other particular domain of value. In my view, such a sequel would throw out the baby with the bathwater, because it ignores the fact of architectonic politics, with which I opened this essay. All regimes embody a relatively complete vision of the human good, and our shared ideals ought to be comparable in scope to our shared actions. The challenge for Aristotelian pluralism is to fashion a positive account of the political common good that is both limited *and* architectonic. To show why this is not an oxymoron, I will first discuss the sense in which politics should be limited, and then sketch a broader "order model" of architectonic politics that makes room for governance pluralism.

3.1 Two Kinds of Limits

There is more than one way for politics to be morally limited. Natural law theorist John Finnis has claimed that the "specifically political" common good is limited in two important senses (Finnis 1998). Firstly, it is concerned only with the virtues of justice and peace, leaving the rest of the virtues to individuals or families. Secondly, politics and law demand only "external compliance," not the full interior realization of virtue. Notice that these are quite different kinds of limits, which we might liken to two different dimensions of a map: how much territory it encompasses versus how much detail it shows. When Finnis excludes essential virtues like moderation or piety from citizens' shared concern, he asserts a limit as to breadth/scope, like a map of only one province rather than a whole country. On the other hand, by restricting political demands to "external compliance," he asserts a limit as to depth or detail, like a map that shows only large cities or main roads. In combining the two types of limit, Finnis denies to politics both the overall plan of the good life and the virtuous actions at its heart. But why would anyone choose a map that lacks both scope *and* detail?

The notion that the public good is severely limited in breadth/scope is both implausible in itself and incompatible with an architectonic politics. Recall that any regime is architectonic to the extent that it orders persons or practices toward some "relatively complete" vision of the good life This need not imply a bureaucrat in every bedroom, but it does entail that the normative order of the regime affects most or all domains of life. An architectonic "political map" covers the whole territory of human concern, more or less. If Finnis could make good on the claim that citizens focus only on a limited set of virtues or pursuits, he would rule out any such broad vision. But the attempt is bound to fail.

In addition to the earlier empirical arguments about the reach of modern government, we may add the specifically Thomistic objections of Michael Pakaluk (2001). He points out that justice concerns all human relations and draws on the full complement of other virtues, so Finnis's restriction of politics to "justice and peace" does not meaningfully restrict its moral scope. Furthermore, the "complete" political community is involved in the very constitution of "incomplete" communities, such as families, schools, or firms. Assigning virtues to a subordinate community such as the family does not fully remove them from political influence; it only makes that influence less direct. When Tocqueville noted that Americans were democrats not only in government, but also in family, in industry, and in literature, he was observing the pervasive reach of ruling principles beyond the narrowly political. It is realism, not anachronism, to recognize that basic political laws and values shape and color the indefinitely numerous areas of life under the regime's oversight. Stephen Macedo, himself no Aristotelian, has rightly observed this fulsome breadth of influence under liberalism quite as much as in premodern regimes: "Basic liberal principles . . . wash across and seep into the whole of our lives, not determining all our choices but limiting them all and structuring and conditioning our lives as a whole" (Macedo 1990, 54).

On the other hand, the depth and detail of citizens' shared "political map" can vary considerably, and this variety is perfectly compatible with the "always-architectonic" thesis. In real-world politics, modes of favoring dominant principles range from detailed control (e.g., taxing and shaming cigarette smokers) to abstract rules of conduct (e.g., contract procedures) to untrammeled freedom of choice (e.g., over one's religion). Regimes like Sparta or Islamist States favor a centralized moralism, with a full set of enforceable prescriptions for life, no assembly required. But other regimes promote their broad vision through hands-off, decentralized governance, in the style of ancient Athens or modern liberal States. They define a broad order of authoritative values, then leave the details to persons on the scene. One can make sufficient room for pluralism by applying this second sort of normative limit, which leaves open most key political questions (aside from scope): *what* visions or values citizens endorse and *how* best to advance them together.

4. AN ORDER MODEL

Relying on limits as to normative depth or detail, I will sketch an alternative to the all-encompassing political common good, which I call an "order model." I find this perspective echoed, though not fully elaborated, in the work of influential neo-Aristotelians such as Yves Simon and Alasdair Macintyre.[8] The distinctive claim of their minority report is that citizens aim primarily at a just public order *among* communities and their goods, and not at the full flourishing of every component of society. Politics wields coercive and directive authority to rank, or more generally to order, the whole gamut of human goods, but many or most of these are not the business of citizens *qua* citizens to realize directly. As MacIntyre puts it, the common endeavor of any political community is "an ordering of goods, goods to be achieved by excellence within specific and systematic forms of activity, integrated into an overall rank-order by the political activity of those particular citizens." The internal ends of a business or a school are subject to political scrutiny (only) insofar as their role in the larger order is in question. What citizens rightly pursue is a civil tapestry that weaves many forms of solidarity with goods of their own into a larger pattern of justice and the good life. A model based on public order is surely not the only way to reconcile the architectonic and the pluralistic character of politics, but I think the account is both descriptively plausible and normatively attractive.

At the core of this model is the notion of politics as "a type of practice through which other practices are ordered" (MacIntyre 1998, 241). This phrase of MacIntyre's implies a multileveled hierarchy of practices, with politics at the top. By the term *practice*, he means "any coherent and complex form of socially established cooperative human activity" (MacIntyre 1981, 187) built around its own internally shared standards and common goods of excellence. The genres of practice (sports, liturgical prayer, automobile manufacturing, painting, etc.) are as various as their institutional settings (families, teams, clubs, firms, churches, etc.). Politics is like other practices in that it has its own proper principles, values, and skills (patriotism, canvassing for votes). The activities and standards of the various practices are relatively autonomous and self-contained, but not entirely. Politics is unlike all other practices, in that its goal is precisely to consider the worth and needs of other practices, and to forge an order between them. Sub-political practices depend on one another and on politics to supply what they lack—not only material resources, but also a legal setting, and a guiding framework of values. For example, an orchestra depends on a whole infrastructure of music appreciation and public support in dealing with external actors, and its own internal organization will draw on political ideas such as equality or anti-discrimination to settle questions left open by the demands of great music. This exposure to outside influence need not corrupt the orchestra or its central musical mission, nor render it an arm of the State. Indeed, appropriate support is essential for the orchestra to thrive as an autonomous but dependent association.

On the always-architectonic view, it is the distinctive task of politics to establish such order between these domains as will frame a complete way of life. Which persons or practices should enjoy more or less of what the public has to distribute, and at which points in the calendar or life course? In a crisis, which concerns are essential and which peripheral? What core values must all citizens enact in all their doings, and which are left to their free decision? In giving answers to such broad questions, public order will both mold and reposition virtually every domain of human concern. Consider the analogy of an individual and her life. She must find a place for work, family, personal wellness, charity, civic duty, etc, within the framework of her whole life, and the way she pursues each domain will reflect in some way the predominant values driving her decisions about the larger order.

The central tension of this multilayered model of society lies in its attempted combination of hierarchy and autonomy. Politics occupies a ruling position over other goods and practices, but it does not subsume them either epistemologically (they remain separate domains of knowledge) or teleologically (private goals are not reducible to political goals, nor vice versa). Any practice is pursued in large measure for its own sake, and its activities and accomplishments can only be fully enjoyed, understood, and achieved by its own members and its own masters. For instance, the primary goal and social contribution of an art museum is to be a great museum; it serves persons *qua* art lovers, not *qua* practitioners of politics. Art or science that forsakes its own proper ends for overtly political goals will inevitably degenerate into propaganda and manipulation.

On the other hand, the various discrete practices are inevitably susceptible to political influence or coloring. We should not demand, nor even aspire to, an art or science totally devoid of political import (great art can be both an effect and a cause of political action—e.g., Picasso's *Guernica* or Goya's *3rd of May 1808*—though political relevance is not the reason these paintings are great). Whence this pervasive influence, and why affirm it? To survive, the political community must maintain something close to Weber's "monopoly on violence," which gives citizens the collective ability to impart their normative vision on lower-level social units. Yet there is more at work than superior force. The point of the classical distinction between "incomplete" and "complete" communities is just this asymmetry. Families or firms are "incomplete" precisely because they *need* the larger political community even to flourish as the sort of associations that they are. Business corporations depend profoundly on their legal structure to become the massive human enterprises they have become; State help is essential, not incidental to them (Ciepley 2013). Likewise, stable families rely on legal and cultural norms, and raising children requires both more inputs and broader horizons than immediate kin can sustain. The practice of politics at its best infiltrates other domains of life so as to enhance and enrich them. Of course, the same prerogative can serve as a pretext for violation and invasion, but the possibility of abuse does not absolve citizens of their broad ordering task, especially if this ordering will go on whether they like it or not.

A non-totalitarian public order can be said to embody a "relatively-complete vision of the good life" on two conditions. First, we must construe "order" in a broader sense than usual. It involves more than the external coordination of the jurist's "law and order," which emphasizes compliance, not inner assent. An architectonic order also aims to configure society "from the inside," by proposing its own scale of ends and values as worthy of the allegiance of persons and groups in their own conduct. Major violations of those values even in private settings (like racial discrimination in the workplace) can be seen as violations of public order. Second, we must recognize that an authoritative ordering of goods and values sets the moral tone of the regime far more decisively than does the nitty-gritty of implementation. As MacIntyre notes, "What discriminates one kind of character from another is how goods are rank ordered by the agent, and [. . .] each rank ordering of goods embodies some conception of what the good life for human beings is" (MacIntyre 2006, 36). For a social order as for an individual, to consistently value goods on one or another scale is to embody a certain vision of the good. A public order of culture and institutions will offer some scale of goods, and so it will embody such a vision, even when it does not police the details. I now consider objections against the whole project of architectonic pluralism, whether in my "order model" or in other possible redactions.

4.1. Three Rejoinders: Feasibility, Limits, and Subsidiarity

Feasibility: Given its breadth, the task I am attributing to citizens' common action may seem an impossible burden. If no one could ever enjoy sufficient knowledge or consensus to carry it out in a just or reasonable way, then misuse is inevitable, and the whole enterprise is misconceived. Here the "pluralism" of the model comes to the rescue, at least in part. The architectonic pluralist's "political map" shows the whole human terrain only in outline. MacIntyre comments that citizens need (only) "sufficient agreement about goods and about their rank ordering to provide shared standards for rational deliberation" (MacIntyre 2006, 39). An architectonic order is hostile to knowledge compartmentalization. Politics may be a game with its own rules, but playing the game well requires familiarity with the other practices under its sway. Yet citizens at large will not know the details of every specialized field in their purview, which would indeed be impracticable. How much do they need to know? A reasonable minimum bar might be: sufficient understanding to evaluate non-political practices. (As Aristotle notes in his defense of democracy [1984, 1282a], broadly educated persons can judge accurately in many fields—such as art, artisanship, cooking, farming, etc.—where they are not themselves skilled performers.) One need not be a technical expert in a field like finance or farming, much less a full-time professional, to understand its needs and contributions with respect to a larger order. Contrariwise, at least some practitioners in those areas need to attend to the place of their field within the larger order. The requisite degrees of mutual knowledge and involvement will vary, of course: citizens at large need little, official regulators rather more.

An architectonic pluralism will also fail if it cannot manage political conflict, especially concerning the jurisdictional decisions that structure the entire scheme. The question of where local common projects are immune from, or susceptible to, political scrutiny is itself a vexed issue. Does the hierarchically superior role of political order and its ends entail that all such decisions come down from the top, from the State and its citizens? Yes and no. For anyone to assert the proper scope or the limits of some association is to make a claim about rightful public order. Hence boundary-drawing and jurisdictional questions are to be resolved from the public perspective of citizens, as custodians of the widest and most authoritative normative order. But as just mentioned, citizens (or State officials acting in their name) should freely acknowledge the limited scope of public competence and principles. Society-spanning values by no means exhaust the relevant goods at stake in particular groups or pursuits. Reasonable solutions may depend on goals and arguments accessible only within a given practice, and one cannot say in advance whose interpretation ought to trump the others. The paradox and promise of an architectonic pluralism would be to keep both sets of reasons, both common goods, in view. In practice, like any other form of polycentrism, a feasible order model would favor enhanced juridical or social power for associations, to keep their concerns and voices politically viable.

Limits: If politics as an ordering practice is genuinely architectonic in the sense of articulating dominant principles that are meant to wash over or infiltrate all of society, one might reasonably doubt that it is also meaningfully limited. As Pakaluk points out, the legitimate intentions of rulers or lawgivers go beyond the letter of the law (Pakaluk 2001, 73–74). For instance, public officials who prudently refrain from micromanaging the energy sector might legitimately hope that solar-power firms will be inventive and efficient as well as egalitarian and environmentally friendly, and will presumably regulate with such ends in mind. Does this not mean that the ostensibly private success of an innovative energy firms is a concern of citizens at large, albeit in an indirect way? If so, the same argument could be extended to the indefinitely many other domains under political oversight, thus razing all the limits to the political common good and returning us to the all-encompassing model.

This objection does not account for the pluralist implications of focusing on common action. The limits of common action delineate the limits of common concern, and the solar firms themselves are not cases of public action. In the strict sense, citizens' shared concern extends only to the soundness of their own regulations, subsidies, and so forth, which do not guarantee the success of any private firm. Public support is indeed designed to encourage the industry, so citizens do share, in some remote degree, in its flourishing. In my recurrent analogy, the political map does show the whole territory. Still, the full flourishing of a firm or industry would not be a matter of the political common good in the strict sense, unless it were transformed into a public agency, becoming a branch or tool of citizens' common action instead of a separate practice in its own right.

But if this is (normatively) possible, what is to prevent an aggressive polity from nationalizing everything? In general, the nature of the goods in question militates against putting too many things in common. MacIntyre emphasizes that key goods (such as deep innovation in energy production) arise only from intact practices, which cannot be well governed by any set of universal rules. Economists, for their part, recognize that some goods lend themselves to central provision (defense), some to private monopolies (toll roads), and some to maximum decentralization (friendship). Yet these categories are highly underdetermined, and my briefly sketched model has little to say about which goods belong where. Healthy, functional social orders have taken many different forms.

Subsidiarity: My order model overlaps the principle of subsidiarity, which appears in the constitution of the EU and in Roman Catholic social doctrine. As conventionally understood, this structural norm dictates that lower-level actors in a hierarchy (such as Luxembourg within the EU, or a family within a State) deserve both support (*subsidium)* and autonomy from higher-level authorities. Is this principle compatible with architectonic pluralism, or are they rivals? Russell Hittinger has argued that the point of subsidiarity is not the efficient realization of social goals, nor decentralization for its own sake, but rather preserving the goods and actions proper to the "group persons" making up a social order (Hittinger 2002). As such, subsidiarity is premised on a social pluralism not unlike the order model I have sketched, which envisions a form of hierarchical complementarity between qualitatively distinct communities. Notice, though, that the principle of subsidiarity in itself is rather empty; it says little or nothing about what the character of those communities should be. The Aristotelian pluralism I have sketched is more definite on one key point: the scope of the political community concerns a whole way of life. Therefore, one can regard architectonic pluralism as one possible fleshing-out of subsidiarity in a version that highlights the world-shaping role of the political community vis-à-vis its constituent persons and groups.

Yet if Aristotelian pluralism is compatible with subsidiarity in the abstract, it does run afoul of one prominent Catholic interpretation of that principle, which marginalizes the architectonic nature of politics, construing the political community in more-or-less instrumental terms. This line of thinking follows from the oft-quoted quasi-definition of the (political) common good as "the sum of those conditions of social life which allow social groups and their individual members relatively thorough and ready access to their own fulfillment" (*Gaudium et Spes* 1965, 26).[9] This language of "conditions" suggests a reductive view of politics as a mere provider of resources, or perhaps a curator of a favorable environment, which assists persons and groups to achieve their own ends, whatever those might be. Insofar as politics is indeed architectonic, citizens' actions cannot be confined to this sort of table-setting. Politics' actions and horizons of value enter into the constitution of sub-political groups, affecting their self-understanding and inner life. Characterizing this deep influence as the mere setting of favorable "conditions" would be misleading to the point of deception. The defenders of subsidiarity should not exaggerate the non-political character of private pursuits, even as they rightly seek autonomy from an encroaching State. The shaping of a whole way of life is part of the political community's function, and will be a major aspect of the "subsidium" (assistance) that it offers, for good and ill, to groups and practices that always need a larger communal home.

CONCLUSION

To conclude, I will briefly comment on the difference an architectonic pluralism might make in practice. Like other modes of polycentrism, it would encourage robust lower-level governance, whether through active regional government, trade unions, or other local control of workplaces and civic institutions. This cuts against the monolithic tendency to view politics, or even the whole moral life, as the product and the care of a single agency. Unlike other pluralisms, a distinctively architectonic pluralism highlights the sense in which citizens do share an overarching moral project in their varied civic pursuits, a project that importantly shapes their own lives and communities. This recognition would allow them to be more forthright in their debates over the good life. I have suggested that every regime, liberal or non-liberal, ancient or modern, embodies some vision of the good, and so is architectonic in practice. Embracing architectonic pluralism would acknowledge this basic reality as a legitimate matter of discussion rather than disguising it under a rhetoric of moral neutrality. Citizens could discard the technocratic posture that treats a torrent of statistics as the relevant public contribution and metric for schools, firms, or whole regional communities. They could ask instead: *How is this institution shaping us? And who do we want to become?* The resulting debate would be no simpler or easier to judge, but it would at least be more honest.

Would not raising the normative stakes of politics foster the temptation to meddle in the very civic associations whose autonomy all polycentrists want to uphold? Likely so, though the temptation to misuse power besets any political system. In an architectonic order model, this temptation would be partially offset by the greater integrity and dignity of non-State practices and associations, as recognized stewards of distinctive common goods, which can serve both practically and morally, as a bulwark against State overreach. All told, an Aristotelian approach to polycentric pluralism would be both more and less intrusive than the politics of contemporary nation-States, but in ways that more fully reflect the real ends and effects of citizens acting together.

NOTES

1. For very useful feedback on earlier drafts, I thank David Thunder, Matthew Wright, the participants in the 2022 RESPUBLICA workshop, and anonymous reviewers.
2. Philip Pettit (2006) gives a similar formulation for quite different reasons.
3. For the original movement see Hirst (1993), and for its recent revival, Levy (2015).
4. Utz defines a *common good* as "goods or values insofar as they are the object of the action of many." (1958 I:132)
5. De Koninck notes that the common good of a given society "is the good of [rational beings] only insofar as the latter are members of the society" (1943).
6. Simon reasons that a common end requires unity of action, and coordination itself requires normative authority of some kind.
7. Wright does acknowledge that politics adds distinctive shared ends of its own, in addition to these aggregated goods. I deny that aggregated goods as such count as part/concern of political common good in the first place.
8. MacIntyre often attributes all-encompassing views to Aristotle, while in his own name he tends to favor more pluralist positions. Compare his *Whose Justice? Which Rationality?* (1988, chap. 7), with *Dependent Rational Animals* (1999, chap. 9).
9. Available in O'Brien and Shannon 1992.

REFERENCES

Aquinas, Thomas. 1947. *Summa Theologiae*. New York: Benziger Brothers.

Aristotle. 1984. *The Politics*, translated by Carnes Lord. Chicago: University of Chicago Press.

———. 1985. *Nicomachean Ethics*, translated by Terence Irwin. Indianapolis: Hackett.
Berlin, Isaiah. 2013. *The Crooked Timber of Humanity*, edited by Henry Hardy. Princeton: Princeton University Press.
Ciepley, David. 2013. "Beyond Public and Private: The Political Theory of the Corporation." *American Political Science Review* 107 (1): 139–58.
De Koninck, Charles. 1943. "On the Primacy of the Common Good: Against the Personalists." In *The Writings of Charles de Koninck*, edited by Ralph McInerny. Notre Dame, IN: University of Notre Dame Press.
Finnis, John. 1998. "Public Good: The Specifically Political Common Good in Thomas Aquinas." In *Natural Law and Moral Inquiry*, edited by Robert P. George. Washington, D.C.: Georgetown University Press.
Hirst, Paul Q. 1993. *The Pluralist Theory of the State*. London: Routledge.
Hittinger, Russell. 2002. "Social Pluralism and Subsidiarity in Catholic Doctrine." *Annales Theologici* 16: 385–408.
Hoipkemier, Mark. 2016. "Law and Friendship: Aquinas and Aristotle on the Virtue of the Common Good." *Archivo Di Filosofia* 84 (1–2): 43–54.
———. 2018. "Justice, Not Happiness: Aristotle on the Common Good." *Polity* 50 (4): 547–74.
Ignatieff, Michael. 1985. *The Needs of Strangers*. New York: Viking Penguin.
Lane, Melissa. 2020. "Politics as Architectonic Expertise? Against Taking the So-Called 'Architect' in Plato's Statesman to Prefigure This Aristotelian View." *Polis* 37: 449–67.
Levy, Jacob. 2015. *Rationalism, Pluralism, and Freedom*. Oxford: Oxford University Press.
Macedo, Stephen. 1990. Liberal Virtues. Oxford: Clarendon Press.
MacIntyre, Alasdair. 1981. *After Virtue*. Notre Dame, IN: University of Notre Dame Press.
———. 1988. *Whose Justice? Which Rationality?* Notre Dame, IN: University of Notre Dame Press.
———. 1998. "Politics, Philosophy, and the Common Good." In *The MacIntyre Reader*, edited by Kelvin Knight, 235–54. Notre Dame, IN: University of Notre Dame Press.
———. 1999. *Dependent Rational Animals*. Chicago: Open Court.
———. 2006. "Rival Aristotles: Aristotle against Some Modern Aristotelians." In *Ethics and Politics: Selected Essays*, Vol. 2, 22–40. Cambridge: Cambridge University Press.
Maritain, Jacques. 1951. *Man and the State*. Chicago: University of Chicago Press.
Murphy, Mark. 2005. "Common Good." *The Review of Metaphysics* 59 (1): 133–64.
O'Brien, David, and Thomas Shannon, eds. 1992. *Catholic Social Teaching: The Documentary Heritage*. Maryknoll, NY: Orbis Books.
Pakaluk, Michael. 2001. "Is the Common Good of Political Society Limited and Instrumental?" *Review of Metaphysics* 55: 57–94.
Pettit, Philip. 2006. "The Common Good." In *Justice and Democracy: Essays for Brian Barry*, edited by Keith Dowding, Robert Goodin, and Carole Pateman, 150–69. Cambridge: Cambridge University Press.

Pope Leo XIII. 1892. "Encyclical Letter 'Au Milieu Des Solicitudes.'"
Simon, Yves. 1962. *A General Theory of Authority*. Notre Dame, IN: University of Notre Dame Press.
Utz, Arthur. 1958. *Sozialethik*. Vol. I. Heidelberg: F.H. Kerle.
Vatican, Pontifical Council on Justice and Peace. 2006. *Compendium of the Social Doctrine of the Church*. London: Continuum.
Verpaalen, Antoine. 1954. *Der Begriff des Gemeinwohls bei Thomas von Aquin*. Heidelberg: F.H. Kerle.
Wright, Matthew. 2019. *A Vindication of Politics*. Lawrence, KS: University of Kansas Press.

Chapter 3

Polycentric Justice

John Thrasher

Justice, John Rawls famously argued, is the "first virtue" of social institutions. Justice, in this sense, structures social cooperation. More precisely, principles of justice provide a framework for evaluating the social rules that govern society, understood as a "cooperative venture for mutual advantage" (Rawls 1971, 4). As he puts it, "[a] set of principles is required for choosing among the various social arrangements which determine this division of advantages and for underwriting an agreement on the proper distributive shares" (4). Principles of justice structure the basic rights, the duties, and the distribution of the benefits and burdens of social life.

Justice is a solution to a fundamental problem in political philosophy. The exercise of political power involves coercion. In a society of free and equal citizens, coercion needs justification to distinguish it from mere force. There are two classic solutions to this problem. Both rely on justifying the use of political power, but they rely on different sources of that justification. One justifies the use of political coercion by referencing an end that the exercise of such power is meant to fulfill. Politics is justified insofar as it achieves or aims at some otherwise valuable or attractive situation for society. This can take many forms, but from Plato to Rawls, one common goal is justice, or a just society. Insofar as political power is used in pursuit of justice, its legitimacy is secure.

Another approach is to see the legitimacy of political power as the result of some procedure. Again, this can take many forms, but agreement and consent are at its core. If everyone in the society agrees or consents to using certain kinds of political power, it is natural to see the exercise of that power as legitimate. Democratic government has this as its basis of legitimacy, but in its most general form, we find the idea of political contractualism. Coercion can be legitimate and publicly justified if it is in accordance with the rational agreement of those to whom it is meant to apply.

These two solutions to the basic political problem are unified in the work of John Rawls, who uses a contractual mechanism of public justification to authorize a conception of justice. Since Rawls, it has become natural to see these two forms of justification as being tightly linked so that public justification establishes a conception of justice that becomes the ultimate basis of legitimacy and standard of evaluation at the highest political level.

I argue that this link is neither necessary nor natural and that we see the clear tensions between contractualism and justice in the context of polycentric theories of governance. Polycentrism highlights the importance of diversity and experimentation in a political order, which helps us see the incongruity between justice and contractualism (see also the chapter by Paniagua and Pourvand 2024, in this volume). Justice as a global standard of legitimacy and a universal evaluative norm is ill-suited to a polycentric system of governance. While polycentric orders need legitimacy in the traditional sense and higher-level regulative norms, both are better accomplished through contractualism, which is not focused on justifying a universal conception of justice. A polycentric-friendly version of contractualism will justify less-substantive procedural norms and institutional rules instead. The insight to which polycentrism leads us is that contractual public justification can generate a standard of legitimacy *without* relying on justice as a basic norm. Or so I argue.

The argument proceeds as follows. In Section 1, I argue that justice and the justification of political authority have traditionally been linked, especially in contractual theories of justification. Early contract theories directly authorized the sovereign to rule, while later theories indirectly authorized the sovereign to act on the basis of a conception of justice that the contractual theory directly authorizes. This elegant solution to the problem of political legitimacy faces a challenge in the high levels of diversity and pluralism found in modern, liberal societies. It is implausible that a determinate conception of justice could meet their diverse and sometimes conflicting interests and values. I introduce this problem in Section 2. In Sections 3 and 4, I examine how polycentrism highlights this problem and poses a potential solution. Although all the strategies of using polycentrism to solve the problem of diversity are instructive, none are without drawbacks. In Section 5, I argue that the real problem is the strategy of indirect authorization through justice used by modern contractual theories of public justification. I argue, instead, that those concerned with diversity and liberalism should embrace a form of polycentricism that abandons the indirect authorization strategy. The implications and paths forward are discussed in the conclusion.

1. JUSTICE AND JUSTIFICATION

The basic political problem is to authorize the use of political power so there is a principled distinction between illegitimate and legitimate coercion. Legitimacy, in this sense, authorizes the rightful exercise of sovereign power. There are two main methods of establishing legitimacy: locating it substantively in some right-making property (e.g., the good, God's will, justice) or imbuing some decision-making procedure with legitimacy, which then confers legitimacy on the outcomes of that procedure. The most general form of the latter approach is a social contract, a general procedure based on an agreement that authorizes legitimate sovereign authority.

We see this clearly in classical social contract theories. The contract's purpose for Hobbes is to authorize and select the sovereign, and justice derives from sovereignty. Of justice in the state of nature, Hobbes writes:

> To this warre of every man against every man, this also is consequent; that nothing can be Unjust. The notions of Right and Wrong, Justice and Injustice have there no place. Where there is no common Power, there is no Law: where no Law, no Injustice. Force, and Fraud, are in warre the two Cardinall vertues. (Hobbes 1651, 196, XIII)

The third law of nature, regarding justice, is "That Men Performe Their Covenants Made," but this law, being a law of reason and a condition of peace, requires more than just words (Hobbes 1651, 220, XV). Justice can only have force when the sovereign is established in the commonwealth.

> Therefore before the names of Just, and Unjust can have place, there must be some coercive Power, to compell men equally to the performance of their Covenants, by the terrour of some punishment, greater than the benefit they expect by the breach of their Covenant; and to make good that Propriety, which by mutuall Contract men acquire, in recompence of the universall Right they abandon: and such power there is none before the erection of a Common-wealth. (Hobbes 1651, 220, XV)

For Locke, the story is somewhat different. Justice has meaning in the state of nature and, in that sense, it can be understood independently of the contract. Nevertheless, its adjudication and enforcement are left to each individual in the state of nature, which makes the expectation of justice being done "very uncertain." Each individual is "constantly exposed to the invasion of others" (Locke 1681, 350, II, 123). The contractual agreement, for Locke, involves, as it does for Hobbes, everyone laying down their natural right to be a judge and executioner of the natural law of justice. Once the sovereign commonwealth is established, it becomes the umpire that decides matters of justice. He writes:

> all private judgment of every particular member being excluded, the community comes to be umpire, by settled standing rules, indifferent, and the same to all parties; and by men having authority from the community . . . Those who are united into one body, and have a common established law and judicature to appeal to, with authority to decide controversies between them, and punish offenders, are in civil society one with another: but those who have no such common appeal, I mean on earth, are still in the state of nature, each being, where there is no other, judge for himself, and executioner; which is, as I have before shewed it, the perfect state of nature. (Locke 1681, 324, II, 87)

In both Locke and Hobbes, the establishment of the sovereign makes justice, in the political sense, possible. Much the same is true in the other contract theorists of the early modern period. These theories directly authorize a sovereign who defines justice or acts based on it (depending on the theory). However, this approach to authorizing the sovereign procedurally creates a serious problem. The person of the sovereign "is but a man" who can preempt the reason and interests of the members of the Commonwealth. As Locke noted, this makes the sovereign more than just first among equals and seems to irresponsibly empower the sovereign in a way that may endanger those who initially authorized him. Doing so is more foolish than staying in the state of nature. As Locke (1681, sec. 93) notes, "This is to think, that men are so foolish, that they take care to avoid what mischiefs may be done them by pole-cats, or foxes; but are content, nay, think it safety, to be devoured by lions." The solution is to limit sovereignty somehow, which creates puzzles of its own.

In contemporary contract theories, these problems are avoided mainly by authorizing the sovereign indirectly. Instead of justifying a sovereign who defines and provides the normativity for justice, Rawls and later contract theorists use the contractual procedure to justify principles or rules of justice.[1] Justice, identified by modeling justification through agreement, becomes the direct source of sovereignty, which is then understood as the source of political normativity. This approach uses a procedural strategy for authorizing a legitimate sovereign, avoiding the dangers of locating that sovereignty in a person or group by making the sovereign a substantive notion, justice, which is the source of normative political authority.[2] In modern contractualist theories that follow Rawls, justice sets the conditions of cooperation and social stability. The contractors in the original position agree to general principles of justice and only indirectly to a sovereign. Insofar as the political order has a role in Rawls's theory, it is to implement justice.

2. DIVERSITY AND CONTRACTUALISM

This move to indirect authorization effectively fuses justice as a source of normative authority and political contractualism or public justification as a method of authorization. Contractualism becomes a model of public justification that, in turn, authorizes a conception of justice. This combines the substantive and procedural methods of identifying legitimate political power. The appeal is that it seems to capture the advantages of each approach while avoiding their respective difficulties.

However, the problem arises once we allow a diversity of individual evaluative and doxastic perspectives into the contractual model to reflect the underlying pluralism of modern societies. Doing so makes the substantive identification of justice difficult or impossible, since it now requires the agreement of many different types of people with different views and interests. Any substantive conception of justice is unlikely to meet the standard of public justification for a diverse community.

Modern contractualism has used two main strategies to deal with this problem. The first is to restrict the diversity and pluralism of the underlying contractual model to generate a determinate and even unique conception of justice. For instance, Jonathan Quong restricts his conception of public justification to only apply to the "constituency of an ideal liberal democratic society," i.e., citizens who already accept a liberal conception of justice (2011, 6). He calls this the *internal conception* of public justification. We can see this as narrowing the scope of political contractualism to secure a stable, identifiable conception of justice. Adopting a different tactic, Nic Southwood (2010) restricts diversity by introducing an ideal deliberative framework for his contractual model. Michael Moehler (2018) pursues this approach differently by endorsing a multilevel contract theory. He argues that while deep diversity exists on a lower level, contractors can rise to a higher, instrumental level where they can agree on terms of peace using a bargaining model of a contract. This approach faces fewer problems than the internal conception of liberalism. Still, this entire family of theories, what I elsewhere call the *insulation strategy* for dealing with diversity in the model of public justification, faces similar problems (Thrasher 2023). The main issue is with the stability of the conception of justice. When the scope of diversity is narrowed in the contractual model of justification, the stability of that justification can be undermined by the actual diversity in the real society it is meant to model. Only those who share the reasoning of the contractors in the model will see the political order as justified, leaving whatever portion of those who do not, outside of consensus on justice.

The other approach is to allow considerable diversity in the model of public justification but to give up on the goal of identifying a stable or determinate conception of justice as a global evaluative standard. This strategy has been pursued by several recent theorists in different ways. Gerald Gaus (2011) allows considerable indeterminacy in the contractual model, arguing that social evolutionary dynamics will settle on a stable conception of justice. Ryan Muldoon (2017) allows for maximal diversity in the contractual model, using a Nash bargaining procedure to select the determinate conception of justice. His model is dynamic, though, choosing different conceptions of justice as the underlying views of the constituents of the society change. Elsewhere, I have described these approaches to widening the scope of diversity in the contractual model as the "harnessing strategy" for dealing with diversity (Thrasher 2023). Unlike the *insulation strategy*, mobilizing diversity in the model of public justification does not create obvious stability problems. Instead, it creates problems with the publicity of the conception of justice and its identification. It is difficult to know what the specific substantive conception of justice is justified in each society, since it may be, as in Muldoon's theory, a moving target.[3] Or, as in Gaus's theory, the specific set of norms in society that are justified may be a complex amalgam that is difficult or impossible for normal citizens to explicate or identify with.

Both strategies face challenges. Nevertheless, as Rawls noted in *A Theory of Justice*, the solution can't be to retreat to a purely substantive approach to identifying justice that rejects the need for a rationalizable procedure altogether. Those who have embraced this approach in either its perfectionist (Raz 1986), purely intuitionist (Enoch 2013; Huemer 2013), Kantian (Pallikkathayil 2016), religious (see: Vallier 2023), utilitarian (Hardin 1988; Goodin 1995), or republican (Pettit 1999) form ignore the problems that diversity and pluralism pose for identifying a stable conception of justice or reject the need for doing so. However elegant and compelling such theories may be on a philosophical level, they won't be satisfying to those who see the project of political philosophy as having to do with diagnosing and finding high-level solutions to the problems of contemporary social life.

3. POLYCENTRISM AND CONTRACTUALISM

Diversity poses a problem to the indirect authorization structure of modern contractualism. In the face of such a challenge, one might look to institutional approaches that avoid the thorny problems of establishing a political order from the top down, as political philosophers often seek to do, and instead look to build it from the bottom up. In this context, polycentricity becomes a potentially powerful solution.

Paul Aligica and Vlad Tarko define a *polycentric system* as "a social system of many decision centers having limited and autonomous prerogatives and operating under an overarching set of rules" (2012). The key idea is that a polycentric order does not have a single unit with a monopoly on decision-making powers. Decision-making in this context may involve coercion or force depending on the order involved, meaning there is no monopoly on using coercive force in such an order. Nevertheless, polycentric orders are rule-governed orders. The overarching rules of the order structure the powers of the units within it, structuring their autonomy. As Aligica and Tarko articulate:

> Polycentricity emerges as a nonhierarchical, institutional, and cultural framework that makes possible the coexistence of multiple centers of decision making with different objectives and values, and that sets up the stage for an evolutionary competition between the complementary ideas and methods of those different decision center. (Aligica and Tarko 2012, 251)

These orders are complex in that there are many combinatorial possibilities for how the multiple units in a polycentric interact and how the agents work within them. Entry and exit within the system and basic rules for changing the structure of the units mean that polycentric systems tend to be both complex and dynamic (Aligica and Tarko 2013).

For our purposes, the distinctiveness of polycentric orders comes from two factors. The first is that the system is composed of decentralized, semi-autonomous units. The second is that an overarching set of rules governs it. These two factors are related. Within a polycentric system, the system's rules are developed in a process of "co-production" that occurs within and between the units in the system (Aligica and Tarko 2013, 736). This allows flexibility in the rules, the ability to adapt rules to local conditions, and a process for generating internal legitimacy for the rules that makes the enforcement problem easier to solve. As Aligica and Tarko argue, the co-production of rules makes it "likely that the quality of rules increases if the competition between rule creators is increased" (Aligica and Tarko 2013, 736). This process of rule co-production is structured by an overarching set of basic rules and the local social norms within the system.

We can now see how polycentric orders can accommodate and harness evaluative and doxastic diversity. In the social and political context, we can think of the polycentric order as a system of institutions, where institutions are the "rules of the game" constructed by people to organize social interactions (North 1990, 3). We have formal institutions and organizations, and informal institutions and norms within this. Institutions tend to be made, while norms emerge from conventions, although the two often overlap and interact. In a polycentric system, we shouldn't expect that the institutions within it will share rules or norms. This means that a diversity of different types of institutions, reflecting the different norms and values of different people, can coexist within the same order.

Returning to the idea of an overarching set of rules that structures the order, this set of rules *doesn't need to be* a conception of justice of the sort we find in modern contractualist theories. Further, there doesn't seem to be a need for a universal standard of legitimacy. Instead, legitimacy is generated at the level of the institutional units. Rather than applying one consensus evaluative standard for the entire system, "the polycentric approach is concerned with the possibility of creating valued states of affairs from as many normative perspectives as possible" (Aligica and Tarko 2013, 738).

Although polycentricism incorporates diversity nicely, it raises the question of the ultimate legitimacy of the political order in a new way. Even if the legitimacy of the institutional rules within a polycentric order is determined locally, insofar as some or all involve coercion, there is still the question of whether that exercise of coercion is legitimate. Polycentric orders have no substantive basis for their legitimacy—nor could they—so the direct method of authorizing political power will not work. They also can't rely on the traditional indirect contractual approach, since it is unlikely that such a conception of justice will allow for the autonomy and flexibility of a polycentric order or that the diverse constituents of such an order could agree on any stable conception of justice. Given that neither method for authorizing legitimate authority seems consistent with polycentricism, what reason do citizens have for endorsing and complying with the system's rules?

One answer, pursued in different ways by Müller (2019) and Barrett (2020), is to use the indirect contractual approach to justify a political system that is not based on justice but will reliably tend toward justice. On this view, polycentric orders can be legitimate as they reliably move society toward justice. This is a *directional* justification for polycentricism. For Barrett, the best we can hope for in a complex world is to identify progressive social orders in the sense that they reliably tend toward justice in the long term. Polycentric orders, he claims, are a crucial element of such a progressive social order. A progressive social order is not legitimate because it is itself publicly justified or implements a conception of justice that is publicly justified, but rather because we can expect it to move toward justice. In this sense, the justification of the social order is doubly indirect. Müller's argument is different in that polycentric democracy is the least unjust system available and the most likely to lead to justice. As he describes it, polycentric democracy is "a launching pad towards a realistic utopia" (Müller 2019, 178). This is also a doubly indirect justification for the polycentric order based on its likelihood of reliably aiming at justice.

Another approach, what we might call a *constitutive* justification for polycentricism, argues that the ongoing process of public justification with a polycentric system justifies it and generates the appealing properties like impartiality that we have come to accept from a global conception of justice. We find this approach in the final work of Gerald Gaus (2021). Although his argument is complex, the basic idea is that modern liberal democracies are best understood as open societies composed of multiple levels of different types of polycentric institutional arrangements. However, these polycentric orders must be governed by a system of higher-level rules authorized through a system of public justification. For Gaus, public justification occurs at the level of basic moral rules that structure the norms of society. Public justification ensures that these moral rules are stable since they are stable in the face of discussion and disagreement (Gaus 2021, 51). These moral rules form a kind of moral constitution that orders the basic terms of the social order (Gaus 2013). Within that moral constitution, the crucial feature related to justice is a general principle of impartiality, which Gaus identifies as the core element of the Rawlsian theory of justice (Gaus 2021, 140). He argues that a contractual deliberative model paired with a model of social evolution generates justification for ever more general principles of impartiality. In Gaus's later theory, we have a process for generating justification on a high-level principle of impartiality and basic moral rules through a deliberative, contractual model and social evolution.

3. STRATEGIES OF LEGITIMACY

The problem of establishing legitimacy has, as we have seen, a solution in the form of using contractualism to authorize a conception of justice that then supplies the normative authority for political power. This solution, however, is jeopardized by the diversity of modern societies, which makes contractually authorizing a substantive conception of justice difficult (see also the chapter by Paniagua and Pourvand 2024 in this volume). This difficulty is compounded when we introduce polycentricity. We have seen three solutions to this problem.

The first *justice-based* approach we looked at in the first section. Within this approach, there are two strategies. The first, the *insulation* strategy, constraints diversity to generate contractual justification for a conception of justice. The second, the *harnessing* strategy, attempts to use the diversity of society to justify a changing conception of justice. This second strategy effectively gives up on a stable conception of justice, while the first attempts to eliminate diversity to generate a stable conception of justice.

The second type of solution embodied in *justice-aiming* theories argues that diversity is ineliminable and, instead, attempts to indirectly justify a diverse, polycentric order on its likelihood of progressively achieving justice. In so doing, they give up on the need for contractual public justification as a source of legitimacy. Rather than rely on an independent justification module for their conception of justice, they posit a notion of justice at which they argue, the polycentric order will reliably aim. The appeal of this notion of justice indirectly justifies the polycentric order.

The third type of solution is Gaus's *constitutive* approach, which goes the other direction. It relies on public justification and diversity while relegating justice to a high-level principle of impartiality and background moral rules. This is not to say that Gaus jettisons justice as a central evaluative principle completely, but the notion of a publicly justified conception of justice is not meant to govern the lower-level institutions of the polycentric order directly; instead, it serves as a basic guiding principle of the society. With the third procedural approach, the idea of justice is becoming more ephemeral. We might wonder why it is there and whether we need it.

Of these, the justice-preserving *insulation* strategy is the most straightforward. Still, at least in its traditional form, it is also the most problematic since it considerably narrows the scope of liberal justification and, thereby, opens itself up to serious problems with stability. The Gaussian *constitutive* solution is the most subtle, attempting to preserve some version of justice in the background while leaving little to do with the actual functioning of the society. The *justice-aiming* approach is probably the best of both worlds in some sense. Still, its plausibility largely depends on what we think about a) its reliability claims, and b) its necessarily vague conception of justice doing much of the work in the background. This approach is probably right because generating a contractual consensus on a direction of justice is easier than a specific conception. Still, in so doing, it may also lose the normative legitimacy that a stable conception of justice confers. In any case, each of these approaches has its costs.

Brian Kogelmann (2017) proposes a more straightforward solution to this problem, which he calls the *polycentric model*. This is a polycentric model of a Rawlsian "well-ordered society." A well-ordered society, for Rawls, is a society governed by a conception of justice that is publicly justified and recognized as justified, ensures social unity, and supports political autonomy. In the well-ordered society under full justification:

> citizens are in a position to know and to accept the pervasive influence of the basic structure that shapes their conception of themselves, their character and their ends . . . that citizens should be in this position is a condition of their

realizing their freedom as fully autonomous, politically speaking. It means that in their public political life nothing needs be hidden. (Rawls 1996, 68, 4.2)

Kogelmann represents diversity directly in his version of the well-ordered society by modeling citizens as having multiple conceptions of justice, none of which can be uniquely publicly justified. In his polycentric model, each constituency for a particular conception of justice J={j1,j2…jn} has its territorial community where that conception of justice authorizes the political order. Crucially, there is a constraint that all these conceptions of justice are liberal. He writes:

[T]hough there are disagreements about justice in the polycentric model, and each differing conception of justice in *J* gets its own separate governance unit to regulate, all such conceptions are still liberal conceptions—there are no pockets of illiberal peoples in our polycentric order. (Kogelmann 2017, 679)

This model has no overarching conception of justice to unify society. Nevertheless, each sub-community does have a unifying conception of justice to organize it. Quite rightly, Kogelmann (2017, 680) compares this approach to Nozick's (1974) model of a meta-utopia in the third part of *Anarchy, State, and Utopia* and Chandran Kukathas's (2003) model of a decentralized society.

In contrast to the *insulation*, *harnessing*, *justice-aiming*, and *constitutive* approaches we have already seen, we can think of this as a *decentralized* approach to reconciling justice, public justification, and diversity. It is decentralized and separated in that each community's conception of justice organizes it, but not any other community. It also partakes in an *insulation* strategy as it insulates itself from the possibility of any of these communities being illiberal. This reconciles justice, in the Rawlsian sense, with diversity in the contractual justification by limiting the output of decentralized public justification only to conceptions of justice acceptable to a larger, virtual public justification for the polycentric order. As such, we can see that what we have here is a virtual model of public justification that outputs a disjunctive conception of justice J= $\{j_1 v j_2 v \ldots j_n\}$. In many ways, this is similar to Gaus's *constitutive* approach, wherein a permissible, "eligible" set of conceptions of justice and then into an "optimal eligible" set before having some conception of justice chosen by a historical evolutionary process (Gaus 2011, 20; 2021, 19). In Kogelmann's *decentralized* model, this later step is skipped, and each sub-community implements its preferred element from a kind of "optimal eligible" set of conceptions of justice through a polycentric mechanism.

This *decentralized* approach has the advantage of capturing the appealing features of Rawls's theory of justice while not having to either completely insulate the contractual model from diversity or use some non-rational mechanism of selection to pick from a diverse set of different conceptions of justice. Regardless, it is not without drawbacks. Alex Schaefer (2022) raises concerns about the polycentric order's exit possibilities. While citizens have a right to exit in the *decentralized* order, there is no guarantee there is anywhere to exit if they possess an extreme minority view. This is a problem with Kogelmann's model, since it undermines the political autonomy component of a well-ordered society. As Schaefer argues:

> The issue here is a consequence of Kogelmann's strict requirement of full autonomy: citizens must live under their *favourite* conception of justice, according to their *independently derived* rankings. Consequently, just as in the unifying model, citizens will fail to realize their full autonomy. (2022, 5) [emphasis in original]

Schaefer proposes an amendment to the decentralized model to solve this problem. He argues that if we model society-wide public justification as involving agents that are reasonable, in the sense that they see themselves as reciprocal cooperators and who include the other conceptions of justice in their rankings, "the choices and values of other agents with whom they interact factor into their practical reasoning" (2022, 8). He models this as every agent in the contractual model A=a1,a2,a3,...aj having a personal ranking of conceptions of justice that involves the intersection of the "eligible" set of options i-nnJi (Schaefer 2022, 7). If no individuals have rankings of justice that are a part of that larger intersecting set, exit options and full political autonomy should be preserved.

This amendment should be compatible with Kogelmann's *decentralized* approach and largely solve the exit problem. Another, perhaps more serious issue concerns how this approach, even in its amended form, insulates the contractual model from illiberal conceptions of justice. In one sense, Kogelmann's decentralized model is an exercise in fusing polycentricity into an otherwise Rawlsian approach. As far as it goes, there is no problem using the restricted Rawlsian assumptions to do so. However, it poses a problem for using it as a general solution to the problem of contractual legitimacy in a diverse society since it will replicate the fragility of other approaches that use an *insulation* strategy.

We can put the point a little more precisely by thinking of the contractual legitimacy problem as being one of generating a disjunctive or intersecting "eligible" set of conceptions of justice. Polycentricity is merely a way of implementing a series of related communities, given those options. We still have a global norm in the form of justice, albeit a complicated intersecting one. Presumably, the institutions within each community would be bound by its norms of justice, and even more complicated norms of justice would bind some that crossed the boundaries of a given community. What we have, then, is a multiplicity of monocentric orders governed by justice that are linked together. Following the model's assumptions, each community should be stable despite insulation, assuming that sorting people into their preferred communities is effective. However, the problems with the *insulation* strategy concerning stability will be replicated in each community over time as new people immigrate and emigrate, as new ideas emerge, and as the values and beliefs of the people change. Diversity, which was cordoned off through decentralization, will predictably *reemerge*, and we can expect the system to be dynamically unstable. Despite its complications, the decentralized model is still *justice-centric* in the Rawlsian way. This emphasis on justice as an authorizing and governing norm makes reconciliation between justice, justification, and diversity virtually impossible.

4. CONTRACTUALISM AND A POLYCENTRIC CONSTITUTION

We have seen that polycentricity highlights the problems diversity poses for contractual models of legitimacy that rely on justice (Paniagua and Pourvand 2024). All the proposed solutions come with attendant problems. Further, polycentric orders can't completely avoid the fundamental political problem of distinguishing between legitimate and illegitimate uses of coercion. We are left with a dilemma. Either embrace some form of contractual justification that authorizes a conception of justice, which limits diversity and, therefore, polycentricity in some way, or give up on a universal standard of political legitimacy that applies to the society as a whole and embrace polycentricity without a clear standard of normative legitimacy. Neither of these options is particularly attractive.

As I suggested at the outset, the link between contractualism as a method of justification and justice as the output of that justification seems natural. I want to suggest that this link isn't necessary. We can directly generate a standard of legitimacy through contractual public justification without relying on justice as a universal normative authority.

Aligica and Tarko (2013, 738) note that polycentric orders are "concerned with the possibility of creating valued states of affairs from as many normative perspectives as possible." Having a universal conception of justice for a society or a contractual model that limits the normative perspectives will constrain these possibilities. Again, this creates a tension between polycentricity and contractual theories that authorize justice. Gaus, as we have seen, wants to allow for considerable polycentricity as well as endorse the important role that justice plays in a society at a higher level. The question here, which Gaus attempts to answer in the third part of *The Open Society and Its Complexities*, is how to keep things separated: how to keep the spontaneous order and dynamism of the polycentric structure of what he calls the meso and micro level without having the rules of the macro-order unify everything into a monocentric uniformity. This is the inherent danger of a universal or macro norm of justice that constrains the possibilities for experimentation in the system it governs. In this way, even Gaus's *constitutive* approach employs an *insulation* strategy. Gaus's concern seems to be what he calls "Hayek's troubling" claim that the basic terms of the open society can't be rationally justified. But, in Gaus's later *constitutive* work, justice doesn't take the role that it did previously. Rather than being a global norm, it seems to set the moral preconditions of any cooperative, complex society.

The cause of this tension is the role that justice is expected to play. As we have seen, in modern contractual theories, justice is that standard by which political power is judged legitimate. It functions as a super-norm that structures all the lower political rules and norms in society. This is, of course, not the only way to think about justice. Michael Walzer (1983) defends a contextual theory of justice, in which what counts as justice depends on the social "sphere" one is in, in the relevant case. David Schmidtz (2006) argues for a pluralistic conception of justice where justice has at least four elements. Chad van Schoelandt (2020) defends a "functionalist" theory of justice that seems to involve some pluralistic and contextual elements. There are many other logical and actual possibilities (see: Van Shoelandt and Gaus 2018).

The point is that justice does not need to play the normative authorization role in modern contractual theory to be important and valuable. For instance, Geoffrey Brennan and James Buchanan argue that justice in conduct should only be thought of as action by some set of recognized rules. They argue that justice as giving each what they deserve only makes sense in the context of a system of rules. They claim, "[t]he mere presence of rules is sufficient to establish the relevance of desert, and hence the possibility of just and unjust conduct by participants" (Brennan and Buchanan 1985, 110). This may seem too strong, but they couple this idea of justice-within-rules with an idea of justice-between-rules. The rules of institutions are assumed to be agreed to by those within the institution, even while those same people may prefer a different institutional structure.

Why should we assume that the institutional rules are the basis of some consensus as Brennan and Buchanan do? Institutions that had rules that diverged substantially from the values and beliefs of those within them would be fundamentally unstable. The rules will either be ignored or changed. As Elinor Ostrom and her collaborators have shown, the juridical rules may differ from the *de facto* rights in many instances, and it is a theoretical and practical error to read off the *de facto* rights and norms from the explicit rules of an institution (Ostrom 1990; Schlager and Ostrom 1992). Where there is a mismatch between the existing norms and rights and the public rules and rights, it is natural to want to align the institutional rules with the existing norms and rights. Gaus and Barrett (2020) argue that there is (and should be) a deep connection between institutional rules and legal structures and the social and moral norms that support them. This point can be correct without it. It is also true that the rules are in some sense optimal or even thought to be optimal by most of the participants in the institution. Anyone working in a university will be familiar with thinking that any number of university rules could be better, without thinking that either breaking the rules is justified or that the entire university is corrupt and unjust.

This conception of justice is compatible with polycentric governance since justice results from action in accordance with institutional rules that will likely vary between institutions. As Aligica and Tarko argue, in polycentric orders, diversity of values doesn't have "to be funneled into a single normative position"; they don't require us to normalize or harmonize justice across institutions (2013, 739). Justice in accordance with institutional rules can be understood as an *institutional* conception of justice. Polycentricity and diversity are compatible with an institutional conception of justice insofar as there are many different institutions with different types of rules that individuals see themselves as having reasons to work within or endorse.

Is there any sense in which an institutional conception of justice can play the indirect authorization role of justice in contractual theories? Can it function as the source of normative authority and legitimacy? Not in the traditional sense. If justice is determined by acting in accordance with institutional rules, then the legitimacy depends on the rules and the institutions that make them rather than the legitimacy of the rules depending on justice.[4] Since the indirect authorization strategy will not work with this conception of justice, we need to think differently about the relationship between justice and the contractual procedure for generating legitimacy. As we saw in Section 1, direct authorization in traditional social contract theories authorized a sovereign who defined and instituted justice. A polycentric order does not have a sovereign in the Hobbesian sense, so this direct approach won't work either. However, polycentric orders have an overarching set of rules that structure the order as a whole and the relations between units within a polycentric order. Perhaps that set of rules can be authorized by the contractual procedure and play the role that justice or the sovereign did in other theories.

Let's return to the idea of a polycentric institutional order to see what such an overarching set of rules would look like. Aligica describes a polycentric order of self-governance as having two key characteristics:

> At its core is, first, the idea of a meta-level institutional framework of "the rules of the game" constituting social arenas through systems of overarching rules. Second is the notion that social actors interact via voluntary exchanges and voluntary associations within those general rules. (Aligica 2018, 197)

We have two sets of rules, one *within* institutions where people act directly to achieve their direct outcomes, and another *between* institutions. We can divide these two levels into the constitutional and institutional levels. An institutional conception of justice will suffice at the institutional level, but we can't rely on institutional rules to structure the constitutional level. We also have the problem of the authorization or legitimacy of the constitutional level rules. We can use a contractual model to consider what kinds of constitutional rules would be agreed to.

As I have argued elsewhere (Thrasher 2020; 2023), the contractual model of public justification is a multipurpose tool of public authorization; it need not aim only at justice. Instead, it can target a basic constitutional structure or set of rules directly authorizing them. We can think of it as a test of legitimacy that can be, in principle, applied at any level. In his later work, Gauthier (1997) describes political contractarianism as a test of normative legitimacy, though he doesn't develop this idea in detail. In some of his work, Gaus (2011, 276–77) also argues that public justification is a test directly applied to rules of social morality and laws. So, there is a precedent for decoupling contractualism as a method of justification from justice as its target.[5] If this is done in the context of a polycentric order, the source of legitimacy becomes the justified constitutional rules rather than a conception of justice that the constitution then implements.

The exact constitutional rules will vary depending on the details of the polycentric order. Minimally, any constitutional set of rules will require some "rule of recognition" in the sense described by H.L.A. Hart (1961). This basic rule is what Hans Kelsen (1934) called a *grundnorm*, or what Ehrenberg (2020) calls a "basic validity rule"; not a traditional rule, but rather a test or criteria for identifying valid secondary and primary rules. Hart is concerned with a system of law, but a basic rule of recognition can also be used at the constitutional level. The contractual test of legitimacy can be used to authorize a basic rule of recognition and associated rules of change and adjudication. These are the basic requirements for a constitutional order that can serve as a system of overarching meta-rules that govern the complex polycentric order within it.

Although a constitutional order of rules will be morally important, it is not dependent on moral authorization. Again, this distinguishes it from contemporary contractual theories focusing on justice as the fount of legitimacy. Justice in a polycentric society will be largely determined by the constitutional structure and the institutions it makes possible. However, the constitutional order does not implement some prior notions of justice. Given the abstraction and generality of the basic secondary rules of society, there is good reason to think that any contractual model of justification would employ a robust "veil of uncertainty" since the link between general secondary rules and outcomes will not be direct or foreseeable (Brennan and Buchanan 1985, 33–36). Our model agents in the contractual model will come with their various moral, religious, and practical worldviews. Since they are not directly choosing a conception of justice or moral constitution to govern them, diversity among these views should not make agreement on a basic set of constitutional rules impossible or create the need for robust insulation that we see in contemporary, justice-centric, contractual theories.

In this sense, public justification of a constitutional order in a polycentric system is best seen in a realist light. Normative and moral concerns are relevant to the choice of basic rules, but those considerations come into play within the contractual test. This form of realism allows for normative considerations to count but does not require a unified moral or normative standard (Hankins and Thrasher 2022). Contractual public justification in this framework doesn't happen in a vacuum; existing norms and conventions of society will be crucial inputs in the contractual model.

CONCLUSION

Polycentric governance poses unique problems for contemporary political theory in ways that neither the political philosophers nor the polycentric theorists have fully reckoned with. I have tried to isolate the main problem as I see it and show how many of the proposed solutions seem inadequate for the task. The problem arises from the *justificatory strategy* that contemporary political contractualist theories have taken to solve the fundamental question of legitimacy in a free society. Their solution, as we saw, was to use a tool for authorizing a sovereign—the social contract—and use it to authorize justice, which would then play the role of the sovereign. Justice becomes the main tool of legitimacy, and contractualism becomes the method for identifying justice. The problem that polycentricity highlights is that the more diversity and dynamism there is in a society, the harder it is to see how a contractual model can identify any clear and stable conception of justice. The dilemma becomes either reducing diversity and dynamism to secure a clear conception of justice, or rejecting the justice-based approach to legitimacy.

I have argued that the second option is plausible and especially well-suited for polycentric systems. Political contractualism as a method of justification can be unmoored from justice and used to evaluate basic constitutional rules that structure the polycentric order directly. In this approach, contractual public justification can serve as the basis of a realist political contractualist theory that outputs constitutional secondary rules rather than justice or rules of morality. This makes the task of justification less fraught and more robust in the face of diversity. Different kinds of societies will authorize different constitutional orders, given their histories, conventions, and norms. Since the rules for changing the constitutional structure are embedded in the basic secondary rules, there is no expectation that a constitutional order should be static. Rather, the process of self-governance within those rules should be dynamic and allow for change in the face of changing circumstances.

The proposal here is a considerable departure from the alternatives on offer (see also Paniagua and Pourvand 2024). It rejects a form of ideal theory in favor of realism and deprioritizes justice as the goal of all social institutions. Public justification in the form of contractual agreement is still central, but it takes on a different form with a different goal than in other theories. The move to direct rather than indirect political authorization makes it possible to move to an institutional conception of justice, but it also raises other issues. The main appeal of this approach is that it incorporates diversity into its model of public justification and governance by assuming polycentricity. This shows that the importance of polycentricity in political philosophy cannot be ignored. It is not merely an institutional structure that can be used as a module in, for instance, justice-centric political theories. As I have tried to show, the appeal and necessity of polycentricity as a governance structure reframe the entire political project at the highest level.

NOTES

1. Rawls, Gauthier, and their followers do this most clearly, but it is common in most contractual theories. Elsewhere, I have argued that the attempt to justify a unique, determinate conception of justice creates serious problems for both rational choice, bargaining contract theories (Thrasher 2014), as well as Rawlsian theories (Thrasher 2019a). James Buchanan develops a contract theory that focuses on the justification of rules, not a determinate conception of justice (Buchanan and Tullock 1962; Buchanan 1975; Brennan and Buchanan 1985) and largely avoids this problem. His contractual theory is different from Rawls's in many respects, though, especially in its emphasis on the role of democracy and individualism (on this point, see Thrasher 2019b).

2. Robert Nozick (1974) uses a different procedural approach in the first part of *Anarchy, State, and Utopia*. Although similar in overall form to modern contractual theories, Nozick's approach is methodologically and substantively different. We can see his thought experiment of the creation of a minimal state without violating anyone's rights as both a possible proof of such a society and as a standard of legitimacy

or justice from which to judge our own. Although both Nozick's model and contractual theories are counterfactual, they differ in that modern contractual theories are concerned with assessing the reasons we have now for endorsing and complying with social rules and use a counterfactual model to test those. For more on the counterfactual status of contract theories, see D'Agostino, Gaus, and Thrasher, (2021).

3. Whether it is a drawback for justice to be a moving target is open to dispute. Muldoon (2017) sees his dynamic conception of justice as a benefit, not a drawback, of his theory. Alex Schaefer (2023) has argued that focusing on determinate conceptions of justice is a vestige of using fixed-point theorems in economics, and a dynamic conception of justice is preferable. This may be correct; the point here is just that no dynamic theory has reckoned with the problem of publicity. Perhaps, as Brian Kogelmann (2021) argues, publicity is overrated. In any case, it is a lacuna in contemporary dynamic accounts of justice.

4. It is important to note that I am speaking here of "social" justice used to evaluate institutions, not justice as it is treated in the criminal law or as applied to individuals. Individuals will, of course, continue to have and use those conceptions of justice.

5. An earlier precedent can be found in the work of James Buchanan, specifically in the model of constitutional choice developed in *The Calculus of Consent* (Buchanan and Tullock 1962). On the relation of this work to the kind of contractualism discussed here, see (Thrasher and Gaus 2017).

REFERENCES

Aligica, Paul. 2018. *Public Entrepreneurship, Citizenship, and Self-Governance*. Cambridge, United Kingdom: Cambridge University Press.

Aligica, Paul, and Vlad Tarko. 2012. "Polycentricity: From Polanyi to Ostrom, and Beyond." *Governance* 25 (2): 237–62. https://doi.org/10.1111/j.1468–0491.2011.01550.x.

———. 2013. "Co-Production, Polycentricity, and Value Heterogeneity: The Ostroms' Public Choice Institutionalism Revisited." *American Political Science Review* 107 (4): 726–41.

Barrett, Jacob. 2020. "Social Reform in a Complex World." *Journal of Ethics and Social Philosophy* 17 (2): 103–32.

Barrett, Jacob, and Gerald F. Gaus. 2020. "Laws, Norms, and Public Justification: The Limits of Law as an Instrument of Reform." In *Public Reason and Courts*, edited by Mattias Kumm, Silje A. Langvatn, and Wojciech Sadurski, 201–28. Studies on International Courts and Tribunals. Cambridge: Cambridge University Press. https://doi.org/10.1017/9781108766579.009.

Brennan, Geoffrey, and James Buchanan. 1985. *The Reason of Rules. The Collected Works of James M. Buchanan*. Indianapolis: Liberty Fund Inc.

Buchanan, James. 1975. *The Limits of Liberty: Between Anarchy and Leviathan*. Vol. 7. The Collected Works of James M. Buchanan. Indianapolis: Liberty Fund.

Buchanan, James, and Gordon Tullock. 1962. *The Calculus of Consent: Logical Foundations of Constitutional Democracy. The Collected Works of James M. Buchanan*. Indianapolis, IN: Liberty Fund.

D'Agostino, Fred, Gerald Gaus, and John Thrasher. 2021. "Contemporary Approaches to the Social Contract." *Stanford Encyclopedia of Philosophy*. 2021. https://plato.stanford.edu/entries/contractarianism-contemporary/.

Ehrenberg, Kenneth M. 2020. "The Institutionality of Legal Validity." *Philosophy and Phenomenological Research* 100 (2): 277–301. https://doi.org/10.1111/phpr.12536.

Enoch, David. 2013. "The Disorder of Public Reason: A Critical Study of Gerald Gaus's *The Order of Public Reason*." *Ethics* 124 (1): 141–76.

Gaus, Gerald. 2011. *The Order of Public Reason: A Theory of Freedom and Morality in a Diverse and Bounded World*. Cambridge University Press.

———. 2013. "Moral Constitutions." *Harvard Review of Philosophy* XIX: 4–22.

———. 2021. *The Open Society and Its Complexities*. Oxford: Oxford University Press.

Gauthier, David. 1997. "Political Contractarianism." *Journal of Political Philosophy* 5 (2): 132–48. https://doi.org/10.1111/1467–9760.00027.

Goodin, Robert E. 1995. *Utilitarianism as a Public Philosophy*. Cambridge University Press.

Hankins, Keith, and John Thrasher. 2022. "Hume's Politics and Four Dimensions of Realism." *Journal of Politics* 84 (2): 1007–20. https://doi.org/10.1086/716946.

Hardin, Russell. 1988. *Morality within the Limits of Reason*. University of Chicago Press.

Hart, H. L. A. 1961. *The Concept of Law*. Clarendon Press.

Hobbes, Thomas. 1651. *Leviathan,* Edited by Noel Malcolm. Clarendon Edition of the Works of Thomas Hobbes. Oxford: Oxford University Press.

Huemer, Michael. 2013. *The Problem of Political Authority: An Examination of the Right to Coerce and the Duty to Obey*. Basingstoke: Palgrave Macmillan.

Kelsen, Hans. 1934. *Pure Theory of Law*. Clark, N.J. The Lawbook Exchange, Ltd.

Kogelmann, Brian. 2017. "Justice, Diversity, and the Well-Ordered Society." *Philosophical Quarterly* (1950–) 67 (269): 663–84.

———. 2021. *Secret Government: The Pathologies of Publicity*. Cambridge, UK; New York, USA: Cambridge University Press.

Kukathas, Chandran. 2003. *The Liberal Archipelago*. Oxford University Press.

Locke, John. 1681. *Two Treaties of Government,* edited by Peter Laslett. Cambridge: Cambridge University Press.

Moehler, Michael. 2018. *Minimal Morality: A Multilevel Social Contract Theory*. Oxford: Oxford University Press.

Muldoon, Ryan. 2017. *Social Contract Theory for a Diverse World: Beyond Tolerance*. Routledge.

Müller, Julian. 2019. *Political Pluralism, Disagreement and Justice: The Case for Polycentric Democracy.* New York: Routledge. https://www.routledge.com/Political-Pluralism-Disagreement-and-Justice-The-Case-for-Polycentric/Muller/p/book/9780367728892.

North, Douglass C. 1990. *Institutions, Institutional Change and Economic Performance*. Reprinted. Cambridge: Cambridge University Press.

Nozick, Robert. 1974. *Anarchy, State, and Utopia*. New York: Basic Books.

Ostrom, Elinor. 1990. *Governing the Commons: The Evolution of Institutions for Collective Action*. Cambridge University Press.

Pallikkathayil, Japa. 2016. "Neither Perfectionism nor Political Liberalism." *Philosophy & Public Affairs* 44 (3): 171–96. https://doi.org/10.1111/papa.12077.

Paniagua, Pablo, and Kaveh Pourvand. 2024. "Whither stability? Polycentric democracy and social order." In *Polycentric Governance and the Good Society: A Normative and Philosophical Investigation*, edited by David Thunder and Pablo Paniagua. New York: Rowman & Littlefield.

Pettit, Philip. 1999. *Republicanism: A Theory of Freedom and Government*. Oxford; New York: Oxford University Press.

Quong, Jonathan. 2011. *Liberalism without Perfection*. New York: Oxford University Press.

Rawls, John. 1971. *A Theory of Justice*. Revised. Belknap Press.

———. 1996. *Political Liberalism*. Paperback. New York: Columbia University Press.

Raz, Joseph. 1986. *The Morality of Freedom*. Oxford: Clarendon Press.

Schaefer, Alexander. 2022. "Reasonable But Non-Liberal: Another Route to Polycentrism." *The Philosophical Quarterly* 72 (1): 218–28. https://doi.org/10.1093/pq/pqab043.

———. 2023. "Is Justice a Fixed Point?" *American Journal of Political Science* 67 (2): 277–90. https://doi.org/10.1111/ajps.12631.

Schlager, Edella, and Elinor Ostrom. 1992. "Property-Rights Regimes and Natural Resources: A Conceptual Analysis." *Land Economics* 68 (3): 249–62. https://doi.org/10.2307/3146375.

Schmidtz, David. 2006. *The Elements of Justice*. Cambridge: Cambridge University Press.

Southwood, Nicholas. 2010. *Contractualism and the Foundations of Morality*. Oxford University Press, USA.

Thrasher, John. 2014. "Uniqueness and Symmetry in Bargaining Theories of Justice." *Philosophical Studies* 167 (3): 683–99.

———. 2019a. "Constructivism, Representation, and Stability: Path-Dependence in Public Reason Theories of Justice." *Synthese* 196 (1): 429–50. https://doi.org/10.1007/s11229-017-1488-7.

———. 2019b. "Democracy Unchained: Contractualism, Individualism, and Independence in Buchanan's Democratic Theory." *Homo Oeconomicus* 36 (1): 25–40. https://doi.org/10.1007/s41412-019-00085-6.

———. 2020. "Agreeing to Disagree: Diversity, Political Contractualism, and the Open Society." *Journal of Politics* 82 (3): 1142–55.

———. 2023. "Contract, Consensus, and Diversity." In *New Approaches to Social Contract Theory: Liberty, Equality, Diversity, and the Open Society*, edited by Michael Moehler and John Thrasher. Oxford: Oxford University Press.

Thrasher, John, and Gerald Gaus. 2017. "On the Calculus of Consent." In *Oxford Handbook on Classics in Political Theory*, edited by Jacob Levy. Oxford: Oxford University Press.

Vallier, Kevin. 2023. *All the Kingdoms of the World: On Radical Religious Alternatives to Liberalism*. Oxford, New York: Oxford University Press.

Van Schoelandt, Chad. 2020. "Functionalist Justice and Coordination." *Social Theory and Practice* 46 (2): 417–40.

Van Shoelandt, Chad, and Gerald Gaus. 2018. "Political and Distributive Justice." In *The Oxford Handbook of Distributive Justice*, edited by Serena Olsaretti. Oxford University Press. https://doi.org/10.1093/oxfordhb/9780199645121.013.34.

Walzer, Michael. 1983. *Spheres of Justice: A Defense of Pluralism and Equality*. New York: Basic Books.

PART II

The Feasibility of Polycentric Orders

Chapter 4

The Problem of Complexity and the Emergence of Polycentric Political Order[1]

Dries Daems and Alexander Schaefer

This chapter proposes an explanation of polycentric state emergence. Despite a rich body of work on polycentricity—work that clarifies our conceptual understanding (Ostrom 2014; Polanyi 1951; Aligica and Tarko 2012), identifies the special functionality of polycentric systems (Ostrom et al. 1961; Aligica and Tarko 2013; Thiel et al. 2019), analyzes extant polycentric governance structures (Vogler 2020), and examines the normative properties of polycentric systems (Gaus 2016, 2021; Kogelmann 2017; Müller 2019; Schaefer 2022)—there is no theory of how such polycentric governance structures first emerged. We argue, on both theoretical and empirical grounds, that the emergence of polycentric political systems can be partly explained by their greater ability to govern complex social systems effectively.

We begin by carefully defining polycentric political systems and describing some of their functional properties. We then proceed, in the following section, to present the key concept of our theoretical framework: the *complexity problem*. As societies increase in scale and diversify their productive activities, governors face increasingly high information-processing demands. This presents a governance dilemma: the State can either maintain *direct control* at the cost of increased complexity or it can embrace increasing complexity by allowing multiple, semi-autonomous centers of power to arise.[2] Through a variety of possible mechanisms, we argue, societies tend to drift toward one of two basins of attraction: low complexity/high control or high complexity/low control.[3] Having explained the logic of our model, we develop a detailed case study that compares the governance structures of Han China and ancient Rome. We opt for a case study since even the best cross-cultural historical data available is rather sparse and unsuitable for thorough testing or for illustrating the finer details of our account.[4] To conclude, we discuss an important implication of our theory for the prospects of centralized control in the near future.

1. POLYCENTRIC POLITICAL ORDERS

At its most abstract, the concept of polycentricity can describe systems as disparate as scientific inquiry (Polanyi 1951; Tarko 2015), democracy (V. Ostrom 2014), markets (Boettke and Candela 2015), and the common law (Hayek 1973). In all these realms, a network of connected agents independently seeks out solutions to pressing problems. Through an evolutionary process of trial and error, ever-better solutions come to replace dysfunctional and outdated ones.

To elucidate the concept of polycentricity, Paul Dragos Aligica and Vlad Tarko have isolated three essential features (2012, 252–53; 2013, 737):

1. *several centers for decision-making* that act with relative autonomy within their (possibly) overlapping jurisdictions,
2. a single *overarching system of rules* (formally or informally enforced), and
3. the emergence of a *spontaneous social order* as the outcome of an evolutionary competition between different governance units.[5]

Illustrative examples of polycentric political orders include metropolitan governance, American federalism (Candela 2021; V. Ostrom 2014), and the European Union (Vogler 2020). Considering the last example, decision centers include the municipal governments of European states, the national governments, regional coalitions, as well as the European council, commission, and parliament. The jurisdictions of these decision centers clearly overlap: cities can pass ordinances, even while the laws passed at the highest level of the European government, the *overarching system of rules*, will also apply to those cities. This overarching system of rules regulates how citizens and governments of various nations interact with one another. A key feature of this system of rules is that it permits the free movement of goods and people between European nations, allowing for both market competition as well as "Tiebout competition," i.e., voting with one's feet, both of which support spontaneous legal and economic orders (Mueller 2003, 187; Tiebout 1957).

One variable related to spontaneous order identified by Aligica and Tarko is of particular relevance to the present argument. Polycentric political orders permit the flow and aggregation of information in a way that monocentric states cannot.[6] As Hayek (1945) argued in the economic context, rivalrous competition facilitates the use of vast quantities of tacit, dispersed, and inarticulable information. To find the cheapest methods of production, for example, several firms must engage in small-scale experiments, trying out different combinations of inputs and producing slightly different products. The emergent prices, which provide an interface between consumer demand and factor supply, determine which firm has successfully met consumer needs at the lowest cost. This firm will enjoy profits, while other firms will experience losses, reducing their market share over time unless they self-correct. Without the process of experimental entrepreneurship, information about the best and least costly production methods would remain underutilized or even undiscovered (Paniagua 2018).[7]

In the same way, individuals within a political unit possess knowledge that a central government does not. Polycentric political orders permit the use of this information through horizontal and vertical competition. *Horizontal competition* occurs between political units on the same level, often those with non-overlapping geographical jurisdictions. Tiebout competition facilitates horizontal competition, and thus provides information about the desirability of different laws and policies. *Vertical competition* occurs as citizens opt to organize the provision of governmental services on different scales. For instance, policing services can be administered by the municipality or at the federal level. When democratic choice procedures are in place, different levels will compete for voter support. More generally, democratic institutions, which grant decision-making power to the lowest-level units and the individuals, aim to aggregate information about voters' preferences and beliefs. This information is harnessed to provide feedback for political leaders who are experimenting with different policy solutions (Barrett 2020). Citizens who are unhappy with a regime can contest it by rallying political support in its opposition. In its ideal form, democracy thus exhibits impressive epistemic properties (Cohen 1986; Estlund 1997; Landermore and Page 2015).[8] By incorporating contestation, experimentation, and competition, this polycentric paradigm is able to utilize dispersed and tacit knowledge in a manner analogous to the market-price system.[9]

By contrast, a monocentric state, relying on the *direct control* paradigm, possesses much less information about the conditions "on the ground." To some extent, this is an issue with any attempt to manage a situation from the top of a hierarchical bureaucracy. As James Scott explains, "Officials of the modern state are, of necessity, at least one step—and often several steps—removed from the society they are charged with governing. They assess the life of their society by a series of typifications that are always some distance from the full reality these abstractions are meant to capture" (1998, 76).

The monocentric state faces especially severe informational limits in this respect: they lack the bottom-up feedback of the democratic process, as well as any process of internal Tiebout competition to signal the success and failure of heterogeneous policy regimes. The direct control paradigm prevents the endogenous emergence of policy decisions, instead attempting to govern in a top-down fashion. The result is informational poverty.

2. THE COMPLEXITY PROBLEM

What Is Complexity?

Intuitively, many contemporary societies exhibit unprecedented levels of complexity. To take one illustration, Eric Beinhocker has noted that the number of different goods currently for sale in New York City far exceeds the number of species on the planet. This is not the case, not even remotely so, for simpler societies such as the Yanomanö (Beinhocker 2006, 9). Although the types of goods and services exchanged in an economy is a sign of social complexity, it is merely a proxy. What fundamentally distinguishes a simpler society from a complex one?

Social scientists have addressed this question both conceptually and empirically. Scott Page (2015) characterizes complexity in terms of five properties. A system is complex when it comprises:

1. a *large number* of entities,
2. a *network structure* that links these entities,
3. high levels of *interdependence* between these entities,
4. *adaptive behavior* on the part of these agents, and
5. diversity or *heterogeneity* of these agents.

In light of these properties, complex systems exhibit emergent properties, nonlinear dynamics, and constant novelty (see also Paniagua 2023). As a result, intervening in complex systems often produces unforeseen yet significant effects. This places severe limitations on long-term prediction and control.

It is important to point out that when discussing social complexity and societies that are more or less complex, we do not refer to outdated modes of social evolutionary thinking with their Eurocentric and modern-centric overtones. These modes of thinking presuppose a constant and irresistible trajectory toward modern, Western nation-states as paragons of complexity, civilization, and morality (Pluciennik 2005). In fact, all human societies can be thought of as complex social systems aggregating or dispersing flows of energy, resources, and information to sustain their population and maintain or expand their organizational structures (Daems 2021). Although societies do vary in the size and density of their populations, and these populations are more interdependent and diverse in some societies than in others, this has nothing to do with their degree of "civilization" or moral status.

The empirical approach to analyzing complexity supports our conceptual analysis. Many of the features identified by Page have been associated with empirical indicators such as the total population and the availability of communication technologies (Turchin et al. 2018). When large numbers of heterogeneous individuals interact, social complexity ensues.

Social Complexity and Direct Control

Social complexity is highly significant when considering the scope and limitations of political actors. To begin our analysis, consider a State that operates in accordance with the direct control paradigm. Such a State has three key features. First, it issues commands unilaterally from higher levels to lower levels of political administration; the direction of command is from the head of the State to its subordinates. The subjects do not issue commands to the State. Second, it actively opposes alternative centers of power, be these other semi-independent governing units or autonomous, private corporations. Finally, power is organized in a vertical fashion, with few horizontal connections.

In a highly complex society, this sort of state faces severe informational challenges of two types. The first is the *bottom-up challenge*, alluded to above, namely, that of apprehending vast amounts of dispersed and tacit information, while the second is a *top-down challenge*, namely, that of predicting the important, long-term effects of policy interventions.

James Scott (1998) expertly analyzes the bottom-up challenge of state administration. According to Scott, the statistical aggregates used by central planners often abstract away crucial details. Public administrators of states that govern complex societies cannot possibly access, document, and digest the heterogeneous vernaculars of their myriad sub-communities. They have difficulty perceiving complex patterns that individuals on the ground are highly adept at utilizing. Consequently, administrators must rely upon "typifications" that offer, at best, rough summaries of the true state of the world. Relying on such "synoptic facts" is indispensable to statecraft (77). Yet, doing so comes at a cost:

> These state simplifications, like all state simplifications, are always far more static and schematic that the actual social phenomena they presume to typify.

> The farmer rarely experiences an average crop, an average rainfall, or an average price for his crops. (46)

Each time a complete state of the world is distilled into a simple, abstract statistic for use at a higher level of administration, information is lost. Often, this information is more than a distracting detail. As Scott shows, it is impossible to know which pieces of information will be crucial for achieving desirable outcomes and which can be safely set aside. This issue is less severe when the governing unit is closer to the subjects being governed, when the subjects being governed are homogeneous, and when these subjects inhabit relatively predictable and uniform environments. However, upon introducing diversity, interdependence, and larger populations—i.e., upon increasing complexity—the loss of information becomes increasingly severe. In short, in the absence of institutional solutions, bottom-up information loss is an increasing function of social complexity. And, without adequate information about local conditions, the effectiveness of State interventions becomes highly suspect. Success will be evaluated according to abstract metrics that fail to capture crucially important details about the true state of the world.

The second, top-down informational challenge also threatens to undermine the effectiveness of State interventions into society. When systems become complex, they defy prediction. Simple models assuming either a small number of elements or homogeneity fail to provide insight into the dynamics of complex systems (Weaver 1948; Paniagua 2023). The impossibility of using the experimental method to determine predictive laws for society has been recognized at least since Mill (1836/2007). At its most basic, the difficulty of prediction is a result of the combinatorics involved in systematic attempts to determine predictive laws. As Page has pointed out, even if society were to possess only ten relevant variables that could take on three possible values, social scientists would need to run 59,049 separate experiments to determine the effects of changing the values of these variables (2018, 5). If there were a mere one hundred relevant variables, we would require 5.15×10^{47} separate experiments. Although we're often capable of making predictions with respect to a narrow set of proximate effects of a particular intervention—increase the money supply and inflation will go up—we can rarely predict its full social ramifications, especially in the long term (Gaus 2021). This lack of precise predictability impedes control. As a consequence, we observe, once again, an inverse relationship between state effectiveness and social complexity.

Both of these informational challenges point toward a fundamental problem that political institutions face when confronted by an increasingly complex society.

> *The Complexity Problem:* The ability to understand and control social outcomes, that is, to effectively intervene into society, decreases as social complexity increases.

At some point, the complexity problem becomes so severe that the direct control paradigm is no longer workable. In such a situation, the State faces a "choice" between two options. First, it can fight against complexity, which entails restricting the diversity and spontaneity of actors in its society. Scott notes that *all* States, to some extent, engage in simplifying practices; they attempt "with varying success to create a terrain and a population with precisely those standardized characteristics that will be easiest to monitor, count, assess, and manage" (1998, 81–2). Attempts at social simplification become especially critical for states organized around the direct control paradigm. If they succeed at holding social complexity at bay, then the direct control paradigm may remain workable. Otherwise, they must opt for the second option: shifting to a new governance paradigm, which we call the *polycentric paradigm*. Like the direct control paradigm, the polycentric paradigm is an ideal type, approximated to different extents by various real-world States. We now turn to the characterization and examination of this paradigm.

3. SOCIAL COMPLEXITY AND POLYCENTRICITY

The polycentric State differs from the direct control State in several key ways. First, polycentric governance requires that services be provided on multiple scales (Aligica and Tarko 2012, 257; V. Ostrom 2014; Stephan et al. 2019, 41). While a direct control State may establish a hierarchy with unidirectional authority (lower levels answer to higher ones), polycentricity requires that these layers exhibit some degree of autonomy and that lower levels exert some influence on higher levels. The subjects, mid-level functionaries, and high public officials answer to one another.

Second, the polycentric State permits competition between administrative layers (V. Ostrom 1972). If local efforts fail to adequately defend the local populace, defense services can be organized at a higher level, such as a confederation of cities, or a nation. This may be undertaken through a "quasimarket" arrangement, where local governance structures purchase such services from larger providers who reap the advantages of economies of scale (Boettke et al. 2011).

Third, the polycentric state supports alternative centers of power within each scale, be these other governing units or semi-autonomous, private organizations. For instance, in the United States, a national government provides services to state governments. In the European Union, the European government supports national governments in various ways. These states (in the United States) or nations (in the E.U.) offer alternative governance schemes to a population of citizens who select their jurisdiction partially on the basis of their governance competency. In sum, polycentric governance entails a multitude of levels, and competition occurs both vertically and horizontally.

In situations of low complexity, it is unclear whether the polycentric paradigm has any advantages over the direct control paradigm. If citizens are homogeneous in their values/preferences, low in number, relatively autarkic, and reside in stable, uniform environments, then the informational problems noted above will be minimal. In fact, in such a scenario, the polycentric paradigm seems to engender unnecessary costs. Polycentric governance involves a larger, less streamlined government. The various nodes of power must negotiate before many resolutions can pass. This often takes the form of competition among elites vying for power, which can produce collective action problems and suboptimal outcomes (Fukuyama 2011, 431). As more and more agents can contest decisions, reform becomes more difficult. Direct control avoids all these additional costs, since a single individual or small group determines the social choice and hands it down without unnecessary delay or bargaining. Direct control, in other words, exhibits *low transaction costs* compared to polycentricity.

As social complexity increases, however, informational problems come to the fore. In the direct control paradigm, detailed information on the ground struggles to reach high public officials. Polycentricity alleviates this problem in various ways. First, much governance is undertaken by lower-level political units. Because these units have smaller constituencies as well as more lines of communication between their officials and their citizens, the officials and citizens enjoy much greater proximity. Second, insofar as lower administrative levels can affect higher ones, the authority between various levels is bidirectional, allowing citizens or small organizations to directly and indirectly register their preferences and beliefs. For instance, in the United States, citizens at the lowest level of organization select the president directly, but they also choose senators, representatives, and governors who influence the president in various ways. This provides a bottom-up source of information. Historically, of course, few if any societies have been democratic in the sense of granting universal suffrage and holding referenda to directly determine government policies. However, polycentric political structures need not be democratic in this sense. Polycentricity, as we have defined it, mainly requires that lower levels of political structure exert power or influence on higher levels.[10]

Competition is also paramount to generating usable information. Vertical competition occurs when citizens decide whether local, regional, or federal governments best provide public goods and services. This information guides the State in determining the best level at which to provide a public good or service. Horizontal competition occurs as polities strive to attract citizens. Due to high transaction costs, horizontal competition is typically less effective than market competition. Nevertheless, when a governing unit is sufficiently ineffective, citizens will emigrate or, at least, decide not to immigrate. Horizontal competition thus facilitates the exercise of exit power and permits the flow of information from citizens on the ground to higher-level political units (Aligica and Tarko 2013; V. Ostrom 2014).

At the same time, polycentricity can be viewed as a partial solution to the top-down information problem. Most obviously, shifting governance responsibilities to lower-level units will reduce the average complexity of the problems that a government must solve. Within lower-level units, constituencies will be smaller and more homogeneous. Consequently, policy interventions are more predictable, and collective goals are better defined. In addition, processes of competition provide informational feedback by directing power and resources toward political units that engage in successful experimentation. Political units that stagnate or engage in unsuccessful experimentation will, correspondingly, shrink in relative size and power. As a result, even if the effect of policy interventions is impossible to predict *ex ante*, the process of competition will scale up *ex post* successful interventions, while unsuccessful policies will diminish in prevalence. Both vertical and horizontal competition thus contribute to an evolutionary search algorithm that identifies effective reforms.

4. A SIMPLE MODEL OF GOVERNING COMPLEXITY

In light of the difficulties faced by direct control and the advantages of the polycentric paradigm in coping with increasing complexity, we can posit a rough relationship between social complexity and government effectiveness (Figure 1). Direct control (blue curve), we have argued, is a low-cost technology for governing low-complexity societies, at least with respect to gathering and utilizing pertinent information. Accordingly, the marginal value of governance is quite high when social complexity is low. However, the effectiveness of governance begins to decrease as social complexity increases. Perhaps the strains of complexity are not felt at first, but beyond some point, the function will be *strictly* decreasing. By contrast, the polycentric paradigm (red curve) generates unnecessary transaction costs at low levels of complexity. The elaborate processes of competition, preference aggregation, and service duplication are wasteful in the absence of informational challenges. However, polycentric governance, largely due to its decentralized structure, scales far more gracefully than direct control. As complexity increases, polycentric governance is able to access and utilize ever more information at a relatively constant marginal cost.[11] Eventually, there comes a *threshold of complexity* at which polycentric governance yields higher marginal benefits for the society it governs. That is, it better enables relevant information to determine decision-making.

Beyond a certain point of complexity, a direct control paradigm may stifle information flows rather than help to gather and utilize them. This occurs at the point c_1, where the blue curve intersects with the abscissa. There also exists a point where governance itself, including a polycentric approach, may simply become difficult or impossible (Gaus 2021, 122), so even the polycentric governance curve will likely decrease beyond a certain point. However, we restrict ourselves to intermediate levels of complexity, where the relative effectiveness of polycentric governance can be represented by an increasing function of social complexity.

Given these two functional forms, there will exist a critical threshold of complexity, c^*, at which point the polycentric paradigm becomes a more effective governance form than direct control. This is the point at which the *complexity problem* becomes acute: to remain effective, the state must either embrace polycentricity or combat the trend of increasing complexity.

So far, this story has not specified the precise mechanism by which a society chooses its political structure. We have avoided doing so because the model we propose is compatible with a number of mechanisms, several of which may be operative at any given time. For example, elites may have an interest in adopting the most effective political structure. Perhaps they see the value of increasing the wealth and power of their society, or perhaps, as Ahmed and Stasavage (2020) suggest, poor policy choices threaten to spark rebellions. A second and probably more important mechanism involves inter-societal competition. When societies coexist under competitive conditions, those that adopt effective governance structures gain an advantage and are thus more likely to subsist and expand than societies that fail to adopt such structures. Assuming competitive conditions, then, we would predict a positive correlation between complexity and polycentricity and a negative correlation between complexity and direct control. These correlations will hold even in the absence of conscious forethought or deliberate design.

This formalistic description is not a historical narrative. We are not claiming that States first arise as examples of direct control before deciding, in the face of increasing complexity, whether or not to become more polycentric. In fact, some modern States have been polycentric from their conception (Hall 1985). What this analysis does suggest, however, is that polycentric States generally better accommodate social complexity, while direct control States face strong pressure to either drift toward more polycentric forms of

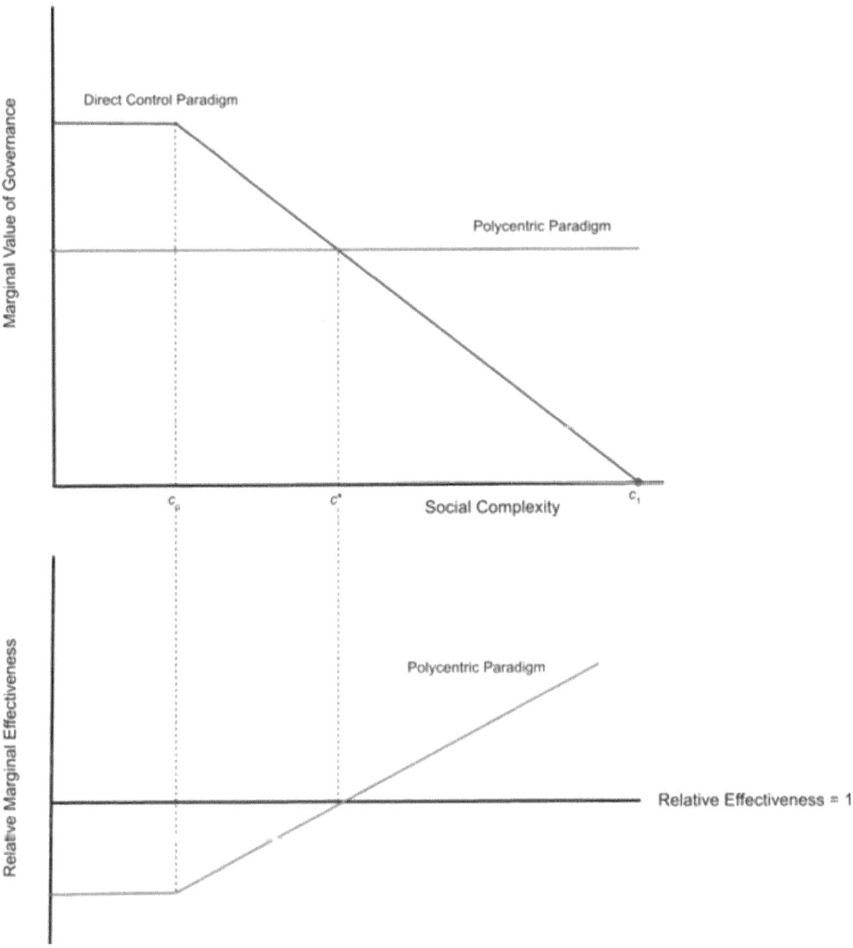

Figure 4.1. Comparative Effectiveness of Monocentric and Polycentric Governance.
Source: One of the authors.

governance or to actively combat the growth of complexity. The direct control State, in other words, must strive to maintain a level of complexity below c^*, lest its power should become clumsy and ineffective.

Can the theoretical apparatus developed thus far shed light on real-world political development? In the next section, we draw on historical work that compares ancient Rome to Han China. The theory developed above allows us to understand better some of the stark differences between the political structures of these two empires.

5. ANCIENT ROME AND HAN CHINA

In this section, we draw on a body of recent work in archaeology and political history that compares Han China to ancient Rome (see, among others, Beck and Vankeerberghen 2021; Scheidel 2016, 2014, 2009; Mutschler and Mittag 2008). The comparison between Han China and Rome illuminates our study for various reasons. First, these two empires were contemporaneous and of roughly equal sizes during the period of comparison (200 BCE–200 CE). Second, hardly any direct interaction existed between the two empires, which resulted in a somewhat clean natural experiment. While goods from China, such as silk garments, were highly sought after by the Roman elite, they mainly reached the Mediterranean through intermediaries operating on the outskirts of the Silk Road (Thorley 1971). While Chinese sources report Roman ambassadors to have visited the Han capital in 166 CE (Leslie and Gardiner 1996), these visits occurred sufficiently late in our temporal window of comparison. For our purposes here, we can consider both polities as only minimally interacting on a restricted scale and in an intermittent fashion. Finally, both states had differing levels of complexity. If we take the composite metric of social complexity developed by the Seshat team (see Turchin et al. 2018 for more details) for China and Rome from 200 BCE to 200 CE, we see the former going from a value of 2.97 to 2.24 and the latter from 1.72 to 3.26. In other words, whereas China started out as more complex at the start of our case study, it was unable to sustain this level, recording a slight decrease in overall complexity, whereas the Roman Empire managed to increase its complexity to a level even higher than Han China's starting value. Ian Morris (2010) corroborates this conclusion with a newly developed measure he calls "social development." Morris used this index to compare Han China to its Western counterpart, attributing higher scores to ancient Rome than to ancient China (100 BCE–500 CE) for three complexity-tracking variables: energy extraction, social organization (i.e., the size of settlements), and communication technology.

Given this disparity in social complexity, the theory laid out above would predict higher levels of polycentricity in the Roman Empire than in the Han Empire. This divergence in level of complexity is important given that we aim to examine the causal relationship between social complexity and polycentric political organization. We wish to know whether polycentric states support higher levels of social complexity and whether monocentric states tend to pursue policies of social simplification.

The roots of Chinese imperialism, as well as the origins of Rome, lie shrouded in myth. We focus on a period in which both empires exhibited a high degree of unity. In China, the Qin emperor's unification of seven regional polities in 221 BCE laid the foundations for the Han Dynasty (202 BCE–220 CE) considered here. In 220 CE, imperial rule under the Han Dynasty came to an end after civil unrest resulted in centuries of disunion and conflict between rival fiefdoms. Although Rome began as a republic, elite rivalries slowly eroded institutional structures from the second century BCE onward (Lintott 2013), culminating in a civil war during the first century BCE. Civil order was restored by Emperor Augustus, setting the scene for imperial rule during the first and second centuries CE.

Recall that the hypothesis we defend here asserts that, at least under competitive conditions, higher social complexity should induce either greater polycentricity or provoke reactionary attempts to stifle that complexity. Examining various aspects of state administration in ancient Rome and Han China confirms this prediction. One preliminary observation is quite striking: while Han China's population was slightly less than that of the Roman empire, the Han state employed *more than ten times* as many public officials (Noreña 2015, 196–97; Scheidel 2015, 167). The reason for this, we argue, is that the Roman Empire relied on municipal governance headed by local elites rather than centrally appointed officials (Noreña 2015, 201). This reflects a massive difference in state organization.

Especially in the eastern Mediterranean, a long tradition of local civic autonomy can be traced back at least to the early Hellenistic period (350–200 BCE), resulting in an intensive competitive interaction space between cities and kings (Ma 1999; Strootman 2011). Within this interaction space, cities competed for favors from the royal courts but also used the constant strife and warfare between the various Hellenistic kingdoms vying for control over the eastern Mediterranean and Near East to gain benefits for themselves, including monetary gifts, tax exemptions, and land donations (Ma 2013).

Moreover, the Hellenistic world was one of unprecedented social and geographical mobility, as specialists, artisans, traders, mercenaries, scholars, and fortune-seekers increasingly roamed from city to city, from court to court, and from festival to festival, throughout the Hellenistic world in search of professional opportunities (Chaniotis 2018, 291–95). Increasing opportunities in the urban centers, along with the normalization of social and geographical mobility, offered genuine alternatives to agriculture and provided real possibilities for the dispossessed to seek employment elsewhere, effectively engendering a Tiebout competition process. The political dominance of the Roman Empire reduced the effectiveness of the competitive interaction space between the local and imperial levels. Still, the Romans maintained many of the existing interaction mechanisms (Colvin 2004). Moreover, the social and geographical mobility, which facilitated Tiebout competition, remained in force as the Roman *oecumene* offered ever-increasing social and economic opportunities in the first two centuries CE (Verboven 2021; Willet 2021).

In contrast to the ancient Roman state, the Han Empire selected its own officials and appointed them to manage the local affairs of its towns. They even had strict rules against assigning officials to towns where they had local connections or preexisting influence (Lewis 2015, 205–06). As Noreña explains, "Throughout the Han Empire . . . the central regime managed to administer its territories and to govern its subjects directly via centrally appointed imperial officials. There is no real parallel in any other premodern empire" (2015, 198).

This stark difference in urban administration reflects very different histories. While large parts of the Roman Empire emerged from a context of self-governing city-states during the preceding Iron Age and Hellenistic period (Boehm 2018; Dimitriev 2005), China's land-owning elites were stripped of power fairly early. Already during the Warring States period, municipal governments were swallowed up by ambitious state-builders (Noreña 2015, 201). Just before the onset of Han rule, during the Qin dynasty, 120,000 of the wealthiest and most powerful families were reportedly relocated to settlements near the capital where they could be more easily surveilled. The relocation process continued during the Han dynasty (Noreña 2014, 194), and within the first hundred years of Han rule, any vestige of feudal institutions had been eradicated (Fukuyama 2011, 132). The power of local elites and the sense of autonomy of cities within the Roman Empire were too great to have permitted the Roman government to achieve such a feat on a grand scale.

Especially in its early years, Han China was ruled by a strong centralized government, exercising strict control over a series of provinces (San 2014, 73). As time went on, the central government weakened and lost its grip over the increasingly powerful elite families. The Han government would eventually come to face major rebellions from regional warlords, resulting in the establishment of a series of regional polities that were only nominally paying homage to the emperor. This decentralization process should not be conflated with the emergence of polycentricity, as the effective transmission of information was cut off in favor of, at best, mere nominal interactions between the centralized government and regional warlords.

The Roman Empire's relative decentralization of political power appears starkly in its relatively distributed population. Urban centers in Rome were smattered across the Mediterranean region, while Chinese urban centers clustered tightly around the capital city (see Figures 2 and 3). This dispersal of towns in imperial Rome is all the more critical when we consider their relative autonomy.

The decentralization of power in the Roman Empire produced several important effects. First, and especially crucial for an empire that relied upon a massive army to maintain control over its provinces, taxation was assessed

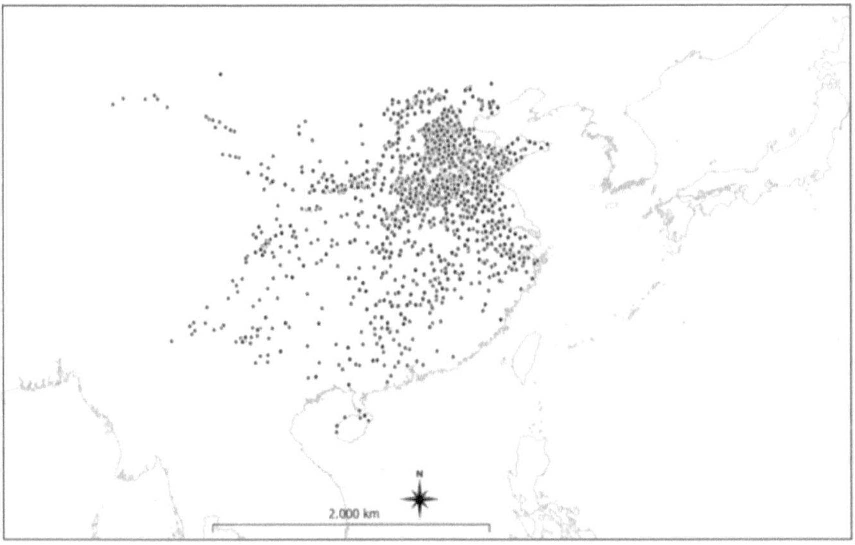

Figure 4.2. Urban sites in Han China.
Source: One of the authors using data from Berman (2017).

and collected at a local and regional level before being passed to the imperial state. This constituted one part of a power-sharing outcome that Walter Scheidel has called "the great bargain" (2014, 164). Under this arrangement, local elites were granted autonomy in exchange for their cooperation in providing the imperial state with tax payments used to support the military and the metropolitan populace of Rome. This arrangement left considerable discretion in the hands of local elites. By contrast, the Han Chinese state was able to undertake direct taxation on land output through the use of its own officials (Scheidel 2015, 164).

Second, local autonomy meant that political organization varied across the Roman Empire, with some provinces or municipalities exhibiting more and some less economic and individual freedom (Eich 2014). Although the evidence does not permit any definitive statements, institutional diversity may have promoted competition between cities and provinces. As noted above, there was a high level of individual mobility between Roman cities. At the same time, Roman elites made massive voluntary investments in public works, perhaps to appease and attract citizens (Lewis 2015, 205). In Han China, by contrast, investments in public buildings were restricted to state officials: "the sanctioned public realm was formally identical with the sites of state activity" (Lewis 2015, 218). The average citizen could not enter nor utilize public buildings. This discrepancy between Roman public works and Chinese state buildings is quite predictable from the perspective of basic

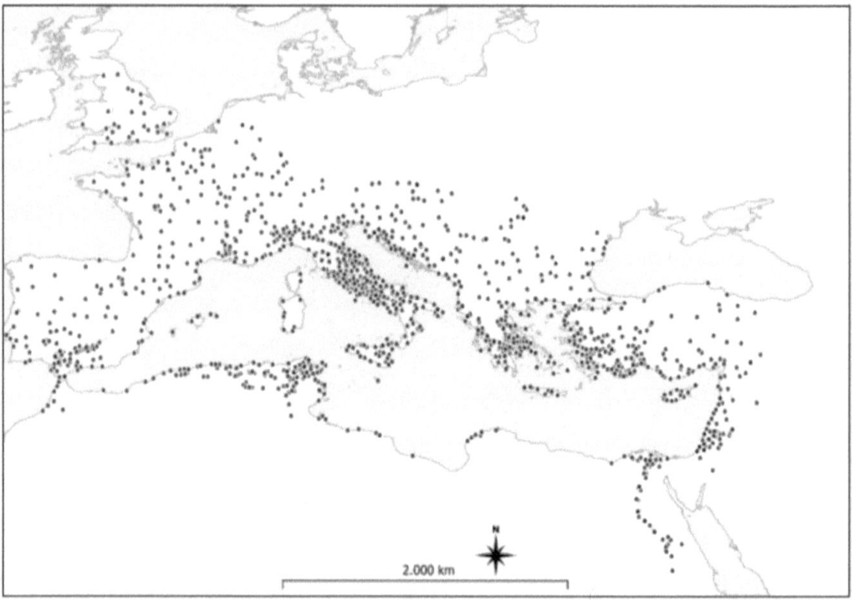

Figure 4.3. Urban sites in the Roman Empire.
Source: One of the authors using data from Hanson (2017).

economic theory: cities within competitive frameworks will offer a greater quantity and quality of services than cities within a monopolistic framework.

A third effect of decentralized political power was a diminished ability to control economic activity. Markets did, of course, exist in Han China, but they were a unique exception to the general lack of public spaces the state provided or permitted. Moreover, markets did not, as in Rome, support a sphere of non-public social activity. As Carlos Noreña explains . . .

> The one exception to [the] general ban on crowds were the official, urban markets. These areas were marked as public spaces through two forms of construction: a central, multistory tower that housed the officials in charge and a grid of stalls in which shops were arranged by the category of goods that they sold. They also followed the pattern of Han public spaces in that they were placed behind walls and open only at stipulated times that were signaled by banners and drums. The beating of drums to signal the opening of the market in the morning and its closing in the evening provided the earliest known form of a major feature of imperial Chinese urban spaces in that a "soundscape" fashioned by the government marked the rhythms of the day. According to Qin law, records of all transactions were to be submitted to officials, so commercial interactions all brought the participants into regular contact with the agents of the government. (2014, 213–14)

Thus, the sole public space in which commoners were permitted to congregate became, in Han China, a platform for social and economic control. In contrast, while still governed by institutional rules, Roman marketplaces appear to be less regulated, less regimented, and often spontaneous (McMullen 1970).[12] It has been noted that the imperial administration lacked the necessary resources to impose new formal institutions and needed local elites to enforce them (Verboven 2021). In a similar vein, Carlos Noreña explains how towns spontaneously formed near the perimeter of the Roman empire in order to exchange goods with soldiers in possession of gold (Noreña 2015, 195). Marketplaces in the Roman Empire were not theaters for state power, as in Han China, but spontaneously emerging centers for capitalist exchange (Runciman 1983; Temin 2013).

In addition to exercising tight control over the venue of exchange, the Chinese imperial state also controlled the price and quantity of goods exchanged by monopolizing most of the relevant industries: salt, iron, tea, wines, and spirits, as well as a monopoly in waterways, foreign trade, and real estate. By contrast, state monopolies in the Roman Empire, though sometimes granted to private merchants, were less extensive and direct than those of the Han State. In its earlier phases, the Roman Empire had very few such monopolies (Broekaert 2019).

For example, consider the market for real estate in ancient towns. Éteinne Balazs reports the stark difference in how this commodity was managed in Rome versus Han China: "Whereas in the West . . . it was the urban patrician class that sold or let sites, premises, workshops, and other commercial or industrial establishments to the artisans and merchants, in China it was the state that was the ground landlord, the state and the officials that built and let shops, warehouses, and other commercial buildings" (1964, 77). According to recent studies, property in ancient Rome was owned primarily by private individuals, priced and distributed by market mechanisms (Temin 2001, 178–79). There are many accounts of Roman citizens who gained or lost fortunes through the private sale or acquisition of property.[13]

A similar contrast between Han China and ancient Rome could be drawn for other crucial commodities, such as cereals, cloth, and iron. These industries were dominated and controlled by the Han State in a way that makes the ancient Roman State, despite its many incursions, look like a laissez-faire pseudo-state. There are, therefore, several examples of how the Han State targeted and crushed rival centers of power. In contrast, the Roman State allowed power, both political and economic, to emerge outside of its ambit. To underline the main point, it was not merely that the Han Chinese State accidentally hampered economic activities through their interventionist policies. For our purposes, the most important fact is that *the State actively and intentionally hindered entrepreneurship and innovation in order to maintain control*. As Balazs writes,

> every means of keeping the merchant class down and holding it in subjection seemed permissible. Compromises, exceptions, favors, pardons—all were allowed so long as they were retracted at the earliest opportunity. Claims, titles, privileges, immunities, deeds, charters were never granted. Any sign of initiative in the other camp was usually strangled at birth, or if it had reached a state when it could no longer be suppressed, the state laid hands on it, took it under control, and appropriated the resultant profits. (41)

The contrast with early imperial Rome is stark. As Michael Rostovtzeff tells us:

> [t]he period of Augustus and of his immediate successors was a time of almost complete freedom for trade and of splendid opportunities for private initiative. Neither as a republic nor under the guidance of Augustus and his successors did Rome adopt the policy . . . of nationalizing trade and industry, of making them more or less a monopoly of the state as represented by the king. Everything was left to private management. (Rostovtzeff 1926, 54)

While some have accused Rostovtzeff of exaggeration (Finley 1973), more recent work has vindicated his analysis of Roman economic organization (Temin 2013, 2001). Market mechanisms played a very important role in determining the distribution of resources. In China, by contrast, private initiatives outside of State institutions were not viable strategies for accumulating wealth; economic power was far more concentrated in the hands of the central State and was largely acquired through State activity. A key consequence of this disparity, as Balazs explains, is that "while the Western town was the seed-bed and after the bulwark of the bourgeoisie, the Chinese town was primarily the seat of government, the residence of officials who were permanently hostile to the bourgeoisie, and thus always under the domination of the state" (44).

An important caveat to the contrast presented here—a contrast between a powerful and centralized Chinese State and a decentralized Roman one—concerns the military. Rome's military was highly centralized and much larger than that of Han China's. During the same period, Rome spent roughly three times more on military expenditures than Han China (Scheidel 2014, 174). However, the vast majority of military affairs were conducted at the periphery of the empire. For this reason, controlling military power did not entail control over cities or towns of the interior. In fact, the need to constantly focus on the perimeters of the empire may help to account for their relative lack of control over the interior.

A second caveat concerns the mechanism at play in determining these disparate political structures. As mentioned above, historical contingency played a significant role in determining the centralized structure of the Han State, as it did in determining the decentralized structure of the Roman counterpart. Many interacting variables were at play in determining these trajectories. The hypothesis we defend here seeks to elucidate a natural affinity between social complexity and polycentricity. Our hypothesis predicts that when effective governance is required for maintaining a society, high complexity will correlate with higher levels of polycentricity. In the case study under consideration, the Roman Empire was committed, even prior to their rapid increase in social complexity, to a form of polycentric governance. This commitment was due to factors that had little to do with social complexity, but they did, nevertheless, permit a flourishing of social complexity without the need for drastic changes in political structure. By contrast, due to the efforts of their Qin forebears, the officials of Han China operated a highly centralized bureaucracy that viewed social complexity as a subversive threat to State control. Consequently, they combatted many of its manifestations.

Our hypothesis is compatible with the observation that historical processes can push societies into suboptimal governance structures, especially in the short run and when competitive pressures are low. Nevertheless, we predict a positive correlation between complexity and polycentric governance due to the greater effectiveness of polycentric governance under conditions of complexity. The comparison between Han China and ancient Rome provides insight into one possible mechanism linking greater governance effectiveness to a greater likelihood of implementation: centralized States have both a capacity and an interest in combating the emergence of complexity, as the Han Chinese State so vigorously did. Polycentric States, on the other hand, are unable to resist social complexity, especially under competitive conditions. All in all, the comparison between Han China and ancient Rome supports our hypothesis.

CONCLUSION

The model developed earlier in this paper offers an information-theoretic, functionalist explanation of the emergence of polycentric governance structures. It identifies a critical force that could drive a State toward a decentralized set of competing jurisdictions, namely the difficulty of governing an increasingly complex society. The same model explains why centralized states might resist increasing complexity by suppressing entrepreneurial activity, technological progress, and cultural diversity. The direct control paradigm can only be maintained when such sources of complexity are kept in check.

However, this is a highly abstract model that identifies only one fundamental relationship that affects governance institutions: complexity and polycentricity. Is this relationship strong enough to make a difference amidst a host of other causal factors? Does this highly abstract model aptly describe real-world processes? Our analysis, supported by a comparative case study of ancient Rome and Han China, suggests an affirmative answer to these questions. The Han Chinese State actively suppressed private concentrations of power and new technologies that might have disrupted the balance of power. By curtailing social complexity, the central State was able to reduce unpredictable dynamism, which might force a delegation of power to local leaders. The ancient Roman State, by contrast, lacked the capacity to suppress sources of complexity and, consequently, was unable to achieve or maintain the degree of centralized power exhibited by the Han State.[14]

An important point has been neglected throughout this chapter, namely the dual role of technology as an impetus to greater social complexity and a tool for increasing State capacity. Communication technologies, for instance, increase the interconnectedness of various nodes in a society, and this, in turn, increases the dynamism and volatility of social activity. At the same time, such technologies make it far easier for a centralized State to receive and transmit information. Some technologies, such as facial recognition technology, will likely enhance the capacity of States to acquire information and thus manage their populations. Others—for instance, social media or cryptocurrencies—will have the opposite effect, contributing more to social complexity than State capacity. The overwhelming trend, some suggest, is for social complexity to grow faster than State capacity (van Creveld 1999, 377–94). If this is correct, our theory has a clear prediction: States seeking to maintain or reprise centralized control will suppress economic, technological, and cultural dynamism.

NOTES

1. We would like to thank David Schmidtz, Vlad Tarko, Justin Bruner, and Thomas Christiano for their comments on the chapter. In addition, the chapter took shape with the help of feedback from Pablo Paniagua, Matthew Jeffers, Mario Juárez García, Jan Vogler, Abigail Devereaux, Cameron Harwick, and Anthony Gill. We also thank Danai Kafetzaki for help with the analysis and figures.

2. Importantly, while it is convenient to anthropomorphize the State and describe this dilemma as a choice faced by some unitary actor, unconscious forces and historical contingency are often more important than deliberate choice. Although it is

consistent with our model for a political leader to consciously choose between control and complexity, we do not claim this is the primary mechanism by which polycentricity typically emerges.

3. We elaborate on two possible mechanisms below (16–17).

4. We do, however, leverage the limited data available to provide a robustness check on our empirical case study. In particular, we've relied upon the Seshat data set. We use some of the indicators identified in the data set as proxies for polycentricity, while others explicitly measure social complexity. Our hypothesis is that these indicators should correlate, which is, indeed, what we find. More details on this large-scale data analysis can be found at: https://zenodo.org/records/10526926.

5. See also Stephan, Marshall, and McGinnis (2019, 41).

6. Ahmed and Stasavage (2020) make a similar point about information flows, but instead of highlighting polycentricity, they emphasize representative or council-based governance. Similarly, Vogler (2023) analyzes the effectiveness of imperial rule in terms of informational asymmetries that exist between local and centralized governance units.

7. The idea of *discovering* new information rather than merely utilizing extant information is an animating idea in recent work on experimentalist governance (Sabel and Zeitlin 2012; Eckert and Börzel 2012). On the relationship between interactions and knowledge, see also Paniagua (2018).

8. Some are far less sanguine about the epistemic value of democracy (Brennan 2017; Somin 2013). But see Christiano (2015).

9. The two processes outlined in this paragraph—Tiebout competition and democratic choice—align with Hirschman's (1970) two famous modes of organizational reform: exit and voice. The competitive, polycentric view of democracy outlined here also coheres nicely with Robert Dahl's concept of "polyarchy," though Dahl mentions its competitive or epistemic properties only in passing (e.g., Dahl 1984, 230).

10. In this sense, polycentricity is closer to Dahl's "polyarchy" than it is to pure democracy (Dahl 1984).

11. It is quite possible, in fact, that the polycentric governance technology exhibits increasing effectiveness as complexity increases.

12. See also Dio Chryostomum 35.15 2006, 35.15, 405–07.

13. For example, according to Pliny the Elder, L. Tarius Rufus lost a sizeable fortune in his property dealings. See Pliny the Elder's Natural History 33.135 and 18.7 (discussed in Morris 2015, 57). Marcus Licinius Crassus acquired much of his fortune through the provision of firefighting services. His tactic was to arrive with his brigade at buildings already ablaze and offer to extinguish the fire only under the condition that the owner would sell him the property at a rock-bottom price (Plutarch and Perrin 1916, 317–19).

14. It's worth noting that our story further corroborates a documented empirical connection between social complexity and higher levels of local or individual autonomy (Maurya and Sahu 2022; Ahmed and Stasavage 2020).

REFERENCES

Ahmed, Ali T., and David Stasavage. 2020. "Origins of early democracy." *American Political Science Review* 114.2: 502–18.

Aligica, Paul D. 2019. *Public Entrepreneurship, Citizenship, and Self-Governance*. Cambridge: Cambridge University Press.

Aligica, Paul D., and Vlad Tarko. 2012. "Polycentricity: From Polanyi to Ostrom, and Beyond." *Governance* 25 (2): 237–62. https://doi.org/10.1111/j.1468-0491.2011.01550.x.

——— 2013. "Co-Production, Polycentricity, and Value Heterogeneity: The Ostroms' Public Choice Institutionalism Revisited." *American Political Science Review* 107 (4): 726–41.

——— 2014. "Institutional Resilience and Economic Systems: Lessons from Elinor Ostrom's Work." *Comparative Economic Studies* 56 (1): 52–76. https://doi.org/10.1057/ces.2013.29.

Balazs, Etienne. 1964. *Chinese Civilization and Bureaucracy: Variations on a Theme*, Translated by H.M. Wright and Arthur F. Wright. New Haven: Yale University Press.

Bang, Peter Fibiger, and Karen Turner. 2015. *Kingship and Elite Formation*. Oxford: Oxford University Press.

Barrett, Jacob. 2020. "Social Reform in a Complex World." *Journal of Ethics and Social Philosophy* 17(2): 103–32.

Beck, Hans, and Griet Vankeerberghen. 2021. *Rulers and Ruled in Ancient Greece, Rome, and China*. Cambridge: Cambridge University Press.

Berman, L. 2017. *V6 Time Series County Points* (V1 ed.). Harvard Dataverse. https://doi.org/10.7910/DVN/Q9VOF5.

Boehm, Ryan. 2018. *City and Empire in the Age of the Successors—Urbanization and Social Response in the Making of the Hellenistic Kingdoms*. Berkeley: University of California Press.

Boettke, Peter J., and Rosolino A. Candela. 2015. "Rivalry, Polycentricism, and Institutional Evolution." In *Advances in Austrian Economics*, edited by Christopher J. Coyne and Virgil Henry Storr, 19:1–19. New York: Emerald Group Publishing Limited. https://doi.org/10.1108/S1529-213420150000019001.

Boettke, Peter J., Christopher J. Coyne, and Peter T. Leeson. 2011. "Quasimarket Failure." *Public Choice* 149 (1–2): 209–24. https://doi.org/10.1007/s11127-011-9833-8.

Brennan, Jason. 2017. *Against Democracy: With a New Preface by the Author*. Princeton, NJ: Princeton University Press.

Broekaert, Wim. 2019. "Occupational Associations and Monopolies in the Roman Economy." *Revue belge de philologie et d'histoire* 97 (1): 5–41. https://doi.org/10.3406/rbph.2019.9258.

Candela, Rosolino A. 2021. "Rethinking Federalism: Social Order through Evolution or Design." In *Elinor Ostrom and the Bloomington School: Building a New Approach to Policy and the Social Sciences*, edited by Jayme S. Lemke and Vlad Tarko. Newcastle upon Tyne, UK: Agenda Publishing: 153–70.

Tiebout, Charles 1956. "A Pure Theory of Local Expenditures." *Journal of Political Economy* 64 (5): 416–24.
Christiano, Thomas. 2015. "Voter Ignorance Is Not Necessarily a Problem." *Critical Review* 27 (3–4): 253–69. https://doi.org/10.1080/08913811.2015.1111669.
Cohen, Joshua. 1986. "An Epistemic Conception of Democracy." *Ethics* 97 (1): 26–38. https://doi.org/10.1086/292815.
Colvin, Stephen. 2004. *The Greco-Roman East: Politics, Culture, Society*. Cambridge: Cambridge University Press.
Creveld, Martin van. 1999. *The Rise and Decline of the State*. Cambridge: Cambridge University Press. https://doi.org/10.1017/CBO9780511497599.
Daems, Dries. 2021. *Social Complexity and Complex Systems in Archaeology*. London: Routledge.
Dahl, Robert A. 1984. "Polyarchy, Pluralism, and Scale." *Scandinavian Political Studies* 7 (4): 225–40. https://doi.org/10.1111/j.1467-9477.1984.tb00304.x.
Dio Chrysostom. 2006. *Dio Chrysostom. 3: Discourses 31–36*, translated by J.W. Cohoon. Reprint. The Loeb Classical Library 358. Cambridge, MA: Harvard University Press.
Dmitriev, Sviatoslav. 2005. *City Government in Hellenistic and Roman Asia Minor*. Oxford: Oxford University Press.
Eckert, S., and T.A. Börzel. 2012. Experimentalist governance: An introduction. *Regulation & Governance* 6(3): 371–77.
Eich, Peter. 2015. "The Common Denominator: Late Roman Imperial Bureaucracy from a Comparative Perspective." In *State Power in Ancient China and Rome*, edited by Walter Scheidel. Oxford: Oxford University Press 90–149.
Estlund, David. 1997. "The Epistemic Dimension of Democratic Authority." *Modern Schoolman* 74 (4): 259–76. https://doi.org/10.5840/schoolman199774424.
Feng, Li. 2001. "'Offices' in Bronze Inscriptions and Western Zhou Government Administration." *Early China* 26: 1–72.
Finley, M. I. 1973. *The Ancient Economy*. Sather Classical Lectures. Berkeley: University of California Press.
Fukuyama, Francis. 2011. *The Origins of Political Order: From Prehuman Times to the French Revolution*. London: Profile Books.
Gaus, Gerald F. 2016. *The Tyranny of the Ideal: Justice in a Diverse Society*. Princeton: Princeton University Press.
— 2021. *The Open Society and Its Complexities*. Philosophy, Politics, and Economics. New York: Oxford University Press.
Hall, John. 1985. "Capstones and Organisms: Political Forms and the Triumph of Capitalism." *Sociology* 19 (2): 173–92.
Hanson, John. 2017. *An Urban Geography of the Roman World, 100 BC to AD 300*. Oxford: Archaeopress.
Hayek, F. A. 1945. "The Use of Knowledge in Society." *American Economic Review* 35 (4): 519–30.
——— 1984. *Rules and Order: A New Statement of the Liberal Principles of Justice and Political Economy*. Law, Legislation, and Liberty, vol. 1. Chicago: University of Chicago Press.

Hirschman, Albert O. 2004. *Exit, Voice, and Loyalty: Responses to Decline in Firms, Organizations, and States*. Cambridge, MA: Harvard University Press.

Kogelmann, Brian. 2017. "Justice, Diversity, and Well-Ordered Society." *Philosophical Quarterly*, 269(67): 663–84. https://doi.org/10.1093/pq/pqw082.

Landemore, Hélène, and Scott E. Page. 2015. "Deliberation and Disagreement: Problem Solving, Prediction, and Positive Dissensus." *Politics, Philosophy & Economics* 14 (3): 229–54. https://doi.org/10.1177/1470594X14544284.

Leslie, Donald, and Gardiner, Kenneth. 1996. *The Roman Empire in Chinese Sources*. Rome: Bardi.

Lewis, Mark Edward. 2015. "Public Spaces in Cities in the Roman and Han Empires." In *State Power in Ancient China and Rome*, edited by Walter Scheidel. Oxford: Oxford University Press, 204–29.

Lintott, A. 2013. *Imperium Romanum: Politics and Administration*. Routledge.

Loewe, Michael. 2006. *The Government of the Qin and Han Empires: 221 BCE–220 CE*. Indianapolis: Hackett Publishing.

Ma, John. 1999. *Antiochus III and the Cities of Western Asia Minor*. Oxford University Press.

———. 2013. 'Hellenistic Empires.' In *The Oxford Handbook of the State in the Ancient Near East and Mediterranean*, edited by Peter Fibiger Bang and Walter Scheidel. Oxford: Oxford University Press, 324–57.

MacMullen, Ramsay. 1970. "Market-Days in the Roman Empire." *Phoenix* 24 (4): 333–41.

Maurya, Garima, and Sohini Sahu. 2022. "Cross-country variations in economic complexity: The role of individualism." *Economic Modelling*, Vol. 115, 105961.

Mill, John Stuart. 2007. "On the Definition and Method of Political Economy." In *The Philosophy of Economics: An Anthology*, edited by Daniel M. Hausman. Cambridge: Cambridge University Press. https://doi.org/10.1017/CBO9780511819025.

Morris, Ian. 2010. *Social Development*. Online. http://pzacad.pitzer.edu/~lyamane/ianmorris.pdf.

——— 2015. "Foragers, Farmers, and Fossil Fuels." In *Foragers, Farmers, and Fossil Fuels*. Princeton, NJ: Princeton University Press.

Müller, Julian F. 2019. *Political Pluralism, Disagreement and Justice: The Case for Polycentric Democracy*. New York: Routledge.

Mutschler, Fritz-Heiner, and Achim Mittag. 2008. *Conceiving the Empire: China and Rome Compared*. Oxford: Oxford University Press. http://www.myilibrary.com?id=186571.

Noreña, Carlos F. 2015. "Urban Systems in the Han and Roman Empires: State Power and Social Control." In *State Power in Ancient China and Rome*, edited by Walter Scheidel. Oxford: Oxford University Press, 181–203.

Ostrom, Vincent. 1977. "Some Problems in Doing Political Theory: A Response to 'A Critique of Democratic Administration and Its Supporting Ideation,' by Robert T. Golembiewski." *American Political Science Review* 71:1488–531. http://hdl.handle.net/10535/4197.

——— 2014. "Polycentricity: The Structural Basis of Self-Governing Systems." In *Choice, Rules and Collective Action: The Ostroms on the Study of Institutions and*

Governance, edited by Filippo Sabetti and Paul Dragos Aligica. Colchester, UK: ECPR Press, 45–60.

Ostrom, Vincent, Charles M. Tiebout, and Robert Warren. 1961. "The Organization of Government in Metropolitan Areas: A Theoretical Inquiry." *American Political Science Review* 55 (4): 831–42. https://doi.org/10.2307/1952530.

Page, Scott E. 2015. "What Sociologists Should Know About Complexity." *Annual Review of Sociology* 41: 21–41. /annurev-soc-073014-112230

——— 2018. "The Imperative of Complexity." *Cosmos + Taxis* 5 (2): 4–12.

Paniagua, Pablo. 2018. "Money and the emergence of knowledge in society." *Review of Social Economy* 76:1, 95–118.

——— 2023. "Complexity defying macroeconomics." *Cambridge Journal of Economics*, 47:3, 575–92.

Pliny, and John F. Healy. 1991. *Natural History, a Selection*. Penguin Classics. New York: Penguin Books.

Pluciennik, Mark. 2005. *Social Evolution*. Duckworth Debates in Archaeology. London: Duckworth.

Plutarch. 2007. *Plutarch's Lives, Vol.3,* Translated by Bernadotte Perrin. Cambridge, MA.: Harvard University Press.

Polanyi, Michael. 1998. *The Logic of Liberty: Reflections and Rejoinders*. Indianapolis: Liberty Fund.

Rostovtzeff, Michael Ivanovitch. 1926. *The Social and Economic History of the Roman Empire*. New York: Biblo & Tannen Publishers.

Runciman, Walter G. 1983. "Capitalism without Classes: The Case of Classical Rome." *British Journal of Sociology*, 157–81.

Sabel, Charles F., and Jonathan Zeitlin. 2012. "Chapter 12: Experimentalist Governance," in David Levi-Faur (ed.) *The Oxford Handbook of Governance*. Oxford: Oxford University Press. https://doi.org/10.1093/oxfordhb/9780199560530.013.0012.

San, Tan. 2014. *Dynastic China: An Elementary History*. New York: The Other Press.

Schaefer, Alexander. 2022. "Reasonable but Non-Liberal: Another Route to Polycentrism." *Philosophical Quarterly* 72 (1): 218–28. https://doi.org/10.1093/pq/pqab043.

Scheidel, Walter. 2010. *Rome and China Comparative Perspectives on Ancient World Empires*. New York; Oxford: Oxford University Press. http://www.vlebooks.com/vleweb/product/openreader?id=Exeter&isbn=9780199714292.

——— ed. 2015a. *State Power in Ancient China and Rome*. Oxford Studies in Early Empires. Oxford; New York: Oxford University Press.

——— 2015b. "State Revenue and Expenditure in the Han and Roman Empires." In *State Power in Ancient China and Rome*, 150–180. Oxford: Oxford University Press.

——— 2016. "Empires of Inequality: Ancient China and Rome." *SSRN Electronic Journal*. https://doi.org/10.2139/ssrn.2817173.

Scott, James C. 1998. *Seeing Like a State*. Yale University Press. https://www.degruyter.com/document/doi/10.12987/9780300128789/html.

Somin, Ilya. 2013. *Democracy and Political Ignorance: Why Smaller Government Is Smarter*. Stanford, CA: Stanford Law Books, an imprint of Stanford University Press.

Stephan, Mark, Graham Marshall, and Michael McGinnis. 2019. "An Introduction to Polycentricity and Governance." In *Governing Complexity*, edited by Andreas Thiel, William A. Blomquist, and Dustin E. Garrick. Cambridge: Cambridge University Press, 21–44. https://doi.org/10.1017/9781108325721.002.

Strootman, Rolf. 2011. "Kings and cities in the Hellenistic Age." In *Political Culture in the Greek City After the Classical Age*, edited by Richard Alston and Onno Nijf. New York: Peeters Publisher, 141–53.

Tarko, Vlad. 2017. *Elinor Ostrom: An Intellectual Biography*. London; New York: Rowman & Littlefield International.

Temin, Peter. 2001. "A Market Economy in the Early Roman Empire." *Journal of Roman Studies* 91: 169–81.

———2013. *The Roman Market Economy*. Princeton, NJ: Princeton University Press.

Thiel, Andreas, Dustin E. Garrick, and William A. Blomquist. 2019. *Governing Complexity: Analyzing and Applying Polycentricity*. Cambridge: Cambridge University Press.

Thorley, John. 1971. "The Silk Trade between China and the Roman Empire at Its Height, Circa A.D. 90–130." *Greece & Rome* 18(1): 71–80. https://doi.org/10.1017/S0017383500017691.

Tiebout, Charles 1956. "A Pure Theory of Local Expenditures." *Journal of Political Economy* 64 (5): 416–24.

Turchin, Peter, Thomas E. Currie, Harvey Whitehouse, Pieter François, Kevin Feeney, Daniel Mullins, Daniel Hoyer et al. 2018. "Quantitative Historical Analysis Uncovers a Single Dimension of Complexity That Structures Global Variation in Human Social Organization." *Proceedings of the National Academy of Sciences* 115 (2): E144–51. https://doi.org/10.1073/pnas.1708800115.

Verboven, Koen. 2021. "Playing by Whose Rules? Institutional Resilience, Conflict and Change in the Roman Economy." In *Complexity Economics: Building a New Approach to Ancient Economic History*, 21–51. New York: Springer International Publishing. https://doi.org/10.1007/978-3-030-47898-8_2.

Vogler, Jan. 2020. "The Political Economy of the European Union: An Exploration of EU Institutions and Governance from the Perspective of Polycentrism." In *Exploring the Political Economy and Social Philosophy of Vincent and Elinor Ostrom*. New York: Rowman & Littlefield International, 148–51.

———2023. "The Complex Imprint of Foreign Rule: Tracking Differential Legacies along the Administrative Hierarchy." *Studies in Comparative International Development* 58, 129–94.

Weaver, Warren. 1948. "Science and Complexity." *American Scientist* 36: 536–40.

Weber, Max. 1978. *Economy and Society: An Outline of Interpretive Sociology*. Berkeley: University of California Press.

Willet, Rinse. 2021. 'Complexity and Urban Hierarchy of Ancient Urbanism: The Cities of Roman Asia Minor.' In *Complexity Economics: Building a New Approach*

to Ancient Economic History, edited by Koen Verboven, 251–94. Palgrave Studies in Ancient Economies. https://doi.org/10.1007/978-3-030-47898-8_8.
Zhao, Dingxin. 2015. "The Han Bureaucracy: Its Origin, Nature, and Development." In *State Power in Ancient China and Rome*, edited by Walter Scheidel. Oxford: Oxford University Press 56–89.

Chapter 5

Whither Stability? Polycentric Democracy and Social Order

Pablo Paniagua and Kaveh Pourvand

INTRODUCTION: THE TWILIGHT OF LIBERAL DEMOCRACY

Since Aristotle (1984) warned that a republic could degenerate into a democracy, which, in turn, could degenerate into despotism, political philosophy has been concerned with the issue of institutional and political stability. In simple terms, the challenge of political stability relates to the notion of holding a society or a political order *together*, with some degree of cohesion and coherence, concerning significant collective action challenges despite complexity and diversity (Enroth 2022; North et al. 2009). In other words, "the problem of social order arises from a recognition of societal complexity and diversity, whence the question of what makes complex and diverse societies hold together" (Enroth 2022, 1–2). This problem "is tied to an awareness of a seemingly new kind of society characterized by irreducible heterogeneity" (2). This perennial question of how to stabilize a just regime has been heightened with the emergence of the Weberian State that monopolizes the power of legitimate coercion and thus anchors society under a single, bureaucratic structure of governance—which we shall call a form of "monocentric" governance (Buchanan 2000; Weber 2019/1920; 1994).[1]

The great power of the contemporary state means it may be a vehicle for great good if governed by a just regime, but it also may be hugely dangerous if its power is abused (Acemoglu and Robinson 2019; V. Ostrom 2007/1974; Tocqueville 2012/1835). As a political form *in practice*, the nation-state has given us both liberal democracy and fascist and communist totalitarianism (Hayek 2011/1960; 2007/1944). These political risks and dangers concerning the concentration of political power for the sake of stability have been highlighted neatly by J.R.R. Tolkien's famous quote from his celebrated novel *The Lord of the Rings*: "One Ring to rule them all, One Ring to find them, One ring to bring them all, and in the darkness bind them." The stakes, then, couldn't be higher in ensuring that the power of the contemporary State is used justly.

Many political philosophers stress that the solution to the "stability problem" is socializing and coalescing citizens into *strongly affirming liberal democratic values* (Rawls 1996; Macedo 1990; Guttmann and Thompson 1998). Virtuous citizens will then maintain a just democratic state. However, this raises the problem of achieving and maintaining de facto consensus in dynamic societies characterized by profound heterogeneity and changing beliefs (Gaus 2011; Sen 2009; Weingast 1997). The probability of stabilizing democracy today via consensus on a substantive set of liberal democratic values seems low in hyperconnected and globalized modern societies.

The stability question has become pressing, particularly in recent years, as liberal democracy has been threatened by the "illiberal populisms" of both left and right (Mudde 2021; c.f. Abts and Rummens 2007; Eatwell and Goodwin 2018; Levitsky and Ziblatt 2019; Paniagua and Vergara 2022). These "illiberal democratic" tendencies question whether a liberal social order governed by a monocentric State will endure over the long run (De la Torre and Srisanga 2021). Anne Applebaum (2020) has even suggested that we face the "twilight of democracy," under which democratic and self-governing practices are deteriorating, giving rise to authoritarian and despotic regimes worldwide.

As we can see, recent events point to the inherent difficulty of relying on citizen virtue to stabilize centralized, liberal nation-states: it is a *high-risk and fragile strategy*. If, for whatever reason, a significant portion of the electorate—which need not be more than a numerical minority of the population—embrace some variant of "illiberal democracy," then the stability of the whole regime is put into doubt. Consider, for instance, the case of Italy during the rise of fascism (1919–1922), in which a minority—but vociferous and violent—group of the population helped pave the way toward an illiberal and populist dictatorship (Scurati 2021).

Moreover, two other considerations suggest that socializing the citizenry into a homogenous set of values would be an undesirable solution to the homogeneity problem, even if it were feasible. First, there are epistemic benefits to diversity. Pluralism and contestation about the good life and justice—including *liberal* conceptions of these values—allow us to *discover* valuable social practices and doctrines. If a diverse social order is analogized to a laboratory, then competing conceptions of the good and right may be seen as falsifiable hypotheses that are subjected to testing (Gaus 2021; Hayek 2011/1960; Mill 2006/1859; Muldoon 2016). Second, the only feasible ways of engendering such consensus may be oppressive to those experimental groups outside it. Even liberal states have a poor record of trying to integrate minorities and diversity.[2]

We propose a different institutional solution to the stability problem—*polycentric democracy*. Such a regime is characterized by plural and overlapping decision-making centers, each of which has some degree of autonomy from the others and none of which reigns supreme over all the others. We argue that such a novel form of democracy might prove more stable amidst deep disagreement, including on liberal and democratic values. Here is our essential claim: polycentric democracy is a better *risk management strategy* than a monocentric State. Suppose the citizens of one particular "decision-making node" adopt "non-liberal" or "undemocratic" values. In that case, that governance challenge *does not* threaten the stability of the whole system, whose institutional support comes from multiple governance centers. This renders a polycentric system more resilient to diversity and changing views than a monocentric one, just as a variegated ecology is more robust than a monoculture (Ostrom 2012a). Such a regime can then afford to be more flexible and tolerant of diversity and heterogeneity than a monocentric one. Greater toleration allows for more "experiments" in forms of life and solutions to social problems, facilitating social learning from which the whole regime can benefit. It also avoids the domination and suppression required to ensure all citizens conform to a particular set of liberal-democratic values. This, we argue, ultimately helps social orders attain dynamic flexibility and political resilience through time, which might be a better form of political stability than non-dynamic ones.

The rest of this chapter will proceed as follows: Section 2 draws on Max Weber and Alexis de Tocqueville to highlight two critical features of the monocentric contemporary state: its drive for uniform and hegemonic legislation and its displacement of intermediate associations (i.e., civil society). We argue that these two features of the contemporary state greatly heighten the risk of political instability, particularly in light of the deep and pervasive disagreement that affects contemporary societies. Section 3 outlines our polycentric alternative. It demonstrates how the "nested resilience" of polycentric democracy makes it more robust in the face of disagreement and strengthens anti-fragile system stability by exposure to disagreement and low-intensity conflict. Section 4 reflects on the broader benefits of polycentric democracy, particularly concerning the experimentation of utopian ideas. Section 5 contains concluding remarks.

1. ONE SOLUTION TO RULE THEM ALL? A WEBERIAN AND TOCQUEVILLIAN CHARACTERIZATION OF THE MONOCENTRIC STATE

The theoretical focus of contemporary philosophers has been principally, if not exclusively, on the monocentric State. They have been concerned with either legitimizing the activities of a centralized State or offering normative prescriptions that such a State is supposed to implement. There has been a general neglect of other forms of political authority, particularly local self-governance (Brennan 2017). Naturally, the monocentric State has dominated intellectual reflections on the question of stability (e.g., Rawls 1999, pt. III). Political philosophy has fallen into a conceptual mistake of conflating the idea of *government* with the *governance challenge.* Government, in the conventional liberal sense of a centralized nation-state, is only one of a range of possible institutional solutions to the challenge of governance.[3]

If we are to outline an alternative to an institution, it is helpful first to define that institution properly. Our definition of the institution we seek to improve can then be used to formulate our desired alternative. That is the purpose of this initial section. Drawing on Weber and Tocqueville, we identify two critical features of the monocentric state: legal uniformity and a tendency to displace intermediate associations. We will then outline how these monocentric State features combined with contemporary societies' pervasive disagreement could produce institutional fragility and, ultimately, political instability, given irreducible disagreement. Our definition of the monocentric State and diagnosis of its problems will then act as a point of contrast for our description of a polycentric alternative in the subsequent sections.

1.1. Weber on the State: Uniformity and Rationalization

Max Weber (2019/1922; 1994) recognized that modernity ignited a process of rationalization under which different fields of human life become dominated by standardization, impersonality, specialization, and enhanced social control (Brubaker 1991, 32–35). The quintessential process of rationalization was the rise of the monocentric nation-state and its bureaucratic apparatus (Weber 1994). The contemporary State, according to Weber, has the following characteristics: (i) the claim to a monopoly of the legitimate use of force within a given territory; (ii) centralization of the material and conceptual means of rule; (iii) planned distribution of the powers of command among various entities; (iv) an administrative and legal order that claims binding authority, and (v) a bureaucratic apparatus—with an administrative staff—oriented to the enforcement and achievement of the political order.[4] This hierarchical structure allows the state to bring uniformity to social life based on formal-procedural rationality (*Zweckrationalität*).

Weber believed this rationalization was necessary to bring predictability and standardization to our social interactions. He sided with Hobbes in recognizing that the nation-state was required to impose order on the social world (Weber 2019/1922).[5] Indeed, our contemporary ideal of equality under the law arose against the background of a Weberian State with the capacity to legislate and enforce the law uniformly in a territory.

1.2 Tocqueville on the State: The Crowding Out of Intermediary Associations

Like Weber, Alexis de Tocqueville (2002/1835) stressed uniformity of legislation as a critical feature of the contemporary State. For Tocqueville, the demand for uniformity was part of the demand for civic equality under democracy. If all citizens had the same standing before the State, they should be treated uniformly. In a democratic age, any legal polycentricity would constitute either privilege for some or neglect of others and would be unacceptable.

Tocqueville stressed that the democratic State's drive for legal uniformity would likely displace or subsume all independent intermediary associations between itself and the citizenry (V. Ostrom 2007/1974). To the extent that intermediary associations were self-governing associations that could adopt differing governance rules, they threatened legal uniformity. Tocqueville famously worried that this displacement would result in "soft despotism." Stripped of the ability to solve their own problems through intermediary associations and bottom-up collective action, citizens would lose their capacity for personal and associational agency, becoming passively reliant on the State, thus eroding citizens' democratic and political skills.[6]

What is essential for this chapter is that the displacement of intermediate association by the State heightens the risks of political instability in two senses. First, to the extent that the central State subsumes all other sources of authority, the health of all other local authorities and institutions depends on the health of the overarching institution. If the central State is captured by bad actors or a poorly motivated electoral coalition, this threatens to sink the whole ship of the political and social order as they were. This looks to be unwise risk management, a case of putting all the proverbial eggs into one basket. It is also worth stressing that, in the case of an electoral coalition, it doesn't require more than a minority of the electorate to take the whole polity in an undesirable direction.

Let us assume, at least for the sake of argument, that in the United States, there is a future vote for a presidential candidate with significantly less respect for democratic and liberal institutions that might endanger liberal democracy in America; similarly, imagine a future referendum in Europe in which some European voters decide to leave the European Union, which might constitute a potential defection from any reasonable interpretation of liberal democratic and free trade economic values. In the hypothetical case of the United States, you need only 25 percent of U.S. citizens of voting age to opt for an authoritarian candidate to endanger the system.[7] In comparison, in the case of Europe, you might need a meager 37 percent of voters to challenge the existing political order.[8] Second, how citizens engage with politics changes under a monocentric state. Politics has become more of a *spectator* sport. As Elinor Ostrom puts it:

> Citizens are effectively told that they should be passive observers in the process of design and implementation of effective public policy. The role of citizenship is *reduced to voting* every few years between competing teams of political leaders. Citizens are then supposed to sit back and leave the driving of the political system to the experts hired by these political leaders. (E. Ostrom 2000, 12)

But this has the following important implications. Demands that may have been met at the local or associational level under a more decentralized social order are now placed at the feet of the monolithic central State. This raises the stakes, particularly in a diverse society, since stability now depends on the central State's capacity to meet heterogeneous political demands at *different scales and sizes*, not all of which may be reconcilable with one another. In other words, the monocentric State has the potential risk of severely marginalizing citizens' efforts and collaboration at better solving their collective action problems at the local level, thus "crowding out" civil society and other forms of local governance that might fit better the size and scale of the problem at hand (Ostrom 2000; Paniagua 2022). To make this point in more concrete terms, consider some contemporary and debated issues in which monocentric States and monocentric forms of policymaking have crowded out (or marginalized) efforts of citizens in crucial areas such as education and school choices environmental policy, pandemic governance, and the definition of marriage, to mention a few.

This marginalization explains at least part of the distrust, polarization, and populism we see in liberal democracies today (Paniagua and Vergara 2022; Rajan 2019). Even a well-meaning centralized State can please only some of its myriad constituencies, leading to resentment and populist pushback from those who feel their demands are unmet or unrepresented. These weaknesses imply that the monocentric State is poorly placed to deal with today's primary source of political instability: deep and pervasive disagreement, which we shall discuss in the following sub-section.

1.3 Deep and Pervasive Disagreement

In the latter part of his career, John Rawls's signature contribution to political philosophy was to lay stress on the problem of deep disagreement. The burdens of judgment involved in considering the truth of complex matters, such as religion, ethics, the good life, and justice, imply that even good-faith actors will disagree fundamentally over these core matters.[9] Furthermore, this is not merely an incidental or contingent feature of liberal democratic societies. It is the "natural outcome of the activities of human reason under enduring free institutions" (Rawls 1996, xxvi). The freedom of expression and association protected by liberal societies give rise to this diversity. This, Rawls saw, poses a profound challenge in terms of stability: How could liberal democracies endure given this deep disagreement, especially when some citizens come to reject cardinal liberal values, such as individual autonomy?

Rawls's initial response was to refashion his theory of justice as a political principle that citizens could affirm for diverse reasons as part of an overlapping consensus (Rawls 1985). However, by the end of his career, Rawls stressed that disagreement extended to justice itself, and the consensus of citizens should be limited to a commitment to *public reason*, the notion that coercive laws should be justified with reasons all citizens could accept (Rawls 1997). However, as the recent decade has shown us, it is hard to see why we will agree on how to conduct politics if we disagree on practically everything else. Indeed, many philosophers have objected to Rawls's public reason proposal (Muldoon 2016; Thunder 2006).[10] Many contemporary political philosophers stress that disagreement is *pervasive* and extends to all domains, including the basic conceptual categories we use to understand the world (Thrasher and Vallier 2018; Muldoon 2021). The search for underlying consensus amidst this diversity looks quixotic at best; thus, "looking for a hidden consensus behind the curtain of reasonable disagreement might be a dead end" (Müller 2019, 85).

Moreover, the challenge is even more profound if the stability problem is viewed in diachronic or dynamic rather than static terms. From a static perspective, the challenge is to find some underlying consensus between a diverse citizenry. Even if those challenges were met, the consensus must maintain itself over time, given changing beliefs and circumstances, including unforeseeable and unpredictable new forms of disagreements.[11] Such a "static" fixed-point stability would look mightily fragile in the face of change (Thrasher 2020).[12] Hence, these crucial considerations suggest it is hard to see how we could form and maintain a consensus on moral values, even liberal-democratic ones, without the "oppressive use of state power" (Rawls 1996, 37).[13] In other words, the social order seems to face a critical tradeoff: either we attain static stability at the expense of coercively reducing disagreement and diversity, or we give up on large consensus and fix stability by allowing deep disagreement and diversity to persist.

As the recent political events from 2016 to 2021 worldwide have shown us, deep disagreement combined with the two risks inherent in monocentric regimes do not bode well for the liberal-democratic state. Suppose the health of a liberal-democratic polity depends on the central State remaining liberal-democratic because it subsumes other associations, but deep disagreement extends to liberal-democratic values. In that case, there is always the possibility that a minority of "illiberal" voters capture the State and take it in an illiberal direction. Suppose deep disagreement leads to a radical diversity of often mutually exclusive political demands pressed against a central State. In that case, it is almost certainly the case that many constituencies in society will be deeply disappointed by the outcomes of the political process. Either quarrels, disputes, and deep disagreements will constantly arise amongst voters, expressing themselves in polarization, fragmentation, deep dissatisfaction with the monocentric state, and eventually, a crisis of legitimacy and political disaffection that could take society down the path of volatile forms of populism, violence, and civil unrest.

In other words, deep disagreement plus a political system requiring uniform "one-size-fits-all" solutions is a recipe for *political fragility*. This fragility has arguably exhibited itself in practice in the recent decade, as liberal democracies struggle to respond to polarization among their populace (Paniagua and Vergara 2022), which might explain why some scholars are concerned that we might be reaching the "twilight of democracy" (Applebaum 2020). Having defined the constitutive features (and significant risks) of the monocentric State and its fragility in the face of deep disagreement, we now turn to outline our polycentric democratic alternative.

2. THE IDEAL OF POLYCENTRIC DEMOCRACY

Following the insights of Elinor and Vincent Ostrom (E. Ostrom 1972; V. Ostrom 2010), M. Polanyi (1951), and Aligica and Tarko (2012), we can conceive of polycentric democracy (hereafter: PD) as a political system or arrangement that possesses the following properties: (i) an overarching and abstract system of rules (i.e., a constitution); (ii) multiple governing authorities *at different scales*; (iii) processes that allow for competition, cooperation, exit and entry procedures, and conflict resolution among the decision centers; and (iv) considerable autonomy for each decision-making center to make and enforce rules within a circumscribed domain of authority (see also Ostrom 2005).[14] Thus, polycentric democracy is one instance of a broader genus of polycentric systems. The market economy and the scientific process are other examples.

In the previous section, drawing on Weber and Tocqueville, we identified legal uniformity and the displacement of intermediate associations as the hallmarks of the contemporary monocentric state. Polycentric democracy does not represent so much a repudiation of the modern state as a reconceptualization of it *away* from monocentricity (Thiel et al. 2021). The equality-driven demand for legal uniformity now finds expression at the "meta" level in the abstract rules that govern the interaction between decision-making centers and resolve their disputes. However, legal polycentricity is given significant latitude over uniformity within the constraint of these meta-rules. In what follows, we argue that such a decentralized state regime is robust and *anti-fragile* in the face of deep disagreement. That is to say, it can not only withstand deep political contestation and disagreement, but it can also potentially be strengthened by it (Ostrom 2012a; Taleb 2012; Taleb and Douady 2013).[15]

2.1 Wither Stability? Political Stability as Nested Resilience

One reason to think that polycentric democracy can be anti-fragile in the face of deep disagreement and diversity is that this is true of polycentric systems more generally. Even though political theorists treat diversity and disagreement as problems, contemporary social science and epistemology have shown that diversity and polycentricity can fruitfully combine to produce various benefits. These include practical problem-solving (Hayek 2011/1960; Page 2007), moral innovation and progress (Gaus 2017), resilient ecosystems (Ostrom 2012a), and radical freedom of association (Kukathas 2003), to mention a few. The critical feature of polycentric democracy, which makes it amenable to stability amidst diversity, is its *nested resilience*, to which we now turn.

Polycentric systems can generate *nested arrangements* and *emergent properties* rather than forming just decentralized or fragmented arrangements that solve only small but separate problems (Ostrom 2012b; Paniagua 2022). Simply, "nestedness" or "nested structures" could be interpreted figuratively as Russian dolls. There are small social or political orders within other larger ones, such that each local set of rules and incentives *aligns with* the rules and objectives of other larger scales. For example, Marshall (2008, 77) conceptualizes "nested arrangements" as cooperative systems that encourage the autonomous functioning of smaller, more exclusive units operating *within* broadly agreed-upon principles.

"Nestedness," then, is an institutional property in which essential governance functions—like monitoring, sanctioning, and the enforcement of rules—are organized into multiple and overlapping layers of governance, enabling the system to generate either emergent properties or a nested solution to complex (multilayered) problems (Paniagua 2022; Paniagua and Rayamajhee 2023). Consider, for example, how the coordinative capacity of the market and its ability to generate social prosperity are emergent and unintended properties of the system (Hayek 2011/1960; Lewis 2012) and how the possibility of local self-governance is an emergent property of polycentric systems that follow certain design principles (Lewis 2021; Ostrom 1990). E. Ostrom recognized that some complex externalities—such as climate change—could only be managed through a bottom-up and concerted effort at *multiple scales of governance* and, thus, in a "nested" manner (Ostrom 2012; Paniagua and Rayamajhee 2023).

Under a polycentric democracy, we do not try to deliberately stabilize the whole system through an *ex-nihilo* conscious, rational consensus on our preferred conception of liberal-democratic values. Macro-level political stability is achieved indirectly as *a side effect* of the efforts of many different (and decentralized) political units, each seeking to maintain their political stability at lesser levels. In other words, overarching stability is the changing and emergent product of myriad micro-level adjustments by the many different decision-making centers to the stability challenges they face. This "diffuses" the macro-level stability challenge by solving it not as a single, unitary problem but as a "nested" problem from the bottom-up. Hence, multi-level flexibility, adaptation, and competition are crucial for systemic-level stability (Ostrom 2012).

For example, consider the restaurant industry. Such an industry looks stable and thriving at the systemic level. However, this higher-level stability is attained through instability at smaller scales (such as regional, local, or street levels), where millions of restaurants go bankrupt monthly (Taleb 2012). Similarly, the aviation industry becomes ever more stable at the systemic level, thanks to the risk of airplane crashes. Airplane crashes are catastrophic and undesirable events that can bring entire companies to bankruptcy. Yet when they occur, they are leveraged as "vital information" at the systemic level, becoming the "epistemic fuel" that ignites the industry's adaptation and improvement process. The aviation industry has successfully used data about actual failures to improve flight safety 139-fold over the last sixty years (Johnson and Gheorghe 2013). Again, industry-level stability is attained thanks to the dynamic adaptation of different units at multiple scales and by fragmenting and tackling other aspects of the problem at various levels.

The principle applies as well with buildings that can attain dynamic stability in the face of earthquakes and other shocks (e.g., wind) by the fact that there are minor micro-movements and oscillations at different scales that help diffuse the shock throughout different and decentralized areas (Reitherman

2012). Dampers are strategically placed in the building structure to control floor vibrations and displacement, mitigating systemic failure risk. To further enhance the building's systemic stability, engineers use clusters of various seismic vibration control technologies at different scales (ibid., chapter 9). Forest fires serve similar purposes in biology and ecosystems. By destroying some trees (local-level damage), other trees and desirable vegetation flourish better, thus increasing systemic stability (Certini 2005).

It has been recently argued that complex externalities, such as modern pandemics, banking instability, and climate change, are complex and multi-layered challenges that could be better managed through nested and polycentric arrangements (Paniagua 2022; Paniagua 2020; Paniagua and Rayamajhee 2023). In all these examples, we can see different ways of applying the principle of "nestedness" or "nested governance" (Ostrom 2012b; Paniagua 2022; Walloth 2016).[16] Moreover, "nestedness" allows management or governance systems to be constantly scaled up (or scaled down) appropriately to better deal with and "match" the scale of the problems they aim to solve, enhancing efficiency (Tarko 2017).

Nestedness then unpacks apparently unitary and complex problems into multi-level smaller problems to tackle the differing aspects of the issue at the most appropriate scale of collective action (V. Ostrom 1994). This helps to solve complex problems from the bottom up in an ascending matter, tackling different aspects and fragments of problems according to their scale and size (Paniagua 2020). Nested governance, then, in the polycentric democratic system, can be explained as "the eventual result of larger, more inclusive organizational [political] units emerging from, and then 'nesting' . . . [within] smaller, more exclusive units that manage to self-organize sooner. Smaller organizations thus become part of a more inclusive system without giving up their essential autonomy" (Marshall 2005, 47).

Let us now consider how nested resilience responds to the challenge of deep disagreement. The most obvious way it does this is by lowering the political stakes. No longer is it the case that one central authority subsumes all others. An "illiberal" turn by a portion of the population does not threaten to "sink the whole ship," as it were. Furthermore, political demands now find expression in multiple jurisdictions rather than solely or mainly in the central state. Politics thus becomes less of a zero-sum, "winner-takes-all" game. My faction attaining a political victory does not imply your faction having to lose since you can still win in another political jurisdiction. One of the key causes of polarization and hostility in politics is at least diminished. As Muller puts it:

> [Polycentric democracy] has the advantage that, in letting different polities follow their own evaluative standards, it also succeeds in defusing disagreement

> on a macro-level. Defusing "deep disagreement" is again a side effect of letting polities discover new "ways of living" [in a nested manner]. . . . Giving (deeply) diverse room for testing their ideas should considerably relax the tensions of society and thus lead to more harmony within society (Müller 2019, 141, 147).

An additional benefit of polycentric democracy, particularly for liberal democratic political elites, is that it is more likely to provide *prompt signals* of disaffection and discontent with, or otherwise rejection of, liberal-democratic values from the citizenry since these sentiments can be expressed forthrightly at myriad local levels. Many more potential canaries exist in the political and social coal mine under a polycentric democracy. This is beneficial because elites will be able to respond sooner to discontent if they become aware of it sooner. Consider what a shock both the Brexit vote and the election of Donald Trump in 2016 were for the Anglo-American political class. Arguably, these landslide results occurred not so much because elites ignored discontent, but because they were unaware of it locally.

Additionally, under a polycentric democracy, there are multiple jurisdictional flora to experiment with potential policy solutions that could alleviate the grievances of the dissatisfied segments of the population. Others can later adopt a successful resolution of the issue in one jurisdiction. Just as local fires strengthen a forest's systemic resilience to fire and plane crashes make the air transportation system safer, so would allowing disagreement to destabilize micro-level jurisdictions *improve*, through time, the system-level stability of a polycentric democracy. In this sense, a polycentric democracy is anti-fragile through a process of nested governance (Paniagua 2020, 2022).

3. THE SYSTEMIC BENEFITS OF POLYCENTRIC DEMOCRACY

Leveraging diversity and nestedness under a polycentric democracy to achieve stability has more comprehensive benefits. First, it avoids assimilation. A polycentric democracy can allow considerable heterogeneity on several important dimensions, including education, religion, social organization forms (consider how the Amish society differs socioeconomically from the broader U.S. population), and language. It thus avoids the repression and social tension accompanying attempts to assimilate the whole population into a moral and cultural consensus. Additionally, under a polycentric democracy, political units can enable experimentation with different normative visions and conceptions of the good life. These can be tried *on a small scale* or at local levels and, after that, be copied, contested, improved, or scaled up if other people desire them after they see them in action. This system of "small scale bets" and "small scale prototypes" helps us explore what institutions work in practice and reduces the significant risk accompanying system-wide social engineering.

Consider, for example, three famous normative institutional proposals: Rawls's (1999a) notion of "property-owning democracy," Nozick's (2013) "libertarian utopia," and Habermas's (1996) proposal for "deliberative democracy." These three proposed systems would require substantial changes to the prevailing institutional regime in liberal democracies—welfare state capitalism. They thus involve very high risks and irreducible uncertainties by tweaking a significant portion of existing socioeconomic regimes. The problem is not simply that these proposals may turn out to be less just than anticipated, but that they might be significantly worse than the status quo, as attested to by the many failures in radical social engineering in the twentieth century.[17]

The advantage of polycentric democracy resides precisely in *minimizing* these "normative risks." Radical normative visions can be subject to experimentation at more minor scales, in which we can later see their real consequences at lower political and social costs. Political entrepreneurs and philosophers will deploy their *own* (and no one else's) human capital, money, effort, and intellect to make their socioeconomic plans work and demonstrate their desirability to the rest of the citizenry. Under these circumstances, failure neither imperils the whole system nor undermines or threatens the lives and well-being of a large portion of the population. Mistakes are comparatively small and contained. Thus, they generate vital information and evidence to learn from, so their damage is mitigated while social learning is maximized. Only in such a manner can radical political and economic ideas be tried and tested in practice while protecting the entire system from downside risk and systemic failure.

Consequently, under a polycentric democracy, we could gradually and slowly alter our existing institutions and socioeconomic systems according to how experiments have worked out in practice and the various revealed preferences of citizens and their changes in the face of new proposals. In Popperian terms, polycentric democracy constrains the utopians to engage in *piecemeal social engineering* (Popper, 2002). This minimizes the risk of moral, populist, and political catastrophe, a vital risk that nation-states have often failed to contain in the last centuries (Mudde 2021; Rummel 1997; Scurati 2021).[18]

4. CONCLUDING REMARKS

We noted that the monocentric liberal-democratic state's drive for legal uniformity and its displacement of intermediate associations mean its long-run stability is a static and high-risk affair. The health of the whole society depends on the health of one overarching institution, which would be the site of many political demands, often incompatible ones because these demands could not find expression at lower institutional levels. Once we additionally consider the problem of deep disagreement, then the monocentric liberal-democratic state looks much more fragile than many have assumed. This is how we have diagnosed the problem of populism and polarization affecting contemporary liberal democracies.

We then outlined our alternative: polycentric democracy. The great advantage of this approach is that decentralizing political power is a better risk management strategy. We are no longer betting the health of the whole society on one highly important institution in the central state. Dynamic stability is the function of the operation of plural and overlapping institutions. This is not only more robust to an "illiberal" turn among segments of the population. Additionally, by allowing a more significant expression of political discontent at multiple levels, this system gives many more advance warnings of discontent and political dissatisfaction, and by allowing multiple jurisdictions, it will enable more variegated attempts to reformulate policies to try to resolve this discontent at their proper size and scale.

We propose polycentric democracy as a reasonable and pragmatic solution to the challenges of polarization and populism. It would prove helpful to conclude by making some remarks as to how this solution may be implemented. We do not conceive of polycentric democracy as an institutional blueprint to be realized wholesale. The question, then, becomes one of which changes would count as a marginal move *toward* such a polycentric regime. The institutions that come closest to a polycentric democracy today are federal systems, such as Swiss institutions. However, existing federal institutions fall short of a polycentric democracy for two key reasons. One, jurisdictional boundaries are usually fixed, or significant restrictions exist on creating new jurisdictions. Therefore, desirable policy changes would make it easier for citizens to develop new jurisdictions, outline conditions under which those jurisdictions can deviate from the central state's rules, and provide conflict-resolution guidelines.

Finally, the hope is that others will follow one set of policy changes in this direction in an iterative fashion. After some new jurisdictions form, an unanticipated conflict between them and the state might arise, creating the opportunity to clarify conflict resolution procedures further. Greater clarity might incentivize the creation of more jurisdictions, which would create further challenges that need resolving. Still, successfully resolving those challenges would make the creation of new jurisdictions even more accessible, and a positive cycle would ensue. This gradual transition toward polycentric democracy might be the most reasonable and resilient way forward to save liberal democracies from polarization, political disaffection, deep disagreement, and their catastrophic demise.

NOTES

1. "Monocentrism" or "monocentricity" is understood here in a Hobbesian manner as the form of governance in which there is a single consolidated decision-making center that has the ultimate authority over all important decisions related to a community or group (V. Ostrom 1994). Thus, polycentric governance is distinguished from monocentric governance by the fact that *it lacks a uniquely designated final authority* over all important decisions related to the governance of a group or community. In such an arrangement, the overarching and shared rules can be agreed upon and enforced by the different decision-making centers themselves, "without an ultimate center for decision-making" (Thiel et al. 2021, 26).

2. Consider, for example, the Australian state's policy of forcibly taking aboriginal children away from their natural-born parents into adoption by white couples. For a brief discussion, see Kukathas (2003,193).

3. Governance *is not* government, but rather *a process* that needs to be maintained by sets of rules and institutional arrangements so as to achieve certain political and social goals such as order. Thus, *governance* is here defined as a "process by which the repertoire of rules, norms, and strategies that guide behavior within a given realm of policy interactions are formed, applied, interpreted, and reformed. A useful shorthand expression . . . is that 'governance determines who can do what to whom, and on whose authority'" (McGinnis 2011, 171).

4. We here follow Dusza's account (1989, 75–76).

5. Though it is worth noting that Weber was famously ambivalent on this issue, expressing fear that the "iron cage" of bureaucracy would also be a threat to certain expressive forms of individuality. Under this "authoritative power of the State . . . the performance of each individual is mathematically measured, each man becomes a little cog in the machine and, aware of this, his one preoccupation is whether he can become a bigger cog. . . . This passion for bureaucracy, as we have heard it expressed here, is enough to drive one to despair. . . . The great question is therefore not how we can promote and hasten it, but what can we oppose to this machinery in order to keep a portion of mankind free from this parceling-out of the soul, from this supreme mastery of the bureaucratic way of life" (Weber 1924/1909, 412–13).

6. Hence his famous lament at the end of *Democracy in America*: "an immense tutelary power is elevated, which alone takes charge of assuring their enjoyments and watching over their fate. . . . It would resemble paternal power if, like that, it had for its object to prepare men for manhood; but on the contrary, it seeks only to keep them fixed irrevocably in childhood. . . . It willingly works for their happiness; but it wants to be the unique agent and sole arbiter of that; it provides for their security, foresees and secures their needs, facilitates their pleasures, conducts their principal affairs, directs their industry, regulates their estates, divides their inheritances; can it not take

away from them entirely the trouble of thinking and the pain of living?" (Tocqueville 2002/1835, Volume 2, Part IV, Chapter 6, 663).

7. To put things in perspective, only 25 percent of U.S. citizens of voting age opted for Donald Trump: only sixty-two million voters opted for Donald Trump, out of 245 million Americans of voting age. Total voter turnout was 138 million. Trump famously lost the popular vote to Hillary Clinton, he but won overall because of institutional quirks of the electoral system in the United States.

8. Similarly, only 37 percent of the registered British voters opted to leave: the Brexit vote was seventeen million. This was 52 percent of those who voted in the referendum but only 37 percent of registered voters (turnout among registered voters was 70 percent.) Note that the 37 percent figure overstates the support for Brexit insofar as not all British citizens who are of voting age and eligible to vote are registered to do so. The percentage would be even lower if the denominator was the number of citizens eligible to vote rather than those registered to do so.

9. Indeed, they will even disagree on what constitutes "truth."

10. The literature is now vast. But for one critique, see Enoch (2015) and the literature cited therein.

11. Consider who, say, fifty years ago could have predicted the disagreements in the West today over issues such as: the status of gender and sexuality, abortion, nationality, migration, vaccinations, etc.

12. Tellingly, the original Rawlsian theory conceived of the problem of how to stabilize a *closed society* cut off from the rest of the world. But this stipulation simply defines away—or assumes a way by mere definition—much of the real-world sources of instability: immigration, new ideas, international politics, trade, new technology, etc.

13. The policies of the Communist Party of China may exemplify this kind of strategy. They try to maintain political consensus and stability of the social order by comprehensive state regulation and suppression of news content, internet use, and cultural content such as films.

14. These decision centers can either be "states within a federal order, free cities—cities with high degree of municipal autonomy—or special experimental zones. For lack of a better name, let us call these decision centers 'polities'" (Müller 2019, 138).

15. A complex adaptive system is anti-fragile when it can not only withstand *known and predictable* shocks and stressors, but also learn and improve from *unknown and unpredictable* disorders and mistakes, in order to become more malleable, thus increasing the long-term probability of its survival (Taleb 2012). On the mathematical definition of anti-fragile consult, see Taleb and Douady (2013).

16. Walloth (2016), for instance, argues that complex systems are nested systems: systems that enclose other systems and that are simultaneously enclosed by even other systems at lower scales. According to his theory, each enclosing system emerges through time from the generative activities of the systems they enclose.

17. The obvious examples of famines in Soviet Russia and Maoist China come to mind here. But there are many other examples of damaging, though not quite so catastrophic, attempts at large-scale social engineering, from authoritarian city planning to forced villagization. For a series of case studies, see Scott (1998).

18. Some readers might object that a monocentric regime with enhanced deliberation is a better way of promoting learning than a polycentric one. Citizens can test one another's ideas through deliberation, thereby spotting weaknesses and improving them. These argumentatively refined normative principles could then be quickly implemented throughout the whole of society by a monocentric state, without the messy fragmentation of a polycentric system. While polycentric democracy is open to deliberation, this is as a *complement* to jurisdictional variety than a replacement of it. There are stern epistemic limits to how much we can establish in *a priori* discourse. To establish what works, we need to *see* what works. This requires scope for *empirical experimentation* that a polycentric regime can, in fact, provide bountifully but that a monocentric deliberative regime could do only to a limited degree. To explore the severe limits of deliberative regimes at promoting factual learning and discovery, consult Müller (2019, chapters 3 and 7) and Brennan and Landemore (2021).

REFERENCES

Abts, K., and Rummens, S. 2007. "Populism versus Democracy." *Political Studies*, 55 (2): 405–24.

Acemoglu, D., and Robinson, J. 2019. *The Narrow Corridor. States, Societies, and the Fate of Liberty*. London: Penguin Publishers.

Aligica, P., and Tarko, V. 2012. "Polycentricity: From Polanyi to Ostrom, and Beyond." *Governance*, 25 (2): 237–62.

Applebaum, A. 2020. *Twilight of Democracy: The Seductive Lure of Authoritarianism*. New York: Doubleday.

Aristotle. 1984. *Politics*, trans. Carnes Lord. Chicago: University of Chicago Press.

Bednar, J. 2008. *The Robust Federation: Principles of Design, Political Economy of Institutions and Decisions*. Cambridge: Cambridge University Press.

Brennan, J. 2017. "Elinor Ostrom, Governing the Commons." *In* J.T. Levy, ed. *The Oxford Handbook of Classics in Contemporary Political Theory, 1st edition*. Oxford University.

Brennan, J., and Landemore, H. 2021. *Debating Democracy: Do We Need More or Less?* Oxford: Oxford University Press.

Brubaker, R. 1992. *The Limits of Rationality*. London: Routledge.

Buchanan, J. 2000. *The Limits of Liberty: Between Anarchy and Leviathan*. Indianapolis: Liberty Fund.

Certini, G. 2005. "Effects of Fire on Properties of Forest Soils: A Review." *Oecologia*, 143 (1): 1–10.

De la Torre, C., and Srisa-Nga, T. 2021. *Global Populisms*. London: Routledge.

Dusza, K. 1989. "Max Weber's Conception of the State." *International Journal of Politics, Culture, and Society*, 3 (1). 71–105.

Eatwell, R., and Goodwin, M. 2018. *National Populism: The Revolt Against Liberal Democracy*. London: Penguin Press.

Enoch, D. 2015. "Against Public Reason." Pages 112–42, *in* D. Sobel, P. Vallentyne, and S. Wall, eds. *Oxford Studies in Political Philosophy, Volume 1*. Oxford University Press.

Enroth, H. 2022. *Political Science and the Problem of Social Order*. Cambridge: Cambridge University Press.

Fotos, M. 2015. "Vincent Ostrom's revolutionary science of association." *Public Choice*, 163 (1/2): 67–83.

Gaus, G. 2011. *The order of public reason: a theory of freedom and morality in a diverse and bounded world*. Cambridge: Cambridge University Press.

———. 2017. *The Tyranny of the Ideal: Justice in a Diverse Society*. Princeton: Princeton University Press.

———. 2021. *The Open Society and Its Complexities*. Oxford: Oxford University Press.

Gutmann, A., and Thompson, D. 1998. *Democracy and Disagreement*. Cambridge: Harvard University Press.

Habermas, J. 1996. Between Facts and Norms: Contributions to a Discourse Theory of Law and Democracy. Cambridge, MA: MIT Press.

Hayek, F.A. 2011/1960. *The Constitution of Liberty: The Definitive Edition*. Chicago: Chicago University Press.

———. 2007. *The Road to Serfdom. The Definitive Edition*. Chicago: Chicago University Press. Originally published 1944.

Hobbes, T. 1960. *Leviathan*. Oxford: Basil Blackwell.

Johnson, J., and Gheorghe, A. 2013. "Antifragility analysis and measurement framework for systems of systems." *International Journal of Disaster Risk Science* 4 (1): 159–68.

Kukathas, C. 2003. *The Liberal Archipelago: A Theory of Diversity and Freedom*. Oxford: Oxford University Press.

Lewis, P. 2012. "Emergent properties in the work of Friedrich Hayek." *Journal of Economic Behavior & Organization*, 82 (2): 368–78.

———. 2021. "Elinor's Ostom's 'realist orientation': An investigation of the ontological commitments of her analysis of the possibility of self-governance." *Journal of Economic Behavior & Organization*, 189 (1): 623–36.

Macedo, S. 1990. *Liberal Virtues: Citizenship, Virtue, and Community in Liberal Constitutionalism*. Oxford: Clarendon Press.

———. 2005. *Economics for Collaborative Environmental Management: Renegotiating the Commons*. London: Earthscan Publications.

Marshall, G. 2008. "Nesting, subsidiarity, and community-based environmental governance beyond the local scale." *International Journal of the Commons*, 2 (1): 75–97.

McGinnis, M. 2011. "An Introduction to IAD and the Language of the Ostrom Workshop: A Simple Guide to a Complex Framework." *Policy Studies Journal* 39(1): 169–83.

Mill, J.S. 2006. *On Liberty and the Subjection of Women*. London: Penguin Press. Originally published in 1859.

Mudde, C. 2021. "Populism in Europe: An Illiberal Democratic Response to Undemocratic Liberalism." *Government and Opposition*, 56 (4): 577–97.

Muldoon, R. 2016. *Social Contract Theory for a Diverse World: Beyond Tolerance*. London: Routledge.

Müller, J. 2019. *Political Pluralism, Disagreement and Justice: The Case for a Polycentric*

Democracy. London: Routledge.

North, D., Wallis, J., and Weingast, B. 2009. *Violence and Social Orders: A Conceptual Framework for Interpreting Recorded Human History*. New York: Cambridge University Press.

Nozick, R. 2013. *Anarchy, State and Utopia*. Second Edition. New York: Basic Books.

Ostrom, E. 2012a. "Why do we need to protect institutional diversity?" *European Political Science*, 11(1): 128–47.

———. 2012b. "Nested externalities and polycentric institutions: Must we wait for global solutions to climate change before taking actions at other scales?" *Economic Theory*, 49 (1): 353–69.

———. 2010. "Beyond markets and states: Polycentric governance of complex economic systems." *American Economic Review*, 100 (3): 641–72.

———. 2005. *Understanding institutional diversity*. Princeton: Princeton University Press.

———. 2000. "Crowding out Citizenship." *Scandinavian Political Studies*, 23 (1): 3–16.

———. 1990. *Governing the commons*. Cambridge University Press.

Ostrom, E., J. Walker, and R. Gardner, 1992. "Covenants with and without a sword: self-governance is possible." *American Political Science Review*, 86 (2): 404–17.

Ostrom, V. 2007. *The Intellectual Crisis in American Public Administration*. Tuscaloosa, AL: University of Alabama Press. Originally published in 1974.

———. 1997. *The Meaning of Democracy and the Vulnerabilities of Democracies*. Michigan: University of Michigan Press.

———. 1994. *The Meaning of American Federalism*. San Francisco: ICS Press.

———. 1972. Polycentricity. Page *in* Workshop in Political Theory and Policy Analysis.

Page, S. 2007. *The difference: how the power of diversity creates better groups, firms, schools, and societies*. Princeton: Princeton University Press.

Paniagua, P. 2020. "Governing the (banking) commons: Polycentric solutions to bank runs," edited by P. Boettke, R. Herzberg and B. Kogelmann. *The political economy & social philosophy of Vincent and Elinor Ostrom*, 115–44. London: Rowman & Littlefield.

———. 2022. "Elinor Ostrom and public health." *Economy and Society*, 51 (2): 211–34.

Paniagua, P. and A. Vergara. 2022. "Gobernanza policéntrica y la crisis de la democracia liberal." *Estudios Públicos*, 167 (1): 77–105. DOI: https://doi.org/10.38178/07 183089/1232210406.

Paniagua, P., and V. Rayamajhee. 2023. "On the Nature and Structure of Externalities." *Public Choice*, forthcoming.

Polanyi, M. 1951. *The Logic of Liberty: Reflections and Rejoinders*. Chicago: Chicago University Press.

Popper, K. 2002. *The Poverty of Historicism*. 2nd Edition, Routledge Classics. London: Routledge.

Rajan, R. 2019. *The Third Pillar: How Markets and the State Leave the Community Behind*. New York: Penguin Press.

Rawls, J. 1996. *Political Liberalism*. New York: Columbia University Press.

———. 1999. *A Theory of Justice: Revised*. Cambridge: Belknap Press.

———. 1985. "Justice as Fairness: Political not Metaphysical." *Philosophy & Public Affairs* 14: 223–51.

———. 1997. "The Idea of Public Reason Revisited." *University of Chicago Law Review* 64: 765.

Rayamajhee, V., and P. Paniagua. 2021. "The Ostroms and the Contestable Nature of Goods: Beyond Taxonomies and Toward Institutional Polycentricity." *Journal of Institutional Economics*, 17 (1): 71–89.

Reitherman, R. 2012. *Earthquakes and Engineers: An International History*. Virginia: ASCE Press.

Rummel, R. J. 1997. *Death by Government: Genocide and Mass Murder Since 1900*. London: Routledge.

Scott, J.C. 1998. *Seeing Like a State: How Certain Schemes to Improve the Human Condition Have Failed, New Haven, CT:* Yale University Press.

Scurati, A. 2021. *M: Son of the Century*. London: Fourth Estate.

Sen, A. 2009. *The Ides of Justice*. Cambridge: Harvard University Press.

Taleb, N. 2012. *Antifragile: Things That Gain from Disorder*. New York: Random House.

Taleb, N. 2018. *Skin in the Game: Hidden Asymmetries in Daily Life*. New York: Random House.

Taleb, N., and R. Douady. 2013. "Mathematical definition, mapping, and detection of (anti)fragility." *Quantitative Finance*, 13 (11): 1677–89.

Tarko, V. 2017. *Elinor Ostrom: An intellectual biography*. London: Rowman & Littlefield.

Thiel, A., W. Blomquist, and D. Garrick, eds. 2021. *Governing Complexity: Analyzing and Applying Polycentricity*. Cambridge: Cambridge University Press.

Thrasher, J. 2020. "Agreeing to Disagree: Diversity, Political Contractualism, and the Open Society." *Journal of Politics*, 82 (3): 1142–55.

Thrasher, J., and K. Vallier. 2018. "Political Stability in the Open Society." *American Journal of Political Science*, 62 (2): 398–409.

Thunder, D. 2006. "A Rawlsian Argument against the Duty of Civility." *American Journal of Political Science*, 50 (3): 676–90.

Tocqueville, A. 2002. *Democracy in America*. Chicago: Chicago University Press. Originally published in 1835.

Tullock, G. 2005. *Bureaucracy*. Indiana: Liberty Fund.

Walloth, C. 2016. *Emergent Nested Systems: A Theory of Understanding and Influencing Complex Systems as Well as Case Studies in Urban Systems*. Zug: Springer International.

Weber, A. 1910. "Der Beamte." *Die neue Rundschau*, 21 (1): 1321–39.

Weber, M. 2019. *Economy and Society*. Cambridge: Cambridge University Press. Originally published in 1922.

———. 1994. *Weber: Political Writings*, edited by Peter Lassman and Ronald Speirs. Cambridge: Cambridge University Press.

———. 1924. *Gesammelte Aufsätze zur Soziologie und Sozialpolitik*. J.C.B. Mohr: Tübingen, 412–16. Available at: https://nbn-resolving.org/urn:nbn:de:0168-ssoar-50766-3. Originally published in 1909.

Chapter 6

Self-Governance Solutions to Social Dilemmas

A Polycentric Approach

Vlad Tarko

INTRODUCTION

Tragedies of the commons are the typical example in which self-interested individual actions do not aggregate into beneficial collective outcomes, as judged by the community members themselves. They are the main counter-example to Adam Smith's logic of the invisible hand, according to which self-interested consumer and producer behavior in markets leads to efficient aggregate outcomes (again, as judged by the people themselves).

Gordon Tullock referred to such problems as "social dilemmas," highlighting the prevalence of conflict and the difficulty of solving such issues purely by means of voluntary cooperation (Tullock 2005). But Tullock also emphasized that conflict is costly, and "[r]egardless of the outcome . . . the use of resources for this purpose is offsetting and therefore inherently wasteful. Social contrivances for reducing such investment of resources are, on the whole, desirable" (5). One of the key points made by Vincent and Elinor Ostrom throughout their work is that self-governance is the fundamental process by which we can discover such beneficial "social contrivances," i.e., institutions for solving social dilemmas.

The reason the invisible hand works in markets but doesn't in cases that lead to tragedies of the commons is the lack of capacity to prevent free-riding.[1] In the case of markets, free-riding is unlikely because markets deal with the exclusion of free riders in private or club goods, i.e., goods that cannot be obtained without paying. As such, the producers' incentives to deliver the goods are aligned with the value of those goods to consumers, and producers can cover their costs. By contrast, when free-riding is possible, producers are only paid for a fraction of the value delivered to consumers (including both paying and free-riding consumers), which lowers the incentives to deliver the goods and often makes it impossible to fully cover the production costs (leading to reduced supply).

Examples of tragedies of the commons include over-grazing pastures, ocean over-fishing, depleting groundwater resources, deforestation of communal forests, global warming, under-production of flood protection, free-riding on public irrigation systems (and lack of contributions to repairs), traffic jams on public roads with no congestion pricing, shirking and laziness in worker-managed enterprises (e.g., in universities), under-production in collectivized communist farms, voter rational ignorance in democracies, the difficulty of revolutions in autocratic regimes, etc. We can ultimately frame any social problem as a type of tragedy of the commons in the sense that they are situations in which it is relatively easy to create the problem (and there are individual-level incentives to generate the problem), and it isn't easy to organize a solution and profit from delivering a solution.

Market failures can also be understood this way because all market failures have theoretical private solutions: In principle, the involved parties can solve negative externalities by negotiating the allocation of rights and compensation schemes (Coase 1960; Paniagua and Rayamajhee 2023). Information asymmetries can be, in principle, solved by certification markets and reputation mechanisms (Aligica, Boettke, and Tarko 2019; Stringham 2015). Monopoly power can be, in principle, fought by organizing a countervailing monopsony power.

In practice, such solutions don't always work because the transaction costs involved in organizing on the side of the problem and on the side of the solution can differ substantially. If it's easy to pollute but challenging to organize the Coasean compensation and property rights arrangements that fix pollution, we end up with an inefficient amount of pollution. If, due to more or less legitimate privacy and fairness concerns, health insurance companies cannot discriminate based on various health conditions, we end up with lower-than-efficient levels of health insurance. If consumers are many, dispersed, and rationally ignorant, while producers are few and well-organized, we end up with rent-seeking and regulatory capture that enhances market power. Furthermore, oligopoly in the product market translates into fewer available employers, i.e., oligopsony power over their workers. In such circumstances, if workers can also free-ride on the benefits negotiated by labor unions, the capacity to fight employer oligopsony with labor union monopoly is diminished (Olson 1965).

In all such cases, governments appear as a possible solution because (a) they involve lower organizational costs than the purely private solutions, and (b) they can eliminate free-riding by forcing compliance. Indeed, in his "Tragedy of the Commons" paper, Hardin (1969) argued that we only have two possible solutions: privatization or government control. Considering that the nature of the examples typically precluded privatization, the argument was a de facto argument in favor of centralized government control. Vincent Ostrom was particularly dismayed by Hardin's paper because it ignored a vast body of literature created in the 1950s and 1960s on successful communal (non-state) governance. Nonetheless, Hardin's paper managed to set the terms of the debate for decades. The Ostroms would often find themselves in this kind of battle with simplistic theoretical arguments that ignored the ample availability of real-world counter-examples (Tarko 2017).

Following the Coasian revolution in law and economics, property rights economics adopted a more sophisticated argument than Hardin's (Alchian and Demsetz 1973; Barzel 2002; Barzel and Allen 2023; Demsetz 1967; Paniagua and Rayamajhee 2023). At its best, property rights economics opens the door for explorations of various bottom-up processes by which property rights regimes are created. At its worst, it is used merely to argue that the task of government is to set up property rights such that markets can then operate without free-riding and, hence, solve the problems. This perspective leaves out the critical political economy question: What incentives and knowledge does the government have to actually set up a good property rights regime rather than an exploitative one? Or, in the case of the more simplistic solution proposed by Hardin, what incentives and knowledge does the government have to manage a commons properly?

Government solutions of any kind, including setting up property rights regimes, always come with the danger of government abuse. The concept of self-governance helps try to pinpoint the conditions under which governments are more likely to solve problems rather than make matters worse. The institutions that secure self-governance are expected to provide a general framework for solving any social dilemmas and adapting to changes. As Vincent Ostrom (1997) has argued, the stakes of this debate are high: "Democratic societies are necessarily placed at risk when people conceive of their relationships as being grounded on principles of command and control rather than on principles of self-responsibility in self-governing communities" (4).

Vincent and Elinor Ostrom's work follows in the footsteps of property rights economics but rejects the simple market versus-government dichotomy, focusing instead on the concern with self-governance. Elinor Ostrom titled her Nobel address "Beyond Markets and States: Polycentric Governance of Complex Economic Systems" (E. Ostrom 2016). What is beyond both markets and states? What does "polycentric governance" mean, and how does it help us better understand complex economic systems?

The "beyond markets and states" idea can be understood in two different ways, both of which find ample support in Elinor Ostrom's work. First, civil society can be understood as a third sector that can play an essential role in solving various social problems. Alongside her husband, Vincent Ostrom, and her many collaborators and students, Elinor Ostrom aimed to recapture and reformulate Alexis de Tocqueville's insights into the role of social norms, civil society organizations, and informal institutions. In her study of how communities succeed or fail at governing common property (E. Ostrom 1990), she has found strong support for the idea that informal mechanisms of monitoring, enforcement, and building trust are essential alongside formal institutions.

A second meaning of "beyond markets and states" refers to the intellectual framework that sees markets and governments as distinct and independent of each other, each having its own separate areas of competence and responsibility. This is fundamentally at odds with the actual complexity of modern-day states. As such, the theories that try to understand the operation of markets as purely economic phenomena or the theories of governments as purely political phenomena will have limited applicability. In the words of economist Richard E. Wagner, our situation is better described as an "entangled political economy" (Wagner 2016). This means that profit opportunities are often related to political actions, and political actions often have private economic reasons behind them.

In this chapter, I first briefly illustrate how these ideas can be applied to the problem of water governance. Groundwater governance and irrigation face the potential tragedy of the commons, and worldwide experience shows that such problems are more likely to be solved in communities with more significant degrees of self-governance. Next, I delve deeper into the concept of self-governance, as developed by authors like Robert Dahl and James Buchanan, then discuss how informal norms fit into a theory of self-governance. I conclude by discussing how the concepts of polycentricity and entangled political economy allow us to move from the analysis of small-scale communities to large-scale federal and international organizations.

1. WATER GOVERNANCE

To illustrate this perspective focused on the importance of self-governance, let us review the question of water governance, and in particular, groundwater. This was one of the key areas studied by Elinor Ostrom. This issue is both simpler than the big questions in political philosophy and complex enough to highlight some of the key difficulties.

Aquifers are large, underground supplies of water, which get replenished by rain at a particular rate. Extracting too much water from them (faster than their replenishing rate) can lead to disaster, affecting a large number of people over a large area. The aquifers are fascinating to study precisely because regular economic theory predicts disaster.

First, their sizeable geographical expanse implies that many people can independently build wells and extract water. As such, the conditions are ripe for a tragedy of the commons—everyone takes as much water as they can before the aquifer dries out. A person acting responsibly would simply harm themselves, without saving the aquifer. The aquifer is sustainable only if almost everyone is acting responsibly.

Second, the aquifer is an interesting combination of rival and non-rival goods. The *quantity* of water is rivalrous, meaning that if one person extracts some water, that water is no longer available for someone else. By contrast, the *quality* of the water is a non-rival public good. If the water is safe to drink, everyone benefits, and a person's benefit does not substract from another person's benefit. Another public good element is *informational*: finding out exactly how much water actually is in the aquifer is far from trivial and may require expensive scientific research. Because this information is a public good, there's an incentive to free-ride: rather than contribute some money to sponsor the research, everyone has the incentive to wait for others to do it, and if not enough contributions are made, not enough resources will be available for a high-quality study.

What can be done to solve all these problems? Given the very large geographical expanse of these aquifers, it is not feasible for a single private actor to own them, which presumably would lead to more careful use. A single actor with monopoly power over the entire aquifer would also be problematic. For the same reason, it is not feasible for the government to own it, as it would essentially imply government ownership of all the land in the area. The best avenue must be some form of regulation, but monitoring will be difficult. This means that some combination of social norms and formal rules must be in place. When conflict occurs, which will occasionally happen, a method for quick and fair resolution must be available. The government will probably be in the best position to pay for the scientific study of the aquifer and regulate pollution so that water quality is not affected.

The bottom line here is that this is a highly complex issue, which may involve the need for cooperation across multiple jurisdictions, and which involves a combination of several different problems. Each of these problems requires a different type of approach, and failure in one area will affect the other areas. In practice, even high-capacity and relatively efficient governments often fail in this area. For example, aquifers in both California and Arizona are poorly managed, with governments allocating water rights in a way that encourages inefficient agricultural activities, such as growing crops (like peanuts) that require unusually high amounts of water. Incentivizing people to grow peanuts in the desert is like encouraging people to grow bananas in Canada.

This type of complexity is the norm rather than the exception. For example, forest management, another area studied by Elinor Ostrom, similarly involves dealing with several different types of goods that must be managed simultaneously. While wood is a rivalrous good, the protection trees offer against mudslides is a public good, as is the environment for hunting and other activities (Tarko 2017, ch. 3–4).

What about irrigation? At first glance, irrigation systems should be easier to manage than aquifers. But appearances can be deceiving (Tarko 2017, ch. 3–4). While the size of aquifers is determined by nature, individuals decide the size of an irrigation system. That adds a layer of complexity because, ideally, the optimal size should be selected somehow. Furthermore, irrigation may be an added complication to the aquifer problem if the water for the aquifer is used in agriculture.

What makes irrigation a commons problem is that (a) they have significant economies of scale, meaning that many farmers should cooperate to build a joint irrigation system, and (b) irrigation systems need constant maintenance and repair, and farmers may be tempted to free-ride on others' efforts while reaping the continued benefits from the water system.

How big should the irrigation system be? Self-governing irrigation systems are built in a bottom-up fashion by farmers cooperating on the initial project, as well as on the continued maintenance of the system and of monitoring and enforcing rules against water theft. Such irrigation systems, as found everywhere worldwide, are expanded until the benefits from the economies of scale become overwhelmed by the costs of coordinating and cooperating among too many people. As such, the scale is chosen based on the nature of the social interactions in that community. In other words, the optimal scale is not driven just by technology (although technology matters), but also by social factors such as trust and the available formal and informal institutions for conflict resolution.

A key source of conflict in irrigation system management is related to fairness concerns, as the system may deliver unequal amounts of water to everyone. One key fact discovered by Elinor Ostrom, and which matches the psychological research on fairness, is that *what matters the most is for the benefits to be proportional to the efforts* (Tarko 2017, pp. 121–126). In other words, fairness does not mean equal outcomes but outcomes proportional to the contribution. Systems that establish fairness in this sense work with the fewest number of conflicts. Also, what counts as "fair" is culturally determined, and the exact conditions also differ in subtle but important ways. "No single set of rules defined for all irrigation systems in a region could satisfy the particular problems in managing each of these broadly similar, but distinctly different, systems" (E. Ostrom 2009).

In contrast to self-governing irrigation systems, governmental systems tend to be much larger. Aid agencies and NGOs with a development mission have often promoted such systems out of honest, good intentions. Unfortunately, most of them have failed and have universally worked much less efficiently than the self-governing ones. In her Nobel Prize interview, Elinor Ostrom noted that after studying "several hundred irrigation systems in Nepal," they discovered that "local groups are very effective" and that "farmer-managed irrigation systems are more effective in terms of getting water to the tail end, higher productivity, lower cost, than the fancy irrigation systems built with the help of Asian Development Bank, World Bank, USAID, etc." (E. Ostrom 1990). The farmers usually had much better knowledge of local conditions than outside governments and organizations, and they had a strong vested interest in solving the problem. Well-intentioned outsiders, by contrast, lack such knowledge, and situations like the following continue to happen: "Millions of dollars have been poured into the development of irrigation works in the dry zone of Sri Lanka" (E. Ostrom 1990).

The main reason the top-down irrigation systems tend to fail is ignoring the maintenance problem and the difficulty of monitoring when the farmers are not co-producers of the system (but instead simply users of the system).[2] Technological considerations usually set the scale of the top-down systems. As such, the expectation is that these systems would work better than the self-governing ones because they would take better advantage of economies of scale. The assumption is that farmers don't build the larger systems themselves due to a lack of resources. In reality, the most significant reason is social—the difficulty of coordinating, building trust, and solving conflicts among an overly large group of people.

On top of this, in the government systems, the monitoring and enforcement is supposed to be done by government agents, but such agents need to have the same vested interests in the system's success that the local farmers have. The agents can also be corrupted or self-interested. When this happens, the trust in the system plummets even more, and the fairness problem is accentuated. Turning the farmers from co-producers into simply system users makes all the managerial problems more difficult. The possibly more significant economies of scale and better technology (due to more resources from outside sources) are not enough to overcome these social-political problems.

From the point of view of economic theory, it is interesting and relevant to compare co-production to team production (Aligica and Tarko 2013). Alchian and Demsetz proposed the concept of team production to explain why firms have hierarchical structures in which managers monitor workers (Alchian and Demsetz 1972). The idea is that most goods are produced as part of a collaborative team, which makes it difficult to measure the labor productivity of each worker purely based on output (the output involves the combined efforts of many workers, which masks the individual efforts of each worker). Such teams face a tragedy of the commons in which each worker is tempted to shirk, leading to decreased output for the team as a whole. The role of managers is to monitor workers more directly and ensure maximum productivity. This also explains why worker-owned and worker-managed firms are unusual or have small sizes. Prominent exceptions include law firms and universities, both of which are cases in which the productivity of individual workers (lawyers and professors) is easier to disentangle from the team production.

The key difference between co-production and team production is that "[w]hereas team production involves cooperation for the goal of producing something for an outside consumer, in the case of co-production the good is consumed by the members of the production team. For this reason, the problem of monitoring can be solved more easily in the case of co-production because the agents have a vested interest in having the good produced in the appropriate quantities and qualities" (Aligica and Tarko 2013). For example, in the case of typical manufacturing, workers are motivated primarily by their wages and not by benefits from the product. By contrast, in the case of an irrigation project, the contributors to the project are motivated primarily by their own use of the irrigation system. This does not *eliminate* the temptation for free-riding, but it provides a more substantial reason against it.

One way of understanding the failure of top-down irrigation systems, as compared to the relative success of the bottom-up systems, is that the top-down systems are built on the wrong assumptions: "Advocates of centralization confuse co-production with team production and, consequently, inappropriately apply the firm model to public administration" (Aligica and Tarko 2013). The firm model assumes workers have no intrinsic motivations but need external rewards and/or punishments. In contrast, the managers and owners of the firm are motivated by the enterprise's success because they are residual claimants[3] (and hence they have the incentive to monitor the workers properly). This is the exact opposite of the case for co-production. The top-down managers are not residual claimants of public projects, while the co-producers do have intrinsic motivations. Consequently, while, in the case of firms, it is unusual to see successful worker-managed firms, the opposite holds for public or common projects.

This Ostromian perspective adds an important *participatory* element to the concept of self-governance. Citizens are not understood as mere passive consumers of public services provided by governments in a direct analogy to the market. In a self-governing system, citizens' participation in the governance of various commons and solving multiple social problems involves more than just voting every few years. Applying models that work well for understanding markets (i.e., governing the production of private and club goods) to the governing of the commons (i.e., common-pool resources and public goods) can seriously backfire and lead to what Elinor Ostrom called "crowding out citizenship" (E. Ostrom 2000). As Vincent Ostrom also put it, "Democratic societies cannot be fashioned without such roots of self-governance. . . . For this reason, the basic architecture of modern societies must, as Tocqueville has argued, draw upon a science of association to fashion rules of social interaction that apply from the level of the village to the level of the nation state and beyond" (Aligica 2003).

2. THE CONCEPT OF SELF-GOVERNANCE[4]

Robert Dahl has highlighted the fundamental problem of self-governance: "to live in association with others necessarily requires that [one] must sometimes obey collective decisions that are binding on all members of the association. The problem, then, is to discover a way by which the members of an association may make decisions binding on all and still govern themselves" (Dahl 1989, 89). Similarly, James Buchanan wrote about the "paradox of 'being governed,'" and pointed out that "the individual does not enter into social contract [with others] for the purpose of imposing constraints on himself," but in order to "secure the benefits of behavioral limitations on their part" (Buchanan 1975, 136; see also Buchanan 1994).

Living with others brings significant benefits, but it requires building consensus about how to govern collective affairs and about what counts as a collective or private affair—i.e., about the legitimate scope of collective decision-making and, conversely, the extent of the private sphere. Building such a consensus is often far from trivial. It takes time and effort to discuss matters and to negotiate various possible schemes for compensating losses, and, ultimately, consensus might still be impossible due to some irreconcilable values.

We can define *self-governance* as "the capacity of a community to live under rules of its own choice and to produce social-economic outcomes that most members of the community find desirable" (Tarko 2021b). Self-governance is valuable because it enables a more economically efficient system, i.e., a system that maximizes preference satisfaction not only concerning the delivery of various private goods and services but also concerning the overall nature of society. As philosopher Tom Christiano put it, "[t]he citizens ought to play the role of defining the basic aims the society ought to pursue and the legislative institutions ought to be concerned with reconciling the different aims of citizens and defining broad means for implementing these aims" (Christiano 2005). In a democratic system, self-governance can be undermined in several ways:

- *External interference*: an external party, which may have its own interests (at odds with the interests of the community), establishes and enforces some rules upon the community, even if most people in the community disagree with those rules (e.g., the federal government may impose various rules upon states and local jurisdictions, or regulatory agencies establish rules that most people dislike) (Aligica, Boettke, and Tarko 2019), or it imposes uncompensated costs on the community (e.g., a community may be subjected to pollution from a nearby source or a jurisdiction may be required to provide financial aid to another) (V. Ostrom, Tiebout, and Warren 1961);
- *Internal polarization*: the community may suffer from extreme disagreements concerning some public issues, and whatever rules they establish or decisions they adopt, a significant fraction of the community will end up subjected to a rule or decision they disagree with (e.g., conflicts in a local community regarding the use of public property, such as whether to facilitate industrial development at the expense of the natural environment; or large-scale conflicts about moral issues like abortion, sexuality, foreign policy, immigration, or income inequality);
- *Special interests*: the dilemma of "concentrated benefits and dispersed costs" is created by the fact that those suffering the dispersed costs find it more challenging to organize than those enjoying the concentrated benefits—as a result, well-organized minorities can establish rules that harm the less-well-organized majorities (Olson 1965, 1982);
- *Lack of competence*: the community may agree to implement certain policies that, in fact, lead to the opposite consequences than those desired. Furthermore, in the aftermath of such errors, the lack of competence may lead the community to misidentify the true causes of the problem and compound the error by adopting additional failing policies (Brennan 2016; Caplan 2003, 2008; Somin 2013).

Ideally, all the above self-governance problems would be minimized, but in practice, trade-offs are present. For example, decentralization allows the satisfaction of a greater diversity of social preferences (Inman and Rubinfeld 1997; V. Ostrom 1987), but it also generates larger externalities between jurisdictions, and it makes collective decisions about larger-scale problems more difficult (Buchanan and Tullock 1999; Tarko and O'Donnell 2018). Decentralization also doesn't address some pervasive causes of moral polarization, which can occur at all scales rather than clustering geographically. In such cases, relying on overlapping civil society organizations and non-territorial governance (Aligica, Boettke, and Tarko 2019; Tucker and de Bellis 2015) may be better alternatives, but such approaches increase heterogeneity and often decrease social trust (Aligica 2013; Gaus 2018). Gerald Gaus refers to the heterogeneity of values as the "fundamental diversity dilemma" facing all societies aiming to be self-governing (Gaus 2010; Gaus and Hankins 2017).

Similar trade-offs affect our reliance on the administrative state. Relying on experts to devise better policies may improve competence, but it can also create problems if the experts have their own normative agendas, which may differ from the values of the community at large or if special interests capture experts (Aligica, Boettke, and Tarko 2019; Tarko 2021b).

One way of looking at the "paradox of being governed" is by exploring the relation between self-governance and state capacity. Self-governance typically enhances political legitimacy, which, in turn, allows the creation of greater state capacity (Geloso and Salter 2020; Johnson and Koyama 2017). The question, however, is whether state capacity can also be built in the absence of self-governance and political legitimacy and used by rulers for more nefarious purposes. Empirically, there is indeed a positive correlation between measures of self-governance, like the liberal democracy measure from the *Varieties of Democracy* data set, and measures of state capacity (O'Reilly and Murphy 2020), as shown in Figure 1. However, the relationship is indeed problematic: The variance in state capacity for low-self-governance countries is higher than for high-self-governance countries. While no

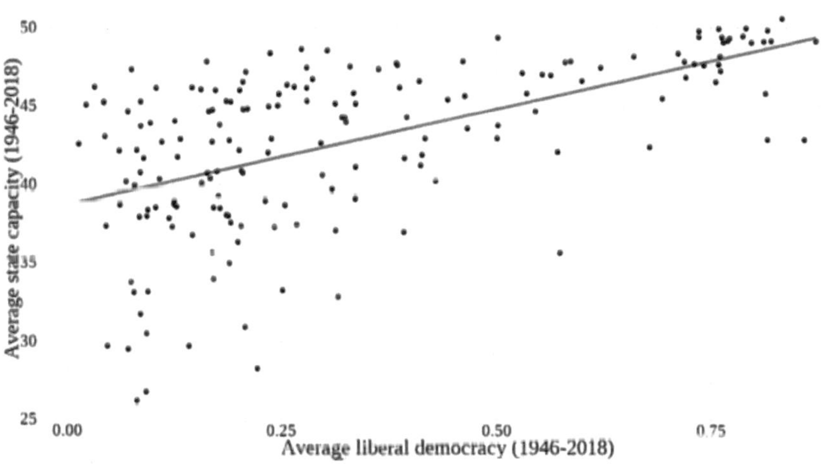

Figure 6.1. Relationship between liberal democracy and state capacity.

Source: Author calculation using the state capacity index created by O'Reilly and Murphy (2020) and the liberal democracy index from Varieties of Democracy (Coppedge et al. 2014).

low-state-capacity countries score well on liberal democracy, there are undemocratic countries with relatively high state capacity.

A possible explanation of this is as follows: If the community trusts its collective choice institutions, greater state capacity helps solve more problems more cheaply and with fewer conflicts. As such, self-governance and state capacity can be seen as part of a positive feedback loop, as the optimistic picture of state capacity asserts. By contrast, higher state capacity is undesirable in the context of low political legitimacy as it would not typically be used to benefit the regular population. Nonetheless, as shown in Figure 1, some undemocratic countries can still build state capacity by relying more on force. The technology of building high state capacity is not restricted to liberal democratic governments.

This highlights Madison's fundamental dilemma of government: "In framing a government which is to be administered by men over men, the great difficulty lies in this: you must first enable the government to control the governed; and in the next place oblige it to control itself" (Federalist No. 51). If a government is strong enough to curb private violence over the territory it controls, it is also strong enough to abuse its power over those it governs (Buchanan 1975; North, Wallis, and Weingast 2009).

3. THE IMPORTANCE OF INFORMAL NORMS

The team production hierarchical model, which emphasizes the importance of top-down monitoring, also goes hand in hand with focusing primarily on formal rules. This goes back to Hardin's original account of the tragedy of the commons, which assumed only two viable solutions (Hardin 1968): privatization or government control and monitoring. The general idea is that a tragedy of the commons is supposed to be solved by implementing certain rules against free-riding and overuse of resources, and because such rules need to be imposed on all (regardless of consent), they need to be imposed by a government. Considering the legalistic nature of government, we're talking about formal rules, not informal social norms.

An important observation made by Elinor Ostrom is that *the tasks of monitoring and enforcing rules themselves suffer from a free-riding problem*. These are called nested social dilemmas (McGinnis 2000, ch. 7 and ch. 16). The original Alchian and Demsetz team production model does *not* suffer from a second-order free-riding problem, because the owners of the firm are residual claimants, and hence they have the proper incentives to monitor and enforce rules inside the firm. In the public realm, government agents are not residual claimants and hence face the second-order social dilemma:

> In the currently accepted theory of collective action, the temptation to free ride—to receive benefits without paying costs—prevents individuals from voluntarily contributing to joint efforts in groups without selective benefits. And creating rules that induce contributions is itself a second-order social dilemma not likely to be solved by those mired in their inability to solve the first-order problem. . . . Enforcing these rules would be a third order social dilemma—costly to those who impose punishments on others and generating benefits of compliance that everyone, even free riders, would receive. (E. Ostrom 2000)

According to standard theory, "[t]he predicted outcome of any effort to solve a second-order dilemma is failure. Yet, participants in many field settings and experiments do exactly this" (E. Ostrom 1998). Ostrom's point here is to argue for a more complex model of rational choice in which we don't rely exclusively on external punishments and rewards. People have other-regarding preferences to some extent, and they also internalize various social values. These are essential for solving second-order (and higher-order) social dilemmas, assuming only external punishments and rewards lead to an infinite regress of nested social dilemmas. The role of intrinsic preferences and beliefs about rules' legitimacy is essential. The nested social dilemmas could not be solved without these: "Without individuals viewing rules as appropriate mechanisms to enhance reciprocal relationships, no police force and court system on earth can monitor and enforce all the needed rules on its own. Nor would most of us want to live in a society in which police were really the thin blue line enforcing all rules" (E. Ostrom 1998). Elinor Ostrom noted that

> (a)t least some individuals in social dilemma situations follow norms of behavior—such as those of reciprocity, fairness, and trustworthiness—that lead them to take actions that are directly contrary to those predicted by contemporary rational choice theory. In other words, *the behavior of many individuals is based on intrinsic preferences* related to how they prefer to behave (and would like others to behave) in situations requiring collective action to achieve benefits or avoid harms. *Intrinsic preferences lead some individual to be conditional cooperators*—willing to contribute to collective action as long as others also contribute. *Intrinsic preferences transform some dilemmas into assurance games* where there are two equilibria and not just one [emphasis added]. (E. Ostrom 2000)

This is a familiar idea, but it has become neglected in modern economic literature. It overly narrows the range of rational choice to focus *exclusively* on external material incentives.

> All long-enduring political philosophies have recognized human nature to be complex mixtures of the pursuit of *self-interest combined with the capacity of*

> *acquiring internal norms of behavior and following enforced rules when understood and perceived to be legitimate*. Our evolutionary heritage has hard-wired us to be boundedly self-seeking at the same time that we are capable of learning heuristics and norms, such as reciprocity, that help achieve successful collective action [emphasis added]. (E. Ostrom 1998)

Recognizing the reality of other-regarding preferences and social norms like fairness is important for understanding both collective action and the results of lab experiments. For example, a puzzling observation is that people cooperate to some extent, even in anonymous one-shot Prisoners' Dilemmas. A common interpretation is that people are irrational—they either don't understand the game or have difficulty calculating the Nash equilibrium.[5] But a different interpretation is that people maximize subjective utility, not objective payoffs (like monetary gains). For example, if maximizing strictly your personal monetary gains while disregarding what happens to other people makes you feel bad in various ways (because of internalizing various norms against selfishness), you are less likely to make that purely selfish choice. People have a certain degree of generosity and fairness and expect the other person to have this as well. As such, cooperation can be rational, i.e., the choice that maximizes people's expected subjective utilities (Tarko 2021a).

The idea that tragedies of the commons can be solved only by adjusting the objective payoffs neglects these powerful mechanisms for enabling cooperation and can interfere with it, leading to what Ostrom calls "crowding out citizenship." Changing the payoffs *can* help: "External interventions crowd in intrinsic motivation if the individuals concerned perceive it as supportive." However, the opposite happens too often: "External interventions crowd out intrinsic motivation if the individuals affected perceive them to be controlling" (E. Ostrom 2000). The bottom line is that "[w]hen intrinsic motivations are crowded out, substantially more resources are required to induce effort than when incentives support a sense of control and reliance on intrinsic as well as material incentives" (E. Ostrom 2000). As such, neglecting the participatory aspect of self-governance leads to higher costs and public sector inefficiencies.

To return to Madison's paradox of government, Elinor Ostrom has similarly warned that:

> officials and policy analysts who presume that they have the right design can be dangerous. They are likely to assume that citizens are short-sighted and motivated only by extrinsic benefits and costs. Somehow, the officials and policy analysts assume that they have different motivations and can find optimal policy because they are not directly involved in the problem. . . . They are indeed isolated from the problems. This leaves them with little capability to adapt and learn in light of information about outcomes resulting from their policies. All

too often, these "optimal" policies have Leviathan-like characteristics to them. (E. Ostrom 2005, 256)

It is important to understand the reasons we have these two distinct types of institutions, both formal rules and informal social norms (Leeson and Coyne 2012). A common misconception is that informal norms are just an imperfect version of formal rules. Rules are clear; norms are vague. However, norms and rules have distinct strengths and weaknesses, and they work best when they form a complementary institutional package. Elinor Ostrom distinguishes formal rules from informal social norms by noting that the latter lack clear predefined explicit penalties (Crawford and Ostrom 1995). This gives credence to the claim that informal norms are just vague rules. But the key idea is that, by lacking predefined penalties, norms are better suited to take context into account. Furthermore, because penalties can differ from person to person, they are better suited to make room for personal interactions (as opposed to one-size-fits-all rules).

Human interactions are generally too complex for us to be able to write down all the possible situations, and formalize the proper behavior for each situation. Moreover, overly formalizing things backfires, both by making it harder to respond to new challenges and by creating unnecessary delays for regular activities. This being said, under-formalizing things can also be a mistake: It gives too much discretionary power to various individuals or to traditions and can make it too dangerous for minority positions to express themselves.

Leeson and Coyne (2012) argue that laws, norms, and contracts have different use cases, which we can identify by looking at their typical costs and benefits. Norms have the greatest accumulated "wisdom" but also the greatest production costs, and they offer the least amount of freedom of choice, partially due to the difficulty of changing norms. Contracts offer some degree of wisdom as a consequence of being based on the mutual agreement between parties (although less than norms, as they embed less experience), and they also offer the greatest flexibility and choice and the lowest production costs.

Table 6.1. Costs and benefits of contracts, norms, and laws. Source: Author, as an interpretation of Leeson and Coyne (2012).

		Contracts	*Norms*	*Laws*
Benefits	Wisdom	Medium	High	Low
	Alterability	Easy	Hard	Medium
	Freedom of choice	High	Low	Medium
Costs	Production costs	Low	High	Medium
	Heterogeneity costs	High	Medium	Low

However, they create significant heterogeneity, which can create problems when social expectations are essential.

Laws offer relatively little "wisdom" as compared to norms or contracts because they allow one group to create rules for others. Nonetheless, they have their advantages, especially in terms of low heterogeneity costs (creating explicit expectations about the rules), and in offering greater freedom of choice than norms. The process of changing laws involves various forms of deliberation and compromise, while norms change via an evolutionary process that is less reflective (E. Ostrom 2014). Even in the case of beneficial norms, people often don't understand the true reasons norms benefit them (Boettke 1996; Henrich 2015). Furthermore, norms typically change more slowly than laws (Williamson 2010).

4. HETEROGENEOUS VALUES, POLYCENTRICITY, AND ENTANGLED POLITICAL ECONOMY

What happens when we move our attention from relatively small-scale issues to larger political problems? The other sense in which we can go beyond the simple dichotomy of markets and states is to recognize the entangled nature of state and private sector. In a paper published as early as 1977, Vincent and Elinor Ostrom tried to highlight the complexity of the relationships between markets and states by pointing out that public goods are, in fact, commonly provided by governments by a variety of methods such as:

> (1) Operating its own production unit. E.g., a city with its own fire or police department. (2) Contracting with a private firm. E.g., a city that contracts with a private firm for snow removal, street repair, or traffic light maintenance. (3) Establishing standards of service and leaving it up to each consumer to select a private vendor and to purchase service. E.g., a city that licenses taxis to provide service, refuse collection firms to remove trash. (4) Issuing vouchers to families and permitting them to purchase service from any authorized supplier. E.g., a jurisdiction that issues food stamps, rent vouchers, or education vouchers, or operates a Medicaid program. (5) Contracting with another government unit. E.g., a city that purchases tax assessment and collection services from a county government unit, sewage treatment from a special sanitary district, and special vocational education services from a school board in an adjacent city. (6) Producing some services with its own unit, and purchasing other services from other jurisdictions and from private firms. E.g., a city with its own police patrol force, which purchases laboratory services from the county sheriff, joins with several adjacent communities to pay for a joint dispatching service, and pays a private ambulance firm to provide emergency medical transportation. (E. Ostrom and V. Ostrom 1977)

One may notice here that some of these methods involve (a) the entanglement between government and market actors, while others involve (b) interactions between different government units. The first situation does not fit well with the simple theories assuming clear distinctions between private goods and public goods, markets, and governments. The second also considers the importance of polycentricity, the phenomenon of having multiple decision centers that overlap, interact, cooperate, and/or compete (Aligica and Tarko 2012).

Polycentricity is generally contrasted with both hierarchical organization and mere fragmentation (Fig. 3) (Aligica and Tarko 2012). In a merely fragmented system, the different decision centers are not embedded in an overarching system of institutions that enables them to solve conflicts, build trust, etc. A polycentric system, by contrast, has avenues for conflict resolution and common norms that establish expectations. Polycentricity is often confused with mere fragmentation because both enable competition, but they are fundamentally different. A key component of Elinor Ostrom's research is concerned with understanding the nature of those overarching institutions that set up a polycentric system and understanding which institutions are likely to lead to resilience and productivity (Aligica and Tarko 2014).

Another common error is to assume there is a hierarchical organization where, in fact, we have a polycentric system. This confusion is due to the fact that both types of systems provide coordination. But they do so in very different ways. For example, Vincent and Elinor Ostrom have highlighted

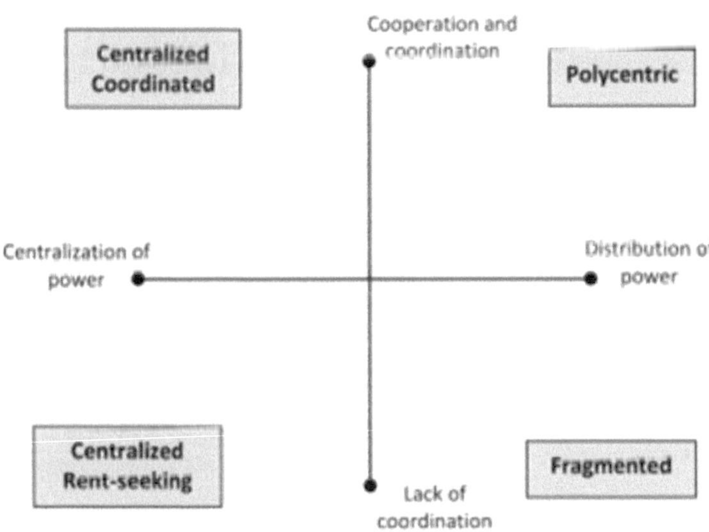

Figure 6.2. Distinction between polycentricity and fragmentation.
Source: Author.

the idea that American federalism is not hierarchical because U.S. states can have state laws that contradict federal laws (e.g., marijuana is legalized in many U.S. states, although it remains against federal law) (Bish 2014; V. Ostrom 1991; Wagner 2005). The assumption of hierarchical organization makes things look simpler and easier to control than they are. Once again, we see a case in which the team production hierarchical model is applied to the public realm instead of a co-production model. An essential fact about polycentric systems is that their social-economic-political order and coordination is *emergent*—meaning that no single actor has complete control over it, but instead, it is the result of many interactions, adjustments, conflicts, and negotiations. As such, seeing the world through the lens of polycentricity is the first step toward understanding its complexity.

Recognizing the importance of polycentricity as a tool for understanding complex social orders has two important origins: (a) James Buchanan's critique of the use of the social welfare function in welfare economics, and (b) Vincent Ostrom's critique of anthropomorphizing states and governments, assigning goals to them instead of recognizing their internal structures and complexity. An earlier, imperfect version of these critiques can be found in John Dewey's *The Public and Its Problems*, in which he noted:

> (t)he moment we utter the words "The State" a score of intellectual ghosts rise to obscure our vision. Without our intention and without our notice, the notion of "The State" draws us imperceptibly into a consideration of the logical relationship of various ideas to one another, and away from facts of human activity. It is better, if possible, to start from the latter and see if we are not led thereby into an idea of something which will turn out to implicate the marks and signs which characterize political behavior. (Cited by V. Ostrom 1997, 40)

We are used to describing collective entities as if they are individuals. We talk about "firms" and "organizations" as having goals. We discuss "states" as having "national interests" and describe international relations as relations between states. We even talk about "society" as if it's an individual—for instance, we are concerned about promoting "general welfare," and we may speak of "national character." It may seem a tedious point to make, but none of these entities have interests—only the individual people within these organizations have goals and beliefs. Is this just a pedantic and useless point? (Tarko 2017, ch. 5).

Vincent Ostrom stressed that "[m]yths and the misplaced use of abstractions to apply to Societies as a Whole need to be recognized for what they are—less than empirically warrantable assertions" (V. Ostrom 1997, 60), and he complained that "[t]he overwhelming amount of political discourse in the mass media, among students and faculty on university campuses, and in casual discussions contains references to 'America,' 'Society,' 'the Nation,' and 'the Government'" (70). He thought that "as intellectual constructs, they are too gross to be useful; they run the risk of being misleading and are the source of serious forms of deception and misconceptions" (111).

Similarly, for Buchanan, "the economy and the government are parallel sets of institutions, similar in many respects, and, of course, intersecting at many separate points" (Buchanan 1979, 146). On the one hand, "'government' is simply that complex of institutions through which individuals make collective decisions, and through which they carry out collective as opposed to private activities" (144). On the other hand, the economy is "that complex of institutions that emerges as the result of the behavior of individual persons who organize themselves to satisfy their various objectives privately, as opposed to collectively" (146).

From this perspective, which refuses to model government as a single, unitary, goal-driven entity, the concept of a social welfare function becomes problematic. In the standard cost-benefit analysis, once the expert "has defined his social welfare function, his public interest, he can advance solutions to all of society's economic ills, solutions that government, as *deus ex machina*, is, of course, expected to implement" (145). When a social welfare function is defined, government is by necessity understood as a goal-driven entity, but then one hampers the analysis of the processes by which policies are actually created and implemented. Government becomes a *deus ex machina* fantasy that fulfills its assigned purpose.

By contrast, when we focus on the political and public administration mechanisms at work, we are led to conceptualize "the government" as a complex polycentric structure comprised of many decision centers rather than a single entity with one goal, i.e., a polycentric system. "The government" no longer has a goal but is an emergent phenomenon.

But if this is so, the role of the economist also changes: "It is wholly beyond his task for the economist to define goals or objectives of the economy or of the government and then to propose measures designed to implement these goals" (Buchanan 1979, 146). Buchanan complains that "[m]ost economists, and, I suspect, most political scientists, view government as a potentially benevolent despot, making decisions in the 'general' or the 'public' interest, and they deem it their own social function to advise and counsel this despot on, first, the definition of this general interest, and, second, the means of furthering it" (145). By contrast, his advice is quite different:

> The role of the social scientist who adopts broadly democratic models of government process . . . [is] to explain and to understand how people do, in fact, govern *themselves*. . . . The social function is not of improving anything directly;

> instead, it is that of explaining behavior of a certain sort which, only remotely and indirectly, can lead to improvements in the political process itself, (145)

The self-governance perspective is also justified pragmatically. Elinor and Vincent Ostrom have noted that Buchanan and Tullock's "principle of conceptual unanimity gave meaning to what [we] had observed and what was accomplished" (E. Ostrom and Ostrom 2004). In a nutshell, the "principle of conceptual unanimity" can be understood as the idea that self-governing groups create institutions in an inclusive fashion, avoiding inflicting severe external costs on some members of their community. Self-organizing groups invent collective choice institutions that lower their decision-making costs to feasibly increase inclusion and reduce the inflicted harm to various community members.

For example, when Elinor Ostrom studied water management in West Basin, California, she found that adjudicating water rights was driven by intuitive considerations of "equity jurisprudence," which can be understood as seeking "to achieve conceptual unanimity in establishing the nature of the problem, in adjudicating water rights, in formulating the rules that were constitutive of water user associations, the way they related to one another, and in monitoring performance" (E. Ostrom and Ostrom 2004). Numerous other studies followed very similar lines and reached similar conclusions (Dietz, Ostrom, and Stern 2003; E. Ostrom 1990; E. Ostrom et al. 1999). The bottom line is that a focus on self-governance is trying to achieve the same thing as an honest cost-benefit analysis. Still, self-governance provides a better and more reliable policy guideline because it has more realistic political economy assumptions. It addresses Gaus's "fundamental diversity dilemma" head-on rather than pretending there are predefined objective criteria about what a society should maximize.

CONCLUSION

Elinor Ostrom addressed some of the biggest questions in political economy, such as the nature of self-governance and the conditions for sustainable development. Part of what makes her work unique is the combination between game theoretical models and extensive empirical fieldwork. Her method of approaching big questions was to find and study in detail specific instances of these big questions, particularly cases in which communities behaved in ways in which theory said it was impossible. The detailed empirical analysis allowed her to gain new insights about why and how self-governance was possible and suggested important changes to our models of economic behavior, such as the necessity of including social norms and other-regarding preferences within our analyses.

As Robert Bish noted, the Ostroms' project tried to respond to two forms of pessimism, one from Max Weber about the inevitability of hierarchical bureaucratic organizations and one from Alexis de Tocqueville about the collapse of democracies due to the gradual loss of civic virtues (see also the chapter by Paniagua and Pourvand [2024] in this volume). Weber "was pessimistic about large-scale bureaucracies, but did not believe there was an alternative. Weber did not seem to have contemplated Vincent's polycentricity, or federalism, as the way to govern a large society" (Bish 2014). The whole point of the research on polycentricity was, indeed, to show, first, that, empirically speaking, large-scale governments *are not* hierarchical, but polycentric, and, second, that, from a normative point of view, we *should not* try to turn them into hierarchical organizations (Tarko 2017). Although this point is still not widely understood, the Ostroms did, indeed, successfully counter Weber's pessimism. The bureaucratic administration is not an inevitability but a *choice* made due to a misunderstanding of the nature of complex institutions.

This brings us to the second issue, namely, citizens' uncritical faith in single-sovereign, mono-centric solutions to social problems, as eloquently articulated by Bish: "Tocqueville did not believe citizens understand how democratic administration and multicentered systems work; hence, citizens seek solutions to problems with a single-sovereign bureaucratic approach. Tocqueville believed that the faith in single-sovereign solutions would eventually suffocate the energy of citizens and destroy democratic administration" (Bish 2014).

The Ostroms, indeed, took this possibility very seriously (V. Ostrom 1997; Vincent and Elinor Ostrom, interviewed by Aligica 2003). Bish recalls that: "Vincent was concerned with what he perceived to be a decline in public participation in civic life, something that went beyond simply participation in governance, and the increasing nationalization of activities that had formerly been left to civic associations or state and local government where citizen participation was much more likely" (Bish 2014). Their attempt to counteract this tendency ranged from their police and water management studies in the United States to the management of common-pool resources worldwide. The study of common-pool resources was part of this broader concern with Tocquevillian self-governance: "My hope is . . . that the examination and analysis of common-pool resources in the field, in the experimental laboratory, and in theory, contribute to the development of an empirically valid theory of self-organization and self- governance" (Elinor Ostrom, interviewed by Aligica 2003).

As the Bloomington School continues after Elinor and Vincent Ostrom's departure, the major challenge, as articulated by Vincent in an interview with Paul Aligica, still continues: "A Tocquevillian science of association—a body of knowledge that helps us to understand the nature of social order, and the forms of social interaction that lead to mutual advantage—is the foundation for choosing among the institutional alternatives open to us. Now, it remains to be determined whether human beings can actually use such methods of discussion, reflection, and choice to fashion the future course of human civilization" (Vincent Ostrom, interviewed by Aligica 2003).

NOTES

1. The free-rider problem is a type of social or coordination failure that occurs when those who benefit directly from resources, public goods, and common-pool resources do not pay for them or underpay. Examples of such goods are public transportation, public services, or other goods of a communal nature. Free-riders are a crucial problem for common-pool resources because they may overuse it by not paying for the good (either directly through fees or tolls or indirectly through taxes). Consequently, common-pool resources may be underproduced, overused, or degraded.

2. Co-production refers to the notion that many services are produced by *both* the producer (regular producer) and the client (consumer-producer). In other words, inputs from both regular producers and consumer-producers are essential. A good example of this is education.

3. The "residual claimants" are the people who capture the profit of an enterprise after all factors of production have been paid, which include: wages paid to workers; rent paid for land, buildings, and other forms of rented capital; interest paid to lenders; and various repairs and current expenses. The residual claimants have a vested interest in running the enterprise as efficiently as possible (i.e., produce the highest value to paying customers with as few resources as possible) because they capture the profits.

4. This section is adapted and expanded from Tarko (2021b).

5. The Nash equilibrium is a situation in which none of the game participants wants to change their decisions—i.e., no one can gain more by individually switching their choice while assuming everyone else's choices remain fixed. A game can have more than one Nash equilibrium. Nash equilibria can also capture the reality of bad equilibria, in which people are stuck in situations no one particularly likes. Prisoners' Dilemma is one such example. Nash equilibria are used to predict the possible outcomes of a game.

REFERENCES

Alchian, Armen A., and Harold Demsetz. 1972. "Production, Information Costs, and Economic Organization." *American Economic Review* 62(5): 777–95.
———. 1973. "The Property Right Paradigm." *Journal of Economic History* 33(01): 16–27.
Aligica, Paul Dragos. 2003. *Rethinking Institutional Analysis: Interviews with Vincent and Elinor Ostrom with Introductions by Vernon Smith and Gordon Tullock.* Mercatus Center.
————. 2013. *Institutional Diversity and Political Economy: The Ostroms and Beyond.* Oxford and New York: Oxford University Press.
Aligica, Paul Dragos, Peter J. Boettke, and Vlad Tarko. 2019. *Public Governance and the Classical-Liberal Perspective: Political Economy Foundations.* New York City: Oxford University Press.
Aligica, Paul Dragos, and Vlad Tarko. 2012. "Polycentricity: From Polanyi to Ostrom, and Beyond." *Governance—An International Journal of Policy and Administration* 25(2): 237–62.
———. 2013. "Co-Production, Polycentricity, and Value Heterogeneity: The Ostroms' Public Choice Institutionalism Revisited." *American Political Science Review* 107(04): 726–41.
———. 2014. "Institutional Resilience and Economic Systems: Lessons from Elinor Ostrom's Work." *Comparative Economic Studies* 56(1): 52–76.
Barzel, Yoram. 2002. *A Theory of the State: Economic Rights, Legal Rights, and the Scope of the State.* New York: Cambridge University Press.
Barzel, Yoram, and Douglas W. Allen. 2023. *Economic Analysis of Property Rights.* 3rd edition. New York, NY: Cambridge University Press.
Bish, Robert L. 2014. "Vincent Ostrom's Contributions to Political Economy." *Publius: The Journal of Federalism* 44(2): 227–48.
Boettke, Peter J. 1996. "Why Culture Matters: Economics, Politics, and the Imprint of History." In *Calculation and Coordination*, London and New York: Routledge, 2001, 248–65.
Brennan, Jason. 2016. *Against Democracy.* Princeton: Princeton University Press.
Buchanan, James M. 1975. *The Limits of Liberty: Between Anarchy and Leviathan.* Indianapolis: Liberty Fund, Inc.
———. 1979. *What Should Economists Do?* Indianapolis: Liberty Fund.
———. 1994. *Ethics and Economic Progress.* Norman: University of Oklahoma Press.
Buchanan, James M., and Gordon Tullock. 1999. *The Calculus of Consent. Logical Foundations of Constitutional Democracy.* Indianapolis: Liberty Fund.
Caplan, Bryan. 2003. "The Idea Trap: The Political Economy of Growth Divergence." *European Journal of Political Economy* 19(2): 183–203.
———. 2008. *The Myth of the Rational Voter: Why Democracies Choose Bad Policies.* Princeton, NJ: Woodstock: Princeton University Press.
Christiano, Thomas. 2005. "Democracy and Bureaucracy." *Philosophy and Phenomenological Research* 71(1): 211.

Coase, R.H. 1960. "The Problem of Social Cost." *Journal of Law and Economics* 3: 1–44.

Coppedge, Michael, John Gerring, Carl Henrik Knutsen, et al. 2024. "V-Dem [Country-Year/Country-Date] Dataset v14," Varieties of Democracy (V-Dem) Project. https://doi.org/10.23696/mcwt-fr58.

Crawford, Sue E. S., and Elinor Ostrom. 1995. "A Grammar of Institutions." *American Political Science Review* 89(3): 582–600.

Dahl, Robert Alan. 1989. *Democracy and Its Critics*. New Haven: Yale University Press.

Demsetz, Harold. 1967. "Toward a Theory of Property Rights." *American Economic Review* 57(2): 347–59.

Dietz, Thomas, Elinor Ostrom, and Paul C. Stern. 2003. "The Struggle to Govern the Commons." *Science* 302(5652): 1907–12.

Gaus, Gerald F. 2010. *The Order of Public Reason: A Theory of Freedom and Morality in a Diverse and Bounded World.* Cambridge; New York: Cambridge University Press.

———. 2018. "Political Philosophy as the Study of Complex Normative Systems." *Cosmos and Taxis* 5(2): 62–76.

Gaus, Gerald F., and Keith Hankins. 2017. "Searching for the Ideal: The Fundamental Diversity Dilemma." In *Political Utopias*, eds. Michael Weber and Kevin Vallier. New York: Oxford University Press.

Geloso, Vincent J., and Alexander W. Salter. 2020. "State Capacity and Economic Development: Causal Mechanism or Correlative Filter?" *Journal of Economic Behavior & Organization* 170: 372–85. doi:10.1016/j.jebo.2019.12.015.

Hardin, Garrett. 1968. "The Tragedy of the Commons." *Science* 162(3859): 1243–48.

Henrich, Joseph. 2015. *The Secret of Our Success: How Culture Is Driving Human Evolution, Domesticating Our Species, and Making Us Smarter*. Princeton: Princeton University Press.

Inman, Robert P, and Daniel L Rubinfeld. 1997. "Rethinking Federalism." *Journal of Economic Perspectives* 11(4): 43–64.

Johnson, Noel D., and Mark Koyama. 2017. "States and Economic Growth: Capacity and Constraints." *Explorations in Economic History* 64: 1–20.

Leeson, Peter T., and Christopher J. Coyne. 2012. "Wisdom, Alterability, and Social Rules." *Managerial and Decision Economics* 33(5–6): 441–51.

McGinnis, Michael D., ed. 2000. *Polycentric Games and Institutions: Readings from the Workshop in Political Theory and Policy Analysis*. Michigan: University of Michigan Press.

North, Douglass C., John Joseph Wallis, and Barry R. Weingast. 2009. *Violence and Social Orders: A Conceptual Framework for Interpreting Recorded Human History*. New York: Cambridge University Press.

Olson, Mancur. 1965. *Logic of Collective Action: Public Goods and the Theory of Groups.* Harvard University Press.

———. 1982. *The Rise and Decline of Nations: Economic Growth, Stagflation, and Social Rigidities.* New Haven: Yale University Press.

O'Reilly, Colin, and Ryan Murphy. 2020. "A New Measure of State Capacity, 1789–2018." https://scholar.smu.edu/centers_oneilcenter_research/62.

Ostrom, Elinor. 1990. *Governing the Commons: The Evolution of Institutions for Collective Action.* Cambridge; New York: Cambridge University Press.

———. 1998. "A Behavioral Approach to the Rational Choice Theory of Collective Action: Presidential Address, American Political Science Association, 1997." *American Political Science Review* 92(01): 1–22.

———. 1999. "Revisiting the Commons: Local Lessons, Global Challenges." *Science* 284 (5412): 278–82. doi:10.1126/science.284.5412.278.

———. 2000. "Crowding out Citizenship." *Scandinavian Political Studies* 23(1): 3–16.

———. 2009. *Understanding Institutional Diversity*. Princeton: Princeton University Press.

———. 2014. "Collective Action and the Evolution of Social Norms." *Journal of Natural Resources Policy Research* 6(4): 235–52.

———. 2016. "Beyond Markets and States: Polycentric Governance of Complex Economic Systems." In *Mainline Economics: Six Nobel Lectures in the Tradition of Adam Smith*. Arlington: Mercatus Center, George Mason University, 191–250.

Ostrom, Elinor, and Vincent Ostrom. 1977. "Public Goods and Public Choices." In *Alternatives for Delivering Public Services. Toward Improved Performance*, edited by Emanuel S. Savas. Boulder: Westview Press, 7–49.

———. 2004. "The Quest for Meaning in Public Choice." *American Journal of Economics and Sociology* 63(1): 105–47.

Ostrom, Vincent. 1987. *The Political Theory of a Compound Republic: Designing the American Experiment.* Third, revised edition. Lanham, MD: Lexington Books.

———. 1991. *The Meaning of American Federalism*. San Francisco, CA: ICS Press.

———. 1997. *The Meaning of Democracy and the Vulnerabilities of Democracies: A Response to Tocqueville's Challenge*. Ann Arbor: University of Michigan Press.

Ostrom, Vincent, Charles M Tiebout, and Robert Warren. 1961. "The Organization of Government in Metropolitan Areas: A Theoretical Inquiry." *American Political Science Review* 55(4): 831–42.

Paniagua, Pablo, and Kaveh Pourvand. 2024. Whither stability? Polycentric democracy and social order. In *Polycentric Governance and the Good Society: A Normative and Philosophical Investigation*, edited by David Thunder and Pablo Paniagua. New York: Rowman & Littlefield.

Pemstein, Daniel, Kyle L. Marquardt, Eitan Tzelgov, Yi-ting Wang, Juraj Medzihorsky, Joshua Krussell, Farhad Miri, and Johannes von Römer. 2024. "The V-Dem Measurement Model: Latent Variable Analysis for Cross-National and Cross-Temporal Expert-Coded Data." V-Dem Working Paper No. 21. 9th edition. University of Gothenburg: Varieties of Democracy Institute.

Somin, Ilya. 2013. *Democracy and Political Ignorance: Why Smaller Government Is Smarter.* Stanford, CA: Stanford University Press.

Stringham, Edward Peter. 2015. *Private Governance: Creating Order in Economic and Social Life.* Oxford; New York: Oxford University Press.

Tarko, Vlad. 2017. *Elinor Ostrom: An Intellectual Biography*. London: Rowman & Littlefield.

———. 2021a. "Elinor Ostrom as Behavioral Economist." In *Elinor Ostrom and the Bloomington School: Building a New Approach to Policy and the Social Sciences*, edited by Jayme Lemke and Vlad Tarko. Newcastle, UK: Agenda Publishing, 47–69. https://ssrn.com/abstract=3739912.

———. 2021b. "Self-Governance, Robust Political Economy, and the Reform of Public Administration." *Social Philosophy and Policy* 38(1): 170–97.

Tarko, Vlad, and Kyle O'Donnell. 2018. "Escape from Europe: A Calculus of Consent Model of the Origins of Liberal Institutions in the North American Colonies." *Constitutional Political Economy*.

Tucker, Aviezer, and Gian Piero de Bellis, eds. 2015. *Panarchy: Political Theories of Non-Territorial States.* New York: Routledge.

Tullock, Gordon. 2005. *The Social Dilemma: Of Autocracy, Revolution, Coup D'Etat, and War.* Indianapolis: Liberty Fund.

Wagner, Richard E. 2005. "Self-Governance, Polycentrism, and Federalism: Recurring Themes in Vincent Ostrom's Scholarly Oeuvre." *Journal of Economic Behavior & Organization* 57(2): 173–88.

———. 2016. *Politics as a Peculiar Business: Insights from a Theory of Entangled Political Economy.* Cheltenham: Edward Elgar Publishing.

Williamson, Oliver E. 2010. "Transaction Cost Economics: The Natural Progression." *American Economic Review* 100(3): 673–90.

PART III

Principles of Polycentric Law and Statecraft

Chapter 7

Panarchy

Non-Territorial Polycentricity[1]

Aviezer Tucker

Much of the history of political philosophy consists of attempts to design the best state. Though all states must satisfy certain basic necessary requirements—like protection against force, collection and disposal of funds, and adjudication of disputes—there is no one and only "best state" that fulfills all these functions optimally under different circumstances and meets the expectations of people with different needs, values, ideas, traditions, and tastes.

As many of the contributors to this volume on polycentricity argue, the very idea of the design of a state that can be implemented from the top down is self-defeating. The attempts of political powers to impose designs against the creative plurality of conflicting views, ideas, interests, and values necessitates the use of force, which undermined most designs because the state is forced to add powerful coercive institutions to the design, and these institutions would be able and interested in gaining independence from any design to undermine it and rule themselves (Nozick 1974, 313–14; Narveson 1988, 139–40; Tucker et al. 2004; Paniagua and Pourvand 2024). Instead of designing a "best state," normative political philosophy may explicate *conditions* under which personal and institutional choices are likely to lead to the emergence of what different people may consider the best states for them.

Panarchy is such a contractarian political theory. It suggests that people and non-territorial states negotiate their relationships and formalize them in explicit and voluntary social contracts. Different states may offer varying levels of services in areas such as public services and security for different prices. *Non-territorial states* reduce to insignificant the costs of mobility between states, thereby maximizing competition between states that offer services to citizens instead of ruling a territory. Non-territorial states are founded on explicit social contracts (constitutions and law codes) rather than on monopoly over territory—sovereignty (Tucker 2016). Panarchic ideas have been invented, reinvented, and developed independently by thinkers from different places and times who mostly were unaware of each other. I co-edited an anthology that collected their writings (Tucker and Bellis 2016). The term *panarchy* was introduced by Paul Emil de Puydt in an article he published in Brussels in 1860 (Puydt 2016/1860). Puydt (1810–1891) was a Belgian polymath who is perhaps best known today as a botanist. He asked how very different kinds of people—conservative monarchists and Republican liberals, Catholics and Protestants, Flemish and Walloons—can co-exist in the same demographically mixed territory. He proposed that they can belong to different, parallel, non-territorial states. Globalization has made much of the world as diverse as Belgium, and the radicalization of politics in the twenty-first century has made compromise as difficult as in 1860 Belgium. Puydt's ideas have, therefore, become even timelier today.

In this chapter, I will build a case for panarchy as an attractive alternative to the modern sovereign State with a territorially defined monopoly of power. I begin by assessing the meaning and potential advantages of the core proposition of panarchy—namely, that citizens and states base their mutual relations on explicit, voluntary, and limited social contracts. I argue that this type of social contract theory is better than contractarian alternatives in the history of political philosophy because it maximizes possibilities for exit and competition between states over services to their customers. Second, I suggest that panarchy could be thought of as belonging to a family of polycentric theories of politics and draw attention to important similarities and differences between panarchy and other polycentric theories of political order. Third, I examine the problem of political monopoly, specifically, the tendency of States to monopolize the production and/or supply of goods and services, resulting in inefficient uses of taxpayers' money; and I argue that by reducing the costs of political exit to close to nothing, panarchy could eliminate the problem of political monopoly. Fourth, I anticipate the Nozickean claim that the State constitutes a sort of natural monopoly, making the case that from a historical perspective, states are not, in fact, natural monopolies. Fifth, I highlight ways in which panarchy could improve the moral quality of the present world order. Finally, I round out the chapter by suggesting that as much as the Westphalian order fitted seventeenth-century technology, recent innovations like information technology, cryptocurrencies, remote work, virtual reality, smart contracts, and the startup are all not-territorial, and they fit panarchy much better than seventeenth-century politics.

1. EXPLICIT SOCIAL CONTRACTS

In panarchy, citizens and States base their mutual relations on explicit, voluntary, and limited social contracts. Political agents choose among states, for example, according to their social contracts (law codes) and their reputations for good service. Political agents literally sign social contracts with States for set durations. Citizens may change their States, just as customers can change their insurance policies. States are founded on social contracts rather than sovereignty and service to citizens instead of monopoly over the use of violence in a territory. Explicit social contracts are voluntary and may have exit clauses. Persons and States are not forced to commit themselves to a social contract they did not sign or see, compose or agree to. Political mistakes and experiments become reversible. The State bases its right to coerce its citizens on their consent formalized in an explicit contract, a law code specifying permissible coercion conditions, just as citizens base their rights to services and protections from the State on the same contract. Voluntary social contracts omit the "original sin–like" character of social contracts that are "accepted" or "approved" hypothetically and implicitly "once and for all," either according to a social origin myth or in a hypothetical, otherworldly thought experiment whose results may well represent mutually inconsistent subjective intuitions. Explicit and voluntary social contracts are better than social contracts in the standard theories of Hobbes's *Leviathan*, Locke's *Second Treatise of Government*, Kant's *The Foundations of the Metaphysics of Morals*, Rousseau's *The Social Contract*, Rawls's *A T,heory of Justice*, and Nozick's *Anarchy, State, and Utopia*: They are neither mythical, nor hypothetical, but explicit and actual, voluntary, and reversible. It is unnecessary to speculate on what would have been an all-important original, once-and-for-all agreement in a hypothetical situation based on what rational and free hypothetical agents *would have agreed on* in otherworldly circumstances as the fundamental principles of any political association, irrespective of the different values and tastes that real, concrete people have here and now.

Panarchy allows political agents to make reversible political mistakes and then exit and contract another State. In panarchy, the incentive for political innovation and improvement comes from competition between States over citizens-customers. One State may offer different social contracts and different policies, just like insurance companies. Socialist social contracts and State models may be expensive, but they provide extensive safety nets. More libertarian social contracts may be more affordable, but they offer limited coverage. States that promote conflicting value systems and traditions may co-exist in the same territory. States with non-competitive social contracts, or whose management is corrupt or incompetent, would go bankrupt or be taken over by more successful ones, by States that wish to save a reformed version of the unsuccessful State, or disperse themselves, just as corporations do. Enterprising and innovative new States would constantly appear spontaneously.

Panarchy has several advantages over democratic territorial monopolies (let alone non-democratic ones). Traditional democracies can function only based on a broad, overlapping consensus when elections decide only a few controversial issues. Any likely result of democratic elections may not satisfy the libertarian French or the socialist American. The costs of migrating from one sovereign State to another, such as giving up on attachments to a geographical region where the emigrant may have family, friends, or a local source of income, are usually high and unaffordable to many.

2. PANARCHY AND POLYCENTRICITY

There are apparent similarities between panarchy and polycentricity, conceived as "a social system of many decision centers having limited and autonomous prerogatives and operating under an overarching set of rules" (Aligica and Tarko 2012, 237). In greater detail: "many centers of decision making, ordered relationships that persist in time; many legitimate rules enforcers, single system of rules, centers of power at different organizational levels, spontaneous order resulting from free entry and exit, the alignment between rules and incentives (rules are considered useful), and the public involvement in rule design (rules about changing rules, connection between rules and consequences relatively transparent)" (253). Both systems reject the monocentric "Westphalian" sovereign nation-state model as neither natural, nor inevitable, and the homogenization of political society as neither possible, nor desirable. Both encourage and endorse overlapping political centers, "competition, cooperation, exit and entry procedures, and conflict resolution among the decision centres" (Paniagua and Pourvand 2024, 11). Both consider freedom of political entry and exit essential, especially for the generation of competition between political units (Aligica and Tarko 2012, 247).

Polycentrism is vaguer, is more complex and general, and has a broader scope than panarchism: "[I]n some cases the decision centers are nonterritorial (they have overlapping jurisdiction), in some cases they are territorially delimitated, and some cases can be in both ways. Hence, the underlying crucial question: Do indeed all those phenomena share something?" (Aligica and Tarko 2012, 249). The broader concept of polycentricity may include much of panarchy as a special case, except for a few properties of panarchy not shared by polycentricity: First, advocates of polycentricity are often committed to some form of democracy (Paniagua and Pourvand 2024). Panarchy makes no commitment to democracy or any other form of government, as long as citizens can enter and exit formal and rule-governed relations in the forms of contracts with any type of government with which they wish to experiment, including unelected technocracy, philosophical aristocracy, hereditary monarchy, or, for that matter, the rule of holy fools and councils of astrologers. Others may wish to live under one of the many types of dictatorships that have proven popular in history. Panarchy is fine with such choices as long as they are voluntary and reversible by allowing exit. Second, panarchy, unlike polycentricity, does not insist on multi-scale decentralization. Non-territorial States may experiment with large and central States and balance economies of scale against difficulties in obtaining sufficient information for effective policymaking, or they may prefer small boutique States with a lot of information but high sunk costs without economies of scale. Empirical trial and error would sort out the successful from the unsuccessful forms of government (cf. Baldwin et al. 2023).

Polycentrism emphasizes that government centers should operate and overlap on different scales, generating multilayered, nested structures with emergent properties and unintended solutions (Paniagua and Pourvand 2024). An obviously possible, though unnecessary, interpretation of "scale" is territorial, considering the governing of a geographical region as the overlapping intersections of local, regional, national, and global governments. This interpretation preserves the historical origins of the idea of polycentricity in the Ostroms' analysis of metropolitan governance (Aligica and Tarko 2012, 241–44). Panarchy, by contrast, does not prescribe political scales, leaving the optimal scales of political units to *experimental discovery* (cf. Baldwin et al. 2023). Panarchism doubts that local administration of public goods—such as garbage collection, sewage treatment, and the construction and maintenance of roads—has to be political, though some panarchic thinkers have considered political hybrids that have local territorial elements combined with non-territorial panarchy (Long 2016; Frey 2016). Kneitschel (2016) presented panarchy as a solution for situations where regional autonomy in a federated system is impossible because different political populations are territorially intermingled and dispersed within each other. In complex demographics, there can be an infinite regress of minority discrimination as each minority on a higher political level becomes a majority on a lower autonomous scale and proceeds to discriminate against minorities on that scale. If those minorities win autonomy on that level, they may proceed to discriminate against minorities on that scale almost *ad infinitum*. Distinguishing polities from territoriality and basing politics on contractual relations between non-territorial states and their citizens who are free to exit makes such regress of discrimination avoidable.

3. EXIT VERSUS MONOPOLY

The current post-Westphalian international political system is based on regional territorial monopolies and nation-states. Each state (except for the Knights of Malta and governments in exile) has a monopoly over a territory and its inhabitants. The definition of a *monopoly* is "a situation in which a seller is the sole source of supply for a good that has no significant substitutes, when the behavior of sellers is less than competitive [and] the seller has significant discretion over the price and whose quantity sold varies inversely with the price" (Bishop 1968). This is an apt description of many territorial governments. Monopolies allow price discrimination, providing an identical product for different prices to different groups, to maximize profits. A monopoly can capture, through price discrimination, the whole market for a product. The state territorial monopoly separates groups of constituents and charges them different prices (taxes) to maximize its revenue (North 1986, 251).

Territorial political monopolies supply goods—like security, adjudication of disputes, etc.—that have a limited number of substitutes. In other words, "the degree of monopoly power of the ruler . . . is a function of the closeness of substitutes for the various groups of constituents" (North 1986, 251). North suggests two possible sources of competition: other states and alternative elites. The fewer the substitutes, the more freedom the State has to become despotic and the more income it is able to extract from society. The State provides greater services for those sections of society with greater access to substitutes such as emigration or competitors within the State. "The former alternative depends upon the structure of competitive political units. The more geographically proximate ones of course have an advantage. The ruler's efforts to gain or keep constituents will be determined by the supply curve of protection and the marginal benefits to be derived from additional constituents" (North 1986, 254).

Immigration opportunities and democracy decrease the monopoly power of the State and increase competition. However, immigration is limited by territorial monopolies that cannot handle the increasing demand for their services. A democratic change of government does not necessarily change policies, control the elected elite, or increase the efficiency of the State. As North noted, the supply curve of the State, like that of all monopolies, is U-shaped. Beyond a certain level of output, the marginal cost of production begins to rise, and the monopoly is unable to meet the increase in demand without a marginal increase in price. "Stagnant states can survive as long as there is no change in the opportunity cost of the constituents at home or in the relative strength of competitor states. This last condition usually implies that the state approaches the status of monopoly" (North 1986, 255–56). Modern nation-states face increases in demand for public services: welfare, education, urban development, crime fighting, health services, and so on. Facing this increased demand, States behave as monopolies that cannot supply an increase in demand without an increase in marginal price (as expressed, in many cases, in higher taxes or debt) because their production power is limited, as expressed in their U-shaped supply curves. Hence, for the monopolist sovereign State, more people are a problem because they generate more demand for more services. Instead, for a service-providing firm, like the States in panarchy, more people are a solution because they generate more demand for services. The modern nation-state is stagnant and inefficient. It has *too few* competitors or substitutes, which forces it to either find new solutions or supply the increase in demand themselves. Instead, some "live on credit," borrowing capital for operational costs.

From the consumer's perspective, the degree of monopoly is inversely related to the degree of consumer mobility. The existing degree of immigration from one territorial monopoly to another is the actual degree of consumer mobility in the political marketplace. Territorial monopolies that may come under increased demand under conditions of increased consumer mobility move to limit such mobility or elasticity in demand through immigration controls. States, oddly in comparison to firms, reject most of their prospective new customers. For a typical company that mass-produces products, marginal customers are cheaper because of economies of scale that generate profit.

A different intellectual route that leads to similar conclusions is through Albert Hirschman's (1970) exit and voice dichotomy. Exiting from all political associations in a world of territorial sovereign States is difficult and expensive, even when possible. Only a small, often privileged, minority is able to exit. As Hirschman analyzed in his famous *Exit, Voice, and Loyalty*, when the quality of service of an organization like a State deteriorates, managers are under pressure to improve it when faced with massive exit of their customers. They can also attempt to dissuade exit by branding it as "desertion, defection and treason" (Hirschman 1970, 17), or in politics, as secessionism (cf. Buchanan 2012). Alternatively, they may be forced to listen to the voice of the disgruntled customers. However, if there is no exit option, or it is difficult or expensive, there is no incentive for managers to improve service or give voice to their customers.

Limited exit possibilities, emigration, and immigration opportunities strengthen bad States because they deprive the opposition of its most vocal voices (Hirschman 1970, 55). As in Hirschman's favorite example, the bad management of the Nigerian railways, poorly managed States can withstand the loss of revenue from the small minority that can exit because their revenue is based on involuntary taxes, on exports of natural resources, or on selling debt. Such regimes even encourage and facilitate exit for their elite opponents; for example, Latin American authoritarian regimes helped their critics move to neighboring States, and the Communist Czechoslovak regime pressured Charter 77 signatories to emigrate to the West while preventing the vast majority of its subjects from leaving. To bring down or reform such low-quality States, massive exit must be possible, as in 1989, when Hungary effectively brought down the Iron Curtain by dismantling its border with Austria and allowing massive emigration to the West from the Soviet bloc. Had there been no regime change in East Germany, massive exit to West Germany would have emptied East Germany of its economically active population, leaving behind only the leaders of the Communist Party and pensioners.

From this perspective, panarchy is a radical facilitator of exit. The possibility of a massive, costless, or very cheap exit would pressure rulers to listen to their political customers. Even democracies can benefit from enhanced exit options for their citizens. As Hirschman noted, when all competing firms provide the same lousy quality products, there is no genuine exit option for the consumer. Exit is particularly useful for victims of conflicts in places like the Middle East. Irrespective of how such conflicts begin, they are sustained by the absence of mass exit options.

4. NATURAL MONOPOLY? THE TERRITORIAL FALLACY

A standard definition of *State* as "the political organization of a body of people for the maintenance of order within its territory by coercion" (Gilbert 1995, 850; cf. Weber 1948, 78) assumes the State is a *natural territorial monopoly* and excludes the possibility of non-territorial States. The idea of a State monopoly over territory and a group of people who reside there has become so entrenched that even philosophers who attempt to defend a minimal State assume, unimaginatively, the territorial definition of the State; for example: "The dominant protective association within a territory satisfies two crucial necessary conditions for being a state: that it had the requisite sort of monopoly over the use of force in the territory, even if this universal protection could be provided only in a 'redistributive fashion'" (Nozick 1974, 113). Similarly, "I use 'the state' to refer, roughly, to the final civil authority (or claimant thereof) in a given geographical domain" (Schmidtz 1991, xvi).

As Wolff (1996, 56–59) noted, Nozick's argument for statist natural territorial monopoly is odd for a libertarian. Nozick argued that when several proto-State protective associations compete, territorial monopolies emerge as a result of contradictions between the regulations of different protective associations: when a citizen of one State or protective association acts toward a citizen of another in a way that constitutes a crime according to the laws of the second State, but not according to the laws of the first State (Nozick 1974, 10–25). Machan agreed with Nozick that a political monopoly is necessary for resolving conflicts of jurisdiction about rights: "a good human community can have only one final authority, having jurisdiction over a homogeneous sphere of human occupancy, and commanding an enforcement agency with loyalty to no other final authority" (Machan 1983, 513).

In Nozick's opinion, conflicts over jurisdiction between mutual protective associations can be resolved only in three possible ways that all lead to the establishment of political monopoly over a territory: First, protective agencies may engage in a war of annihilation in which only one agency survives and establishes sovereignty. Second, the battle may result in a geographical division in which clients of conflicting States concentrate around their centers of power. "In either of these two cases does there remain very much geographical interspersal. Only one protective agency operates over a given geographical area" (Nozick 1974, 16). Thirdly, the conflicting agencies may reach an agreement, refer all disputes to a third authority, or divide the jurisdiction to create a federal structure. "In each of these cases, almost all the persons in a geographical area are under some common system that judges between their competing claims and enforces their rights" (Nozick 1974, 16).

Nozick made several unwarranted assumptions:

1. If protective associations cannot agree, they resolve their disputes violently.
2. War is over territory.
3. Arbitration between States is necessarily federal.
4. Sovereignty resolves the problem of relations between citizens of States with inconsistent laws.

Actually, States and protective associations rarely go to war over jurisdiction. Had Nozick been right, Britain would have gone to war against Brazil over the extradition of the "Great Train" robbers. States do not go to war over conflicts of jurisdiction because the prospective losses considerably outweigh the expected gains. This has been recognized since Aeschylus, Euripides, and Lucretius, who ridiculed Agamemnon for joining the Trojan War, a war of jurisdiction over Helen. David Friedman (1973) suggested in his account of private protective associations a more plausible scenario of jurisdiction conflict resolution between protective associations that involves neither war nor federal arrangement but voluntary arbitration:

> Whoever wins, by the time the conflict is over it will be expensive for both sides. They might even have to start paying their employees higher wages to make up for the risk. Then both firms will be forced to raise their rates. If they do, . . . an aggressive new firm . . . will undercut their prices and steal their customers. There must be a better solution . . . arbitration. In practice, once [free market] institutions were well established, protection agencies would anticipate such difficulties and arrange contracts in advance, before specific conflicts occurred, specifying the arbitrator who would settle them. (Friedman 1973, 157–58. Cf. Rothbard 1996, 221–27)

War, then, is not necessarily over territory, and it does not result inevitably in regional territorial monopolies. Economic and technological progress has made territorial wars increasingly obsolete. When humans were pastoralists, cows and goats were more important than land, and wars took the form of raids for stealing cattle and livestock (oxen were particularly popular). After the Neolithic Revolutions, when people developed agriculture and came to live on and from the land, territory became the most common and non-perishable (but illiquid) form of wealth. Then, war over it made sense. In today's world, the most important forms of wealth are information and capital, not territory. The mobility and liquidity of information and capital following the communication revolution made territorial wars as increasingly obsolete as cattle raids. Conquering a territory makes nobody smarter, but it makes investors withdraw capital and invest it somewhere else; for example, Russia's invasion of Ukraine not only made Russia's position much worse in the world, but even if Putin had achieved his goals, it would have done nothing for improving Russia's position in relation to the American and Chinese superpowers. Accordingly, if war results in a division of power, this division is not necessarily territorial.

Most importantly—and this goes to the heart of what I find wrongheaded about much of contemporary political philosophy—Nozick, like Rawls, attempted to support his conclusions with thought experiments when the historical record not only showed that the results he reported were wrong, but it also made such thought experiments redundant. Thought experiments are poor and sometimes lazy substitutes for real experiments, evidence, and reading history because they leave too much for intuition and implicit background assumptions. When rich historical records and "natural experiments" are available, relying on thought experiments is neither necessary nor desirable.

There have been many historically functioning models of mixed, overlapping, and extraterritorial jurisdictions (cf. Tucker and Bellis 2016). Tribal societies of hunters and gatherers and pastoralists based their political organization on kinship, not territory. The Greek *polis* was essentially a structure of people united by law, not by a relation to a territory. When the Greeks colonized, the future State, the *polis*, its hierarchical political structure, had already existed on the ship, before a territory was chosen. Plato represented this political worldview in *The Laws*, suggesting a constitution for a colony that had no territory. The first Puritan New England communities were based on an explicit covenant, agreed on by the settlers irrespective of the actual site of their settlement. The feudal state system was based on territorial ambiguity. The hierarchical-personal feudal relationships overlapped and were more essential than accidental territories. The division of power between the church, the king, and the vassals was at odds with the modern idea of a single sovereign ruling over a single territory.

The subjugation of society, territory, and nation to a single political monopoly has been historically recent. An international system based on sovereignty became dominant in Europe only following the Westphalian settlement of the Thirty Years' War in 1648 (Held 1997, 86–89). Outside of Europe, various extraterritorial arrangements of mixed sovereignty existed in the Ottoman and Chinese empires. Today, citizens of different States do business with each other and live together in large global hubs. Following the recent invention of decentralized contracts, the adjudication process may be automated in whole or in part without involving any adjudication, jurisdiction, or sovereignty. In sum, there is plenty of historical evidence that the State is not a natural monopoly, and the Westphalian order is nothing more than an episode in political history.

5. MORALITY AND PANARCHY

Current immigration restrictions unbalance the world economy. We live in a world where ideas can travel freely and instantly, and censorship is challenged by technology. The movement of capital across borders has also been liberalized. The movement of goods and trade is not nearly as free as that of ideas, but the trend, especially since the end of the Cold War, has been toward greater liberalization of trade despite the populist rhetoric of the last few years. Political barriers to the movement of people and to their ability to work in multiple geographical locations originated in the destructive and pathological era following the First World War. They contributed to the Great Depression of the thirties, the rise of Nazism, and the Holocaust. Though human and labor movement has become both faster and cheaper than in any other historical period, many of these barriers remain in place. Political barriers to migration create global imbalances when people cannot chase capital and production where they are, though they know where the capital is and have a good idea about the benefits that geographical movement may bestow on them. For example, capital flows often move from riskier to less risky, first-world environments. But workers cannot follow the capital. Vice versa, production shifts to areas with lower labor costs, often from the first to the third world. But first-world workers cannot follow production processes. Barriers to human movement generate imbalances, unemployment, low returns on investment, and scarcity of qualified labor.

Immigration restrictions in the last one hundred years have contributed to ethical catastrophes, most notably genocide, by trapping victims in territories they urgently needed to exit. Without immigration restrictions before and during the Second World War, the scope of the Holocaust would have been far more limited. The current political international system of sovereign States is responsible for global poverty that could have been prevented had people been able to move according to their economic interests. The misery of a great number of people who would have had happier, more decent, and more fulfilling lives had they been able to migrate to better places has political rather than economic roots. The history of immigration to the United States indicates just how much innovation, economic progress, scientific discoveries, and cultural contributions are prevented today by closed or impermeable borders. Heroic, brave, and entrepreneurial individuals, a vanguard of economic rationality and prosperity, who attempt to cross borders to improve their lives and the lives of others, are prevented from realizing their potential by political borders.

Thousands of migrants who die every year of drowning, thirst, and exposure crossing the Mediterranean in rickety boats or the deserts into Texas and Arizona in the United States, and the women who are trafficked into the first world would have had decent lives if sovereign States did not prevent them from simply walking over and finding a job. Emigrants fall prey to smuggling gangs and traffickers who exploit them and sometimes torture and kill them because they cannot legally take a ferry or a bus to where they have reason to believe their fates would be better (Stevis 2015). The *Economist* (2015) described this as "a moral and political disgrace." Yet the same magazine, in the same issue, while calling to accept political refugees from civil wars, also called for separating them from economic migrants, ignoring the obvious utility of economic migrants who come to work and improve the global as well as their household income. The *Economist* presented people who want to work, exactly the kind of immigrants who can create value for others, as criminals who need to be distinguished from refugees, who are not necessarily as economically valuable. The moral case for open borders is compelling (Carens 2013, chapters 11–12).

Apart from irrational atavistic xenophobia, one reason for politically blocking migration is the fear that migrants may make demands on the welfare system that would reduce its quantity as well as quality for current beneficiaries.

Panarchy can eliminate such fears because geographical migrants are not political migrants in a world without sovereignty: their domicile does not affect their access to welfare, and because States that are not territorial monopolies would react to increases in demand as commercial companies do by expanding production and supply to maximize profits, or by creating franchises.

Another reason often mentioned for immigration restrictions is the right of political self-determination. Arguably, nations may lose their fragile identities if people with different languages, cultures, and culinary habits can immigrate (cf. Carens 2013). By separating political affiliation from geographic location and States from territories, panarchy allows open borders without forcing any State to accept anybody as its citizen.

Foreign direct investment in underdeveloped, poorer parts of the world is currently limited by insecurity and corruption. Had investors been able to secure their investments with their own security forces and legal and judicial institutions and frameworks, there would have been far more development and less poverty throughout modern history. A world of competing non-territorial States would lift current sovereign barriers to development. Currently, middle-class pensioners from the north can move to many warmer and more affordable global neighborhoods, but they cannot bring their State services with them, especially personal security and medical benefits. Non-territorial States may be able to offer such services globally. Panarchy would not be heaven on earth, but from a moral perspective, it would create a world considerably better than anything we have had so far in human history.

6. TECHNOLOGICAL AND SOCIAL PREREQUISITES

Political territorialism and sovereignty are necessary in agrarian societies where land is limited and exit is difficult, both because the "pharaoh" has an interest in not letting his people go and because to exit, they have to cross natural barriers like sea and desert. The old empires were based on caging populations who could not leave or could only leave at great peril and expense (Fukuyama 2012). The rise of the nation-state in the nineteenth century coincided with and was facilitated by several technological and business innovations: canals and railways united national territories; the post office and the telegraph united the national territory through information transmission; and universal basic education united the various dialects of national languages and allowed a unified national bureaucracy, education system, and newspapers. Today, airplanes are faster, cheaper, and safer (if less convenient and glamorous) than trains, creating a global transportation system. Electronic communications have been replacing letters and have not just made the post office obsolete, but also unified the globe through the internet and satellite communication, which are immediate and do not distinguish between the geographically distant and the proximate. English has become the universal language of science, the internet, and global television channels. Apart from a thin global elite of polyglots, native English speakers tend to be monolingual, while everybody else speaks their mother tongue and learns English.

The rise of global mega-cities and regions—like the Northeast of the United States, from Washington, D.C., to Boston; Northern California; London; Paris; Berlin; and Hong Kong—where many people with diverse origins, political identities, and allegiances live and work together, have made the nation-state obsolete in the sense that New York and London communicate with, and are affected by, each other, far more than, say, London and Newcastle or New York and West Virginia. People who live in mega-cities have more in common with each other than with rural compatriots. Consequently, territoriality and geographical location matters much less than at any other time in history, as supply chains and commercial networks span the globe irrespective of geography (Friedman 2007). The non-territorial and global communities of inventors, entrepreneurs, and futurist visionaries, who are used to innovation and its implementation, naturally expand their horizons to the political realm and come up with innovative political ideas that come close to panarchy (Frank 2015; Tucker and Bellis 2016; Srinivasan 2022; Rothblatt 2003).

The fact that technological and social prerequisites for panarchy have been accumulating does not imply that they amount to sufficient conditions. A hundred years ago, the steam engine and the telegraph also facilitated the globalization of the world. Still, these inventions were followed by the most horrendous and murderous anti-global phase in human history, which left global trade disrupted, parts of the globe isolated, and the worst territorial wars and destruction of human life in European history, with effects that have lasted for seventy years. From a contemporary perspective, but also from a nineteenth-century liberal perspective, the two world wars of the twentieth century seem anachronistic and pointless since land matters little for prosperity, and natural resources can be a curse for other sectors of the economy and for the democratic accountability of States. The fact that technological facilitators and prerequisites for panarchy have accumulated does not imply that the potential *will* be actualized, only that it *can be* actualized.

The growing capacity of the internet to transmit information, and of computers to process it, reduces the cost and difficulties of running global enterprises such as States. Computers can fulfill some of the traditional functions of government to the extent that they coincide with the operations of credit card and insurance companies; they collect and distribute resources according to a contract. The latest innovations allow computers to enforce contracts through decentralized agreements and payments, issue currency, and set monetary policy through cryptocurrencies.

Estonia has been at the forefront of the digitalization of government, allowing it to be as ex-territorial as the internet. Estonia offers anybody in the world the option of becoming an Estonian "e-resident." In return for paying taxes to Estonia, its e-residents can register their companies there and execute contracts through e-signatures according to Estonian and EU laws and regulations. Estonia pioneered the digitalization of government, whereby much of the interaction between citizens and the State is electronic and can take place anywhere. Two innovations facilitate this process: e-signatures that are safer than ink on paper and electronic identity cards. Estonia, a country of little more than a million residents, expects a tenfold e-residency. Whether or not ten million global citizens become virtual residents of Estonia is not as important as the ability, through computerization, to increase exponentially the number of citizens without significantly increasing the number of government employees. Schnurer (2015) reports that Estonia plans to move its entire government into the cloud, thus making it immune to any physical seizure either by an invading army or by cyberattacks on its computer servers on Estonian territory. Such entrepreneurial governments can become more productive and profitable. In other words:

> The Internet makes the potential scope of this market for extraterritorial services infinitely broad. Governments can now offer different kinds of services to customers located just about anywhere in the world—if only these services can somehow be put online. . . . The more a state goes virtual, and the less its government depends on territory and other physical resources, the more smaller, more nimble competitors such as Estonia would be able to innovate and compete for new customers. Most of the world's governments might not be at this point yet, but Estonia offers an indication of things to come. (Schnurer 2015)

Generally, public services and relations that involve funds and information can be transmitted and exchanged electronically; other services can be ordered locally via the internet, like concierge services offered by major credit cards. Health and education could be supplied locally by contractors, but more significantly and controversially, so could security. The last couple of decades have witnessed a rise of private security companies and the historical return of mercenary armies. Conventional states like the United States and Nigeria hire private armies to fight their wars. More interestingly, corporations and NGOs like World Vision and Save the Children hire security firms to protect their employees (Kinzer 2015; McFate 2014). Such security companies can have the same corporate structure as any service company with local branches. If a State does not have its own security services in a location, it can contract one of those companies. Historically, mercenary armies did not offer reliable services because they could break contracts and work for themselves against their customers or even work for the adversaries of their customers if they outbid them. This problem is likely to be just as relevant if States wage war. But if non-territorial States need to get small security jobs done locally, like escort a citizen out of a danger zone or enforce a contract, a security company will have an incentive to provide a good service rather than sell loyalty to the highest bidder (as long as it is not a monopoly like modern nation-states). Political services attached to social contracts can be bought and sold on internet platforms like insurance, with “likes,” customer reviews, and so on to help customers decide.

The emergence of global social media networks like Facebook has led Balaji Srinivasan (2013, 2022) to suggest that political communities are losing their geographical characteristics by migrating to the cloud. The relevant distance between people is no longer geographical, but geodesic, the number of degrees of separation on a social network. Cloud formations can lead later to the foundation of communities and then to political formations:

> Emigrants would be moving within or between nation states to become part of a community, not to strike out on their own. . . . Unlike so-called secessionists, the specific site of physical concentration would be a matter of convenience, not passion; the geography incidental and not worth fighting over. Today, one of the first and largest international reverse diasporas has assembled in Silicon Valley, drawn by the internet to the cloud capital of technology; in fact, an incredible 64% of the Valley’s scientists and engineers hail from outside the U.S., with 43.9% of its technology companies founded by emigrants. (Srinivasan 2013)

Srinivasan, a Silicon Valley academic, entrepreneur, and investor, outlined the political implications of the new technologies in an online bestseller (Srinivasan 2022; cf. Tucker 2022). Facebook has far more nodes at more places than any historical empire has ever had. Remote work is becoming normal: “during the pandemic, every sector that had previously been socially resistant to the internet (healthcare, education, law, finance, government . . .) capitulated.” In the future, virtual reality may enable distant physical work through robotic avatars. Cryptocurrencies shift monetary policies from central banks to the diffused net. The invention of smart contracts that act automatically when set conditions are satisfied (for example, when a property is listed publicly as owned by a buyer, a bank account automatically sends funds to the seller) may eliminate the need for national sovereign adjudication, laws, and enforcement.

Blockchain technology may record all financial transactions and smart contracts publicly in a ledger to form a grand archive of humanity (Borges’s

Library of Babel comes to mind). “The first draft of history will be the raw on-chain event feed, written directly to the ledger of record by billions of writers and sensors around the world.” Some States and municipalities have already transferred many functions to digital platforms. El Salvador uses a cryptocurrency. Estonia offers e-citizenship; British journalist and Lib-Dem parliamentary candidate Edward Lucas became its first e-citizen. Technology initially facilitated the nation-state. Srinivasan points out that mapmaking clarified fuzzy borders, printing established national tongues, and firearms redistributed power from elites to ordinary people. One may add that canals and railroads, the telegraph, the radio, television, and national mass media built centralized nations. Since the middle of the last century, Srinivasan emphasizes that technology has been decentralized and fragmented. The internet unbundles society into its constituent parts and then re-bundles them, like playlists in music-streaming services, by connecting peers to peers.

Migration to the web has resulted in better products that cost less, from the post office to electronic mail, from taxis to Uber and Lyft, from maps to GPS. Srinivasan recommends a similar migration of States to the cloud. Srinivasan admires the founder of Zionism, Theodore Herzl, not as a nationalist who obsessively sought a territory to found a nation-state (he thought of parts of Latin America or a part of present-day Kenya before being compelled by his more romantic Zionist colleagues to settle on a return to Zion), but as a political entrepreneur whose vision led to a (indeed, *the*) startup nation. Similarly, Srinivasan wants to found political startups on the basis of preexisting geographically distributed communities. Cloud communities should share common goals or an innovative moral principle. Unlike philosophical liberals, Srinivasan does not want to construct states from abstract individuals according to universal constitutions. Like communitarians, he wants laws to represent preexisting communal values: “We can apply all the techniques of startup companies to startup societies. Financing, attracting subscribers, calculating churn, doing customer support.” The networked community, like Zionism, would start with crowdfunding (Herzl preferred “angel investors,” like the Rothchilds and Hirschs, but they turned him down), followed by the creation of a cryptocurrency, electronic passports, encrypted keys for the citizens to access their State, and blockchains that register the State’s data:

> In practice, we say that a user has consented to be governed by a startup society if he has signed a social smart contract that gives a system administrator limited privileges over that user’s digital life in return for admission to the startup society. . . . Signing the social smart contract is . . . taking conscious risk with an on-chain asset in return for admission to a digital ecosystem. (Ibid.)

The sovereignty of network states is the cryptographic private keys of the administrators. Hacking those codes would constitute a political invasion. Diplomatic relations between networked States are mutual recognitions of protocols and formats. Networked States may have different regimes, such as democratic, corporate, theocratic or dictatorial, if a right to exit and take one's cryptocurrency is respected in a prospective age of "pax Bitcoinica." "Post-Satoshian network states will be limited in control to people who've opted into their networks" (Srinivasan 2022).Political competition will encourage diversification and innovative experimentation. To borrow a phrase from insurance law, networked States and their citizens may be "alluring hazards" for legacy States and "Neolithic" populations. They may find it irresistible to do to them what China is doing to Hong Kong or what majorities have been doing to commercially successful minorities throughout history. Visibility can be a vulnerability. Invasions and theft may be legitimized by accusing network States of colonialism, money laundering, tax evasion, or narco-trafficking. Srinivasan considers two solutions: The classical panarchist "nonviolent digital defense through secrecy, pseudonymity, decentralization, and encryption," or alliances with nation-states. But historically, such alliances required either a common enemy or money-laundering and tax-evasion services for foreign elites.

Like others who developed panarchic ideas, Srinivasan wrote in ignorance of the previous formulation of non-territorial, contractually founded states. Lack of familiarity with the tradition that started at least in 1860 with Puydt (2016) is hardly unusual. Even an accomplished philosopher like Moritz Schlick, the Viennese philosopher founder of logical-positivism who came to similar conclusions in his posthumously published book *Natur und Kultur* (1952), was inspired by late-Habsburg ideas for non-territorial national autonomies and Augustine's City of God, but was unaware of Puydt. The Czech dissident Václav Benda envisioned in 1978 a "parallel polis" (Benda 1988) of dissident communities to the late totalitarian state, again without reference to other political theorists. More poetically, China Miéville (2009) published a science fiction novel about two cities (reminiscent of Augustine's City of Man and City of God) that coexist in the same geographical space but whose residents learn to "unsee" each other in shared "crosshatching" streets. Most recently, the political economist and data scientist Trent MacDonald (2019) examined non-territorial States with a thorough knowledge of the panarchic literature. He examined non-territorial States as efficient forms of economic unbundling, like switching from paying cable companies for bundles to paying for individual streaming services.

Less promising, in my opinion, is "seasteading," the creation of floating towns off the territorial waters of California, as a recent attempt to create new States with freer entry and exit regulations. If creative political entrepreneurs could not find a territory on earth, they could move to the sea and allow there, away from any sovereignty, free immigration, labor, and trade. However, such communities would still be territorial. Without a military, they would be easy targets for nation-states who could occupy them merely by blocking the shipping lanes, which would be their lifeline. The excuse for such action could be anything from alleged drug production and dealing to tax evasion. The American government went after banks and exchanges of cryptocurrencies outside of the United States because they operated without a U.S. license and allegedly helped criminals and terrorists to move money across territorial borders, as well as honest businessmen (Halpern 2015). Going after a territorially defined and fully dependent territory is likely to be considerably easier. Panarchy would offer all the benefits of such new States, without having to move anywhere, let alone to the sea or to Mars.

CONCLUSION

A political free market is not heaven on earth. It will not eliminate human misery or generate universal justice. It is simply the best procedure for selecting which States are the best. Panarchy offers a political mechanism for the selection of best States that is absent from all other normative political theories, such as (i) anarchism, which seeks to avoid erecting States altogether, (ii) certain versions of cosmopolitanism, which seek to create a world-state, and (iii) internationalism, which reaffirms the present "Westphalian Order" of nation-states. Unlike a universal world monopoly State, States in free competition are incentivized to reform and improve while their customers gain strong exit and voice options. Unlike present-day nation-states, non-territorial States can offer a greater choice and variety of services, likely curtail mass warfare, and have considerable positive effects on economic growth and rationalization in the world economy.

Some libertarians and anarchists suggest that in a universal free market, the State would be redundant because people could purchase from various firms the services that single States provide today (Rothbard 1996; Sanders 1980). But as Trent Macdonald (2019) argued convincingly, the optimal forms of political bundling and unbundling would be experimented with and discovered rather than inferred abstractly. Panarchy, unlike anarchy, allows persons to voluntarily purchase the kind of political services they desire from a single provider, thus exploring bundling options and reaping economies of scale.

A free and regulated political market is possible because the State is not a natural monopoly and a regulated market can function without a monopolist State. Is panarchy practical or otherworldly, if not a utopia? I do not have sufficient information to answer this question. It is possible to consider where there may be the demand for such States. People who currently are citizens of weak, ineffective, or corrupt States may want to contract a supplementary non-territorial State for higher-quality services. Citizens of relatively effective States that are small may want to contract with a non-territorial State that offers more extensive and global services as a kind of supplementary insurance. An American may purchase a Scandinavian level of welfare coverage. With enough such non-territorial States, it may be possible to chip away at the limits of sovereignty and eventually abolish it altogether. To quote Theodore Herzl out of context, "If you will it, it is not a dream."

NOTE

1. This article is based partly on Tucker (2016b and 2022). Its present composition benefited from support from the European Union under the REFRESH—Research Excellence for Regional Sustainability and High-Tech Industries—project number CZ.10.03.01/00/22_003/0000048 via the Operational Programme Just Transition.

REFERENCES

Aligica Paul D., and Vlad Tarko. 2012. "Polycentricity: From Polanyi to Ostrom, and Beyond." *Governance: An International Journal of Policy, Administration, and Institutions* 25 (2), No. 2: 237–62.

Baldwin, E., A. Thiel, M. McGinnis, and E. Kellner. 2023. "Empirical Research on Polycentric Governance: Critical Gaps and a Framework for Studying Long-term Change." *Policy Studies Journal*.

Benda, Václav. 1988. "Parallel Polis, or An Independent Society in Central and Eastern Europe," translated by Paul Wilson. *Social Research* 55 (1/2): 211–46.

Bishop, Robert L. 1968. "Monopoly." In *The International Encyclopedia of the Social Sciences* 10 (458). New York: Macmillan.

Buchanan, Alan. 2012. "Secession and Nationalism." In Robert E. Goodin, Philip Pettit, and Thomas Pogge, eds., *A Companion to Contemporary Political Philosophy*, 2nd ed., 755–66.

Carens, Joseph H. 2013. *The Ethics of Immigration*. New York: Oxford University Press.

Economist, The. 2015. "Europe's Boat People," and "For Those in Peril," 11, 21–24, April 25, 2005.

Frank, Sam. 2015. "Come with Us If You Want to Live: Among the Apocalyptic Libertarians of Silicon Valley," *Harper's Magazine* 330 (1976): 26–36.

Frey, Bruno. 2016. "A Utopia? Governance without Territorial Monopoly." In Tucker, Aviezer, Bellis, and Gian Piero de, eds. *Panarchy: Political Theories of Non-Territorial States*. New York: Routledge, 234–46.

Friedman, David. 1973. *The Machinery of Freedom: Guide to Radical Capitalism*. New York: Harper & Row.

Friedman, Thomas L. 2007. *The World Is Flat: A Brief History of the 21st Century*. New York: Picador.

Fukuyama, Francis. 2012. *The Origins of Political Order: From Prehuman Times to the French Revolution.* New York: Farrar, Straus & Giroux.

Gilbert, Paul. 1995. “State.” In *The Oxford Companion to Philosophy*, edited by Ted Honderich, 850. Oxford: Oxford UP.

Halpern, Jake. 2015. “Bank of the Underworld,” *Atlantic*, May, 105–16.

Held, David. 1997. “Democracy: From City-states to a Cosmopolitan Order?” In *Contemporary Political Philosophy*, edited by Robert E. Goodin and Philip Pettit. Oxford: Blackwell, 78–101.

Hirschman, Albert O. 1970. *Exit, Voice, and Loyalty: Responses to Decline in Firms, Organizations, and States*. Cambridge, MA: Harvard University Press.

Hobbes, Thomas. 1968. *Leviathan*. London: Penguin.

Kinzer, Stephen. 2015. “National Sovereignty Is So Last Century,” *Boston Globe*, March 29, K6.

Kneitschel, Dictmar. 2016. “Federalism and Non-Territorial Minorities.” In Tucker, Aviezer, Bellis, and Gian Piero de, eds. *Panarchy: Political Theories of Non-Territorial States*. New York: Routledge, 247–255.

Long, Roderick T. 2016. “Virtual Cantons,” in Tucker, Aviezer, Bellis, and Gian Piero de, eds. *Panarchy: Political Theories of Non-Territorial States*. New York: Routledge, 227–33.

McFate, Sean. 2014. *The Modern Mercenary: Private Armies and What They Mean for World Order*. New York: Oxford University Press.

Macdonald, Trent J. 2019. *The Political Economy of Non-Territorial Exit: Cryptosecession.* Cheltenham: Edward Elgar.

Machan, Tibor R. 1983. “Individualism and the Problem of Political Authority.” *Monist* 66.4, 500–16.

Miéville, China. 2009. *The City and the City*. New York: Del Rey.

Narveson, Jan. 1988. *The Libertarian Idea*. Philadelphia: Temple University Press.

North, Douglass. 1986. “A Neoclassical Theory of the State.” In *Rational Choice*, edited by Jon Elster. Oxford: Blackwell.

Nozick, Robert. 1974. *Anarchy, State, and Utopia*. New York: Basic Books.

Paniagua, Pablo, and Kaveh Pourvand. 2024. “Whither stability? Polycentric democracy and social order.” In *Polycentric Governance and the Good Society: A Normative and Philosophical Investigation*, edited by David Thunder and Pablo Paniagua. New York: Rowman & Littlefield.

Puydt, Paul Emil de. 2016 [1860]. “Panarchy,” translated by John Zube and Aviezer Tucker. In Tucker, Aviezer, Bellis, and Gian Piero de, eds. *Panarchy: Political Theories of Non-Territorial States*. New York: Routledge, 21–36.

Rothbard, Murray N. 1996. *For a New Liberty: The Libertarian Manifesto*, rev. ed. San Francisco: Fox & Wilkes.

Sanders, John. 1980. *The Ethical Argument Against the State*. Washington, D.C.: University Press of America.

Schlick, Moritz. 1952. *Natur und Kultur.* Vienna: Humboldt.

Schmidtz, David. 1991. *The Limits of Government: An Essay on the Public Good Argument*. Boulder, CO: Westview Press.

Schnurer, Eric B. 2015. "E-Stonia and the Future of the Cyberstate: Virtual Governments Come Online," *Foreign Affairs*, January 28. http://www.foreignaffairs.com/articles/142825/eric-b-schnurer/e-stonia-and-the-future-of-the-cyberstate.

Srinivasan, Balaji. 2013. "Software Is Reorganizing the World," *Wired*, November 22. http://www.wired.com/2013/11/software-is-reorganizing-the-world-and-cloud-formations-could-lead-to-physical-nations/.

Srinivasan, Balaji. 2022. *The Network State: How to Start a New Country*, self-published. https://thenetworkstate.com/. Accessed June 13, 2024.

Stevis, Martina. 2015. "Rich Smuggling Trade Fuels Deadly Migration," *Wall Street Journal*, April 21, 1.v.

Tucker, Aviezer. 2016a. "Introduction." In Tucker, Aviezer, Bellis, and Gian Piero de, eds. *Panarchy: Political Theories of Non-Territorial States*. New York: Routledge, 1–17.

Tucker, Aviezer. 2016b. "The Best States: Panarchy as Anti-Utopia." In Tucker, Aviezer, Bellis, and Gian Piero de, eds. *Panarchy: Political Theories of Non-Territorial States*. New York: Routledge, 140–65.

Tucker, Aviezer. 2022. Review of: Balaji Srinivasan, *The Network State, American Purpose*, November 18. https://www.americanpurpose.com/articles/the-network-state.

Tucker, Aviezer, Bellis, and Gian Piero de (eds.). 2016. *Panarchy: Political Theories of Non-Territorial States*. New York: Routledge.

Tucker, Aviezer, Maria Ruibal, Robert Cahill, and Farrah Brown. 2004. "The New Politics of Property Rights," *Critical Review* 16, 377–402.

Weber, Max. 1948. *Essays from Max Weber*, translated by H. Gerth and C. Wright Mills. London: Routledge.

Wolff, Jonathan. 1996. *Robert Nozick*. Cambridge: Polity Press.

Chapter 8

Polycentricism, the Rule of Law, and the Intelligibility of Human Rights Law[1]

Pilar Zambrano

Opponents of "monocentric governance" frequently view polycentric structures of governance as a pragmatic solution to the inefficient way in which modern constitutional state institutions cope with diversity (see, for example, Müller 2019; Aligica and Tarko 2013; Paniagua and Pourvand's discussion of polycentric democracy and stability in chapter 5 of this volume; and Tucker's defense in chapter 7 of non-territorial contracts as a better way to tailor policy solutions to citizens' preferences). Other advocates of polycentrism are concerned to promote political legitimacy (e.g., Stringham 2015; Benson 2011; and Auerbach 1984) or else better respond to the requirements of true human flourishing (see, for example, Thunder's arguments in chapter 1).

In this chapter, I will build a case against monocentric paradigms of legal order by showing that they are so far removed from the complexity and pluralism of real legal practices that they are completely unrealistic, even if we consider them as regulative ideals. In addition, I will make the case that a forthrightly polycentric approach to law and legal interpretation better fits the practice of law in contemporary society, and may help us tackle the challenges raised by legal interpretation in a post-statist, globalized world.

The argument will proceed in four stages. First, I contend that the notion of a State monopoly over law is receding in present legal practices, both as a fact and as an ideal. Based on various contributions from contemporary legal philosophy, I offer an alternative, rather more complex description of existing legal practices, which Francesco Viola calls "the legal space," where different kinds of bottom-up and top-down sources of law overlap with each other, with a preeminent role for human rights law (Viola 2017, 24). Second, I argue that a pluralist, bottom-up standard of legal legitimacy should be assessed in the light of the wider standard of fair and efficient coordination under the Rule of Law, while in section 3, I specify this requirement in greater detail by proposing that the Rule of Law not only requires that the language of the law be intelligible, but also and foremost, that judicial decisions be intelligibly connected to the law. Fourth, I take note of the serious challenges the heterogeneous legal space raises for the intelligibility of the law, and hence for the Rule of Law, most notably human rights law, which is applied to diverse legal practices. In light of these challenges, I bring the argument to a close in section 5 by observing the potential contribution that polycentric approaches and conceptual categories may have in helping us more adequately address these challenges.

1. FROM THE LEGAL SYSTEM TO THE LEGAL SPACE: LEGALITY WITHOUT MONOPOLY

Most polycentric theories rest on the premise that the monopoly of law is a core factual and normative element of State-centric political practices. As these practices are generally understood, the political institutions of the constitutional modern state hold the exclusive and exclusionary power to create and apply the law within a given territory, while dominant theories of political and legal authority are understood by polycentrists to view this monopoly as desirable or else unavoidable from the perspective of public order. This fact and this ideal, viewed through a polycentrist lens, impedes the modern constitutional State from coping with the complexity of present-day Western societies and/or harnessing the advantages associated with social complexity.

While I do not wish to challenge the soundness of these arguments against monocentric statism, it is worth noting that the factual premise should be somewhat qualified as a description of law, given that there is a well-established consensus among legal philosophers that legal monopoly is gradually declining, both as a fact and as an ideal. As legal pluralism advances, the age of the "legal system" is being replaced by the new age of the "legal space," conceived as overlapping sources of law not traceable to one sovereign lawmaker (Viola 2019, 24; Amato Mangiameli 2000, 72–80; Periñán Gómez 2018, 81).

One of the most conspicuous signs of this ongoing transformation affects the connection between the judicial principle of legality and the ideal of legal monopoly, in the sphere of activity of the judiciary. The principle of legality is typically understood to require that national courts of justice derive their decisions from the law of the State, or from the set of values, principles, and rules that, as a matter of fact, make up each national legal system. In other words, not any value, principle, or rule, however reasonable, can legally justify a judicial decision: Rather, only the law created through legal procedures by legally authorized institutions.[2]

Nonetheless, even if most national courts of justice continue to affirm this principle of legality, they progressively dissociate it from the ideal of legal monopoly. Foreign case law; observations and recommendations of treaty bodies; decisions taken by regional human rights courts in cases where the State is not a signatory; and all sorts of "soft law" are used to back up their decisions, with no explanation whatsoever for why they take them to be a valid source of law (Caroccia 2017, 87–91; Zambrano 2019, 36).

Put simply, judicial decisions frequently combine domestic norms with various foreign and global norms that were neither created nor incorporated into the relevant legal system by the relevant domestic political institutions. This fact highlights a progressive tendency toward legal pluralism, and a gradual dissociation of the principle of legality from the ideal of legal monopoly.

This tendency cannot be isolated from other political transformations of the constitutional modern State. On the contrary, it is typically explained as a side effect of the replacement of the "Westphalian" system of international relations by the more cooperative one, whereby States renounce their sovereignty, and in doing so facilitate the multilevel governance of global public goods (Paternsman 2017, 3–9).

Take human rights, for example. These are a paradigmatic example of global public goods that have resulted in the emergence of a multilevel type of governance and of a new kind of "global law." In effect, human rights are global public goods because they are valuable to all human beings, independent of their nationality. On the other hand, given that the threats to their flourishing are frequently the very States that theoretically defend them, it seems obvious that their protection can only be properly secured through international coordination. Thus, their governance by the States, the United Nations, and the regional systems of human rights is a paradigmatic example of what we refer to as "multilevel governance of global public goods." Lastly, the international and regional systems of human rights are typical examples of this kind of global law ruling the multilevel governance of public goods (Paternsman 2017, 191–93).

Legal monopoly doesn't really fit into this picture, either as a matter of fact or as an ideal. Breaking it down from the factual point of view, Francesco Viola observed some years ago that the multilevel governance of human rights and legal pluralism gives rise to the age of the "legal space" (Viola 2017, 24), a dimension of legal practice and interpretation constituted by diverse and overlapping sources of law. While the territorial jurisdiction of domestic courts is clearly defined in this age of "legal space," their normative jurisdiction is oftentimes obscure and elusive. This is because the multilevel governance of public goods produces new global or regional legal systems that converge with domestic law in judicial decisions. The legal space requires that judges justify not only their interpretation of the legal sources, but also (and perhaps mainly) their qualification as "sources," as well (Zambrano 2019, 57).

Another important reason for the decline of legal monopoly is the globalization of human interactions across different fields of activity, which cannot feasibly be coordinated through a monopolistic system of law. For example, economic and financial globalization explains the need for common rules on matters that are traditionally linked to the sovereignty of the States, such as tax and financial law. This need has been addressed by international organizations (e.g., World Trade Organization/the Organization for Security and Cooperation in Europe [OCSE]), who issue "soft law" directives that, more often than not, are ultimately incorporated into domestic law (Rozas, Valdés, and Coppa 2017, 67). Consequently, judges often justify their decisions using diverse sources of law, among which the new global law plays an ever-greater role. Therefore, even if the principle of legality still rules the judicial activity of the modern constitutional State, the fact and the ideal of a legal monopoly are gradually declining.

2. THE BOTTOM-UP STANDARD OF LEGITIMACY: FAIR AND EFFICIENT COORDINATION UNDER THE RULE OF LAW

In polycentric theories, a bottom-up standard is used to assess the legitimacy of legal practices. With this standard, the creation and interpretation of the law should involve the civil society, or the agents to which the law applies. However, in the modern constitutional State, the principle of the monopoly of the law involves a top-down way of creating and interpreting the law that does not significantly involve the civil society, or if it does, it does so in a marginal way.

At this point, a pressing question arises: Does the decline of the fact and ideal of the monopoly of the law mean that the legal space better fulfills the bottom-up criterion? Or, to put it a little differently, does the prominent role of human rights law widen the gap between the law and civil society? Any answer to these questions should start by distinguishing between the factual and normative aspects of the bottom-up criterion.

From a factual point of view, one should acknowledge that many supra-national—soft and hard—sources of the international law of human rights arise from a complex interaction between States, international organizations, and the so-called civil society, in which there is a considerable space for bottom-up procedures of legal creation. Therefore, it is at the very least disputable that the sources of human rights law necessarily exclude the participation of civil society (Tramontana 2010, 2). Moreover, there are entrenched conceptual devices that have been created and are presently being used by constitutional and international courts, out of a concern for the identities of the communities to which human rights law applies. Two paradigmatic examples are the concepts of "national margin of appreciation" and "constitutional identity." While the former is used by the European Court of Human Rights as a self-restraint criterion in favor of the domestic courts (Garcia Roca 2021, 245), the latter is used by domestic courts to restrain their use of international and cross-national sources of the law (Jacobsohn 2010, 138–39; Bruggeman and Larik 2020, 23–25). In both cases, a fundamental goal is to safeguard the social identity of the peoples to which the law applies.

This leads us to the normative question: whether a significant participation of civil society in the creation and interpretation of the law is enough for assessing its legitimacy. In this respect, authors as distant in time and traditions as Joseph Raz and Thomas Aquinas have elucidated a more general criterion of legitimacy that, perhaps due to its simplicity, tends to be forgotten. According to it, the law is legitimate when it serves its final end, which is to fairly and efficiently coordinate the actions of a group of people with a view to the attainment of the common good of a given social practice (Aquinas, *Summa Theologie*, I–II, qq. 90 and 96; Raz 1979, 248–49; 1986, 53; 2003, 13; 2006, 1031).[3]

According to this broad criterion of fair and efficient coordination, any global rule is legitimate when the following conditions are met:

a. The goods and values that it attempts to attain are truly global.
b. There is a global community sharing a given practice, whose purpose is to secure those global goods and values.
c. There is an aspect of the practice that seeks coordination, which the global rule affords.
d. The coordination is not only necessary, but also fair and efficient under the Rule of Law.

Given that bottom-up procedures of creation and interpretation of the law involve the agents of the practice that the law purports to govern, they obviously fulfil the first three conditions. Nonetheless, as many authors who are concerned with the steady emergence of different kinds of "populism" in Western constitutional practices remark, civil participation doesn't necessarily secure the legitimacy of the law, which also (and perhaps mostly) depends on the fourth condition: *fair and efficient* coordination under the Rule of Law.

Moreover, many populist theories explicitly claim that the Rule of Law curtails the legitimate space for the participation of civil society in public affairs (Cianciardo 2022, 51–54).

Saving the various discussions regarding which are the conditions of fair and efficient coordination, there is also ample consensus that, at the very least, they comprise the formal *desiderata* of the Rule of Law.[4] Within this frame, the relevant issue is whether and how the participation of civil society in the creation and interpretation of the law—the bottom-up standard—reinforces, at the very least, these formal *desiderata*.

3. CORE FORMAL DESIDERATA OF THE RULE OF LAW: THREE LEVELS OF INTELLIGIBILITY

Among the formal *desiderata* of the Rule of Law, the most basic is the adjustment of all government actions to the sources of the "law," or—what amounts to the same thing—to the set of values, principles, and rules that, as a matter of fact, make up each legal system. This foundation in law has its own requirements.[5]

First, not just any value, principle, or rule, however reasonable, serves to validate a government action. Although it seems redundant, the law in question must be the law in force: that is, the law that has been produced as "law" by legally authorized institutions, through procedures indicated as appropriate to create, modify, or extinguish law. In this light, the principle of legality is not only a way of reinforcing the monopoly of the law of the modern State, but also (and perhaps mainly) a requirement of the *Rule of Law*. As mentioned above, it is this latter function that best explains its endurance in a time of diverse and overlapping legal systems without a single sovereign lawmaker, or what we have been referring to as the "legal space."

Second, the legality of government actions must be intelligible, that is, understandable or accessible to the reasoning of the general public or, at the very least, to the main parties affected by the government's action. Third, in addition to intelligible, the legality of all actions by the government must be public. That is, it must be brought to the attention, if not of the general public, at least of the main parties affected by it.[6]

At the judicial level, the principle of legality involves a fourth condition, which doesn't necessarily apply to other fields of public action: Judicial decisions are not only required to be intelligibly and publicly grounded in the sources of the law, but they also must be publicly argued. Not just any kind of argumentation will suffice to make a judicial decision public, but only one that is intelligible, both in itself and to the reasoning of the general public or, at the very least, to the main parties affected by it.

Among the numerous reasons for demanding an intelligible argument at the judicial level, the most obvious one is that judicial decisions are supposed to resolve interpretative controversies about how to apply the law to the facts in dispute. Furthermore, only when the connection of a judicial decision with the current law is explicitly and intelligibly argued, can it also be said that law is prospective, which is another desideratum of the Rule of Law. If judicial decisions were based on values, principles, and rules that were only intelligible to the judge, they would be unpredictable and, consequently, unable to generate reasonable, forward-looking expectations about the meaning and application of the law.[7]

To summarize, the Rule of Law not only requires that all public actions be founded on the law, but also that this foundation be intelligible, public, and, when it comes to judicial decisions, intelligibly argued. From this, it can be concluded that the formal *desiderata* of the Rule of Law rest, first and foremost, on the intelligibility of the set of institutional facts through which the sources of the law are created; second, on the intelligibility of the language of the sources of the law; third, on the intelligibility of the argumentation of the legality of judicial decisions. The intelligibility in all these three dimensions is, in short, a logical condition of the principle of legality, which is a condition of the formal *desiderata* of publicity and prospectivity of *Rule of Law*, which is a condition of any form of fair and efficient coordination.

4. THE LEGAL SPACE AND CHALLENGES FOR THE INTELLIGIBILITY OF THE LAW

There is broad agreement in the philosophy of legal interpretation that at least three conditions should be met for the law to be intelligible and thus in conformity with the Rule of Law:

a. Institutional facts are intelligible when they comply with the appropriate institutional rules. Applying the law obviously involves identifying the law, which, in turn, involves identifying the acts through which the law was created. This identification requires that the acts creating law abide by the relevant institutional rules (e.g., constitutional rules allocating competence between different branches of government).
b. The language of the law is intelligible when it complies with the appropriate discursive rules. Interpreting the law entails identifying its core legal meaning and distinguishing it from the zone of doubt or penumbra. This identification and distinction require that the language of the law abide by the relevant lexicographical and discursive rules (e.g.,

rules affording meaning to the concept of "liberty" in the Fourteenth Amendment, according to the case law of American constitutionalism).

c. Institutional and discursive rules are the object of shared knowledge. All relevant participants should know how to identify, understand, and use the institutional rules that make institutional facts intelligible, and the discursive rules that make the language of the law intelligible (Marmor 2005, 17–18; 2014, 26).

The third condition doesn't arise from thin air. On the contrary, participants learn how to use rules conferring institutional meaning upon actions, and discursive rules affording legal meaning to legal statements, when they share an underlying understanding of the ends, purposes, or values that both kinds of rules are meant to support. Last but not least, the shared understanding of values springs from shared practices through which these values are instantiated and developed.

At this point, we can establish a simple proviso of intelligibility: the broader and deeper the shared knowledge of values is, the broader the shared knowledge of institutional and discursive rules is, and the easier it is to intelligibly argue judicial decisions. On the contrary, the narrower and more superficial the shared knowledge of values is, the thinner the knowledge of institutional and discursive rules is, and the more difficult it is to intelligibly argue judicial decisions.

The right to a fair trial is a good example of the way in which this proviso works. There are references to it in all three founding constitutional Bills of Rights[8]; in the Universal Declaration of Human Rights of 1949[9]; in the International Convention of Civil and Political Rights[10]; and in each of the three Regional Conventions of Human Rights.[11] Its acknowledgment, in fact, goes back to the famous Magna Carta of 1215 or, much longer before, to the episode of Susan and the Old Men, in the book of Daniel:

> Taking his stand in the midst of them, he said, "Are you such fools, you sons of Israel? Have you condemned a daughter of Israel *without examination and without learning the facts?* Return to the place of judgment. For these men have borne false witness against her." Then all the people returned in haste. And the elders said to him, "Come, sit among us and inform us, for God has given you that right." And Daniel said to them, "*Separate them far from each other, and I will examine them.*" (Daniel 13:1–9, 15–17, 31–62).

To some extent, there appear to be traces of this right in non-Western cultures, too. Wangari Maathai elaborates on this:

> The Oromo of Ethiopia and Kenya deem the scepter tree (also known as the *bokku*) a suitable place for officials of the traditional courts to gather. The judges [that] form the Massai and Kalenjin communities traditionally sat under a tree, and once ensconced beneath it one was obliged to tell the truth—much as placing one's hand on the bible is meant to encourage honesty in a court of law today. (Maathai 2010, 85).

Now, taking all these global anecdotes into account, we can draw the conclusion that there is a long-standing global/transcultural acknowledgment of the right to a fair trial. However, another question is, how do we abide by this abstract right? Does failing to interrogate and cross-question the witnesses of the prosecution amount to its abrogation, as the prophet Daniel claimed as long ago as 167 BC? Or alternatively, are the ceremonies of placing one's hand on the Bible, or sitting under a chosen (perhaps sacred) tree, sufficient guarantees of the honesty of the witnesses?

The Rule of Law requires that any answer to these questions be argued in an intelligible way at the judicial level. Arguing intelligibly involves using the relevant institutional rules affording legal force to the sources of the law, and the relevant discursive rules affording them legal meaning. Nonetheless, the identification of this or that type of rules stands on the particular ways through which, as a matter of historical fact, each community has instantiated (and thus understood) the values endorsed by the right to a fair trial. Thus, the question remains: According to which shared practice and underlying understanding should the interpretation of the global right to a fair trial be argued?

Recall that the main feature of the "legal space" characteristic of our globalized and deeply interconnected systems of law is legal pluralism, where global law at large (and the international law of human rights, in particular) coexists with local legal systems. In this context, the international law of human rights doesn't purport to replace local law, let alone local cultures, except in the very exceptional cases where one and/or the other are inhuman from the perspective of all cultures. In other words, the international law of human rights is not expected to replace local cultures, but instead, it is meant to be trans-cultural. Nonetheless, if shared *practical* knowledge arises from shared practices, the more trans-cultural any rule is, the more detached it is from fully contextualized social practices, and thus the more difficult it is to argue its interpretation in a way that is intelligible to the affected parties.

This condemns us to a deadlock. On the one hand, we need human rights international law for securing global goods. On the other hand, the more global this law is, the less it fits with the particular way in which different communities understand and endorse these rights. If this is so, then the international law of human rights would appear to be more difficult to argue for intelligibly, putting in question its consistency with the Rule of Law. Hence, some authors argue that the main challenge to its legitimacy is, in fact, its global range of application (Seligman 2021, 426–39).

CONCLUSION: THE PROMISE OF THE BOTTOM-UP STANDARD OF LEGITIMACY

We opened this chapter by observing that the monopoly of the law is fading away, both as an ideal and as a fact. This decline is in direct proportion to the rise of legal pluralism and the proliferation of global rules in the age of the legal space, the international law of human rights being a paradigmatic example of the latter. We next argued that the bottom-up standard of legitimacy is subsidiary to the broader one of fair and efficient coordination under the Rule of Law. More specifically, we contended that the relevant issue is not so much—or at least not only—how much room is afforded to civil society for the creation and interpretation of the law, but whether and how this participation of civil society can be consistent with the formal *desiderata* of the Rule of Law, in particular in a complex and pluralist legal environment.

To explore this question, we reviewed the challenges that the legal space raises for the intelligibility of the law, focusing our analysis on the international law of human rights. We pointed out that the global character of human rights law loosens the law's connection with the particular ways in which each community instantiates the rights it is supposed to grant. We argued that this untethering of human rights law from local legal practices undermines its intelligibility and, therefore too, its accommodation to the formal *desiderata* of the Rule of Law. This, in turn, led us to a conundrum: we need the international law of human rights because securing them depends on some form of global coordination. Nonetheless, the more global the human rights law is, the less it is connected to local practices and identities, the less its chances of being substantially intelligible to affected parties and, thus, the less its capacity to fairly and efficiently coordinate international relations.

Having reached this point, we can now address the core question, namely, how, if at all, does the bottom-up criterion of legitimacy help us to address this puzzle? The answer might be found in the epistemic priority of social practices over global rules, which is involved in the criterion of fair and efficient coordination under the Rule of Law. To put it simply, the closer any procedure of legal creation and interpretation is to the nature of the social practice to which the law purports to apply, the higher its chances of enhancing the intelligibility of the law and, by the same token, the formal *desiderata* of the Rule of Law. Given that bottom-up procedures of creating and interpreting the law are obviously closer to social practices than top-down procedures, our second conclusion is that, at least *prima facie,* bottom-up procedures are more legitimate than their top-down counterparts.

Polycentric theorists of law have a leading role to play in turning this *prima facie* assessment into a conclusive one. In so doing, they should explore whether the existing bottom-up procedures within the legal space are enough to secure the Rule of Law, and if not, which institutional transformations or innovations are necessary to this end. This analysis should take into consideration all the salient facts that make up the legal space, facts that we have highlighted in this chapter: legal pluralism; the prominent role of international human rights law in judicial argumentation; the steady detachment of the principle of legality from the monopoly of the law; and the standing (conceptual or institutional) devices that purport to bridge international human rights law with the identity of the communities to which it applies. To the extent that these devices assume that States are the smallest viable units of governance, a promising line of study for polycentric studies might be to explore how to extend those devices to yet smaller units of governance.

NOTES

1. I express my gratitude to David Thunder, Borja López Jurado, Julio Pohl, and Mariana MacMillan, for their insightful formal and substantial observations to a first version of this work, which were incorporated to this final, unquestionably better one.

2. Beyond the debate around the differences between the Rule of Law within the context of a law-making State and the Rule of Law in non-State-controlled contexts (Rule of Law versus state of law ("*estado de derecho*"), no one disputes the idea that they both share the formal *desideratum* of legality (Trujillo 2015, 164). Along these lines, Ferrajoli points out that "current" law is a necessary and undisputed source of any judicial decision in legal practices that purport to avow the *Rule of Law* (Ferrajoli 2016, 24).

3. While some authors of the Natural Law Tradition contend that the political common good is equivalent to respect for human rights, others counter that this is only one dimension of the political common good. John Finnis tailored his position on this issue, as he explains in his postscript to *Natural Law and Natural Rights* (2011, 459). On this debate, and on Finnis's turn, see Ortíz de Landázuri (2020, 564, footnote 38).

4. Beyond the debate about whether the Rule of Law, either in the common law sense or in the more statist, continental sense of the term (which is rendered in Spanish as "law of State," "*estado de derecho*"), contains substantive requirements in addition to the formal ones, the formal requirement of legality—the Rule of Law as opposed to the rule of men—is, without a doubt, central to both conceptions of the Rule of Law (Trujillo 2015, 164).

5. Ferrajoli points out that the "law currently in force" is the necessary and undisputed source of any judicial decision in a Rule of Law, and it defines the "law

currently in force" as the set of legislative normative statements. He also distinguishes the "law currently in force" from the "living law," which would add to the "law currently in force" the practice of its judicial interpretation, in Ferrajoli (2016, 24). At this point, we use the expression "law in force" in a broad sense, that also includes "living law."

6. The European Court of Human Rights is very explicit in stating that the expression "according to law" not only requires that "restrictive measures of individual liberty have some basis in domestic law, but also that they are accessible to the affected person, and formulated in terms precise enough so that the person can foresee its effects" (see, among other cases, ECHR, *Landvreugd vs. The Netherlands*, June 4, 2002, ¶ 54; *Maestri v. Italy*, February 17, 2004, ¶ 30). The requirements of precision, accessibility, and predictability were also enumerated by the Inter-American Court of Human Rights, in *López Mendoza v. Venezuela*, ¶ 199.

7. Ferrajoli points out, along similar lines, that the principle of legality requires judicial decisions to be argued around the value of "truth"—meaning "truth" as the adequacy of the law in force. See Ferrajoli (2016, 33).

8. Thus, the English Bill of Rights of 1689 states that "jurors ought to be duly impanelled and returned, and jurors which pass upon men in trials for high treason ought to be freeholders . . . all grants and promises of fines and forfeitures of particular persons before conviction are illegal and void." Similarly, the American Bill of Rights of 1791 states in its Fifth Amendment that "(i)n all criminal prosecutions, the accused shall enjoy the right to a speedy and public trial, by an impartial jury of the state and district wherein the crime shall have been committed, which district shall have been previously ascertained by law"; while the French Declaration of the Rights of Man and Citizen of 1789, article VII, commands that "No man should be accused, arrested, or held in confinement, except in cases determined by the law, and according to the forms which it has prescribed."

9. Article 10: "Everyone is entitled in full equality to a fair and public hearing by an independent and impartial tribunal, in the determination of his rights and obligations and of any criminal charge against him."

10. Article 14: "All persons shall be equal before the courts and tribunals. In the determination of any criminal charge against him, or of his rights and obligations in a suit at law, everyone shall be entitled to a fair and public hearing by a competent, independent and impartial tribunal established by law."

11. European Convention on Human Rights, article 6; American Convention on Human Rights, article 8; African Charter on Human and Peoples′ Rights, article 7.

REFERENCES

Alexy, Robert. 1989. *A Theory of Legal Argumentation. The Theory of Rational Discourse as Theory of a Legal Justification.* Oxford: Clarendon Press.

Aligica, Paul D., and Vlad Tarko. 2013. "Co-Production, Polycentricity, and Value Heterogeneity: The Ostroms' Public Choice Institutionalism Revisited." *American Political Science Review* 107 (04): 726–41.

Amato Mangiameli, and C. Agata. 2000. *Stati post-moderni e diritto dei popoli.* Torino: G. Giappichelli Editori.

Auerbach, Jerold S. 1984. *Justice Without Law? Resolving Disputes Without Lawyers.* Oxford: Oxford University Press.

Benson, Bruce L. 2011. *The Enterprise of Law: Justice Without the State.* Independent Institute.

Bruggeman, Robert, and Joris Larik. 2020. "The Elusive Contours of Constitutional Identity: Taricco as a Missed Opportunity." *Utrecht Journal of International Law* 35 (1): 20–34.

Caroccia, Francesca. 2017. "Quel che resta del Sistema?" *Ars Interpretandi* 2: 81–102.

Cianciardo, Juan. 2022. "Populismo y *Rule of Law.*" In *Estado de derecho, teoría del derecho e interpretación jurídica*, edited by Eduardo E. Magoja and Luciano Laise, 47–69. Buenos Aires: Abaco.

Dworkin, Ronald. 1986. *Law's Empire.* Cambridge, MA: Harvard University Press.

———. 2006. *Justice in Robes.* Cambridge, MA: Harvard University Press.

———. 2011. *Justice for Hedgehogs.* Cambridge, MA: Harvard University Press.

Ferrajoli, L. 2016. "Contro il creacionismo giurisprudenziale," *Ars Interpretandi* 2: 23–44.

Finnis, John. 2011. *Natural Law and Natural Rights.* Oxford: Clarendon Press, 2nd edition.

Garcia Roca, Javier. 2021. "International Deference, the Vague National Margin of Appreciation and Procedural Review." In *Fundamental Rights Challenges: Horizontal Effectiveness, Rule of Law and National Margin of Appreciation*, edited by M. Izquierdo Sans, Guastavino Nogueira, and C. Martínez Capdevilla, 245–76. Madrid: Springer.

Gardner, John. 2001. "Legal Positivism: 5 1/2 Myths," *American Journal of Jurisprudence* 46: 199–227.

Greenberg, Mark. 2004. "How Facts Make Law." *Legal Theory* 10: 157–98.

Hart, H.L.A. 1994. *The Concept of Law.* Oxford: Clarendon Press. Originally published 1979.

Hershovitz, Scott. 2015. "The End of Jurisprudence." *Yale Law Journal* 124: 1161–204.

Jackson, Vicki. 2010. *Constitutional Engagement in a Transnational Era.* Oxford; New York: Oxford University Press.

Jacobsohn, Gary Jeffrey. 2010. *Constitutional Identity.* Cambridge, MA: Harvard University Press.

Kelsen, Hans. 1960. *What Is Justice? Justice, Law, and Politics in the Mirror of Science.* Berkeley: University of California Press.

Marmor, Andrei. 2005. *Interpretation and Legal Theory.* Oxford: Hart Publishing, 2nd edition. Originally published in 1992.

———. 2009. *Social Conventions. From Language to Law.* Princeton; Oxford: Princeton University Press.

———. 2011. *Philosophy of Law.* Princeton: Princeton University Press.

———. 2014. *The Language of Law.* Oxford: Oxford University Press.

Müller, Julian F. 2019. *Political Pluralism, Disagreement and Justice: The Case for Polycentric Democracy*. New York: Routledge.

Ortíz de Landázuri, Luis. 2020. "Los derechos humanos y el bien común. Una aproximación desde John Finnis." *Persona y Derecho* 83 (2): 553–70.

Periñán Gómez, Bernardo. 2018. "*Ius Globale* 3.0: Hacia la reformulación de la capacidad jurídica individual." In *Derecho global. Positivismo, iusnaturalismo y razón práctica*, edited by Carlos Fidalgo Gallardo, 57–91. Madrid: Civitas.

Raz, Joseph. 1979. *The Authority of Law. Essays on Law and Morality.* Oxford: Oxford University Press.

———. 1986. *The Morality of Freedom.* New York: Oxford University Press.

———. 2003. "About Morality and the Nature of Law." *American Journal of Jurisprudence* 48 (1): 1–15.

———. 2006. "The Problem of Authority. Revisiting the Service Conception." *Minnesota Law Review* 90: 1003–44.

Rozas Valdés, J., and D. Coppa. 2017. "Il Soft law internazionale nel Diritto financier." *Ars Interpretandi* VI: 67–80.

Stringham, Edward Peter. 2015. *Private Governance*. Oxford: Oxford University Press.

Tramontana, Enzamaria. 2017. "*Soft Law* et la Resilienza del Diritto Internazionale." *Ars Interpretandi* VI: 43–66.

Viola, Francesco. 2018. "Il Futuro del Diritto." *Persona y derecho* 79: 9–36.

Zambrano, Pilar. 2019. "Convencionalismo jurídico e inteligibilidad del derecho. El uso como espejo de las fuentes sociales en la teoría jurídica de Andrei Marmor." *Doxa Cuadernos de filosofía del derecho* 42: 35–61.

———. 2021. "Comprender o interpretar el Derecho. El convencionalismo semántico en su laberinto." *Revista Chilena de Derecho* 48 (3): 131–54.

Chapter 9

The Constitution of Liberties

Polycentric Constitutionalism and the Westminster Export Model[1]

W. Elliot Bulmer

This chapter explores the practical application of polycentricity in constitutional terms. It investigates the extent to which polycentrism can be realized within the framework of the modern liberal-democratic constitutional State. Much of modern Western constitutional thought since the French Revolution has been based on monocentric notions: "The People" is often construed as a singular collective actor, expressing a "national will" and possessing nominal sovereignty, in whose name constitutions are made and remade, and from whom all public powers are derived (Arato 2016).

However, monocentric popular sovereignty is not the only foundation for modern constitutionalism. There are other strands of constitutional thought and practice that may be more amenable to polycentric interpretations. In particular, while the British-derived constitutions that spread around the world in the decolonization era mostly copied the majoritarian governance structures of "Westminster Model" parliamentary democracy, they also responded to the needs of divided societies by incorporating an array of innovative approaches to the problem of "deep, pervasive and persistent disagreements" (Müller 2020), including on matters of religion and identity (de Smith 1964).

In contrast to the French republican constitutional tradition—which is based upon a monocentric constituent power rooted in popular sovereignty, and which sees the constitution as the expression of the will of one united sovereign—Westminster Model constitutionalism has recognized that successful constitutions are often the result of negotiations, agreements, and compromises made between multiple actors, each seeking to recognize certain liberties, autonomies, or privileges. Westminster Model constitutions therefore often established liberal-democratic States in a pluralist, rather than unitarist, form. They incorporated bills of rights that not only protected individual freedoms, but also created space (through freedoms of assembly, association, expression, and religion; rights to private and family life; and other such provisions) for distinct communities, such as religious communities, schools, and households, to freely operate according to their own norms, under their own leadership, to realize their own *telos*, while protecting the *modus vivendi* with other groups in a polycentric constitutional order. They are replete with special rights, privileges, exceptions, and peculiarities that may be extended to regions or provinces, ethnic or linguistic groups, or religious minorities. In contrast to the French republican model of a *constitution of sovereignty*, the Westminster Model—while still favoring, where possible, strong, effective, active government (Jennings 1963)—embraced a *constitution of liberties*, through which particular autonomies could be protected.

Moreover, these constitutions were, in many cases, the result of negotiated bargains, giving recognition to multiple "peoples" and to overlapping and abutting spheres of authority. This includes traditional leadership, customary law, religious law, and various forms of both territorial and non-territorial autonomy for particular groups who saw themselves as possessing an internal solidarity and an inherent source of authority that had to be recognized by, but was not derived from, the State.

This chapter consists of three substantive sections. Section 1 examines, briefly, what I mean by polycentrism in the constitutional sense, and it distinguishes this from other, more economic or sociological notions of polycentrism. Section 2 looks at the French republican model of constitutional theory—the monocentric constitution of sovereignty against which the Westminster Model's polycentric constitution of liberties can then be contrasted. The third—and longest—section then defines the Westminster Model, and considers several examples of this polycentric *constitution of liberties* in the Westminster tradition.

The examples are selected to be illustrative of the various modes and forms that polycentric constitutionalism can take, whether in developed or developing countries, in old or new democracies, or on different continents. What unites them all is that they each arise not from a single, unified, sovereign constituent power, but from a compromise settlement, whether that is between communities each having a sense of themselves as distinct collective actors engaged in constitutional negotiations, or between different normative sources of political and legal authority (state law versus traditional law). In each of these cases, the constitution is presented as an instrument that guarantees the rights of particular communities to recognition, representation, or some form of self-government, within the overall constitutional framework. These examples contribute to polycentric theory by providing worked examples of real, if minimal, polycentrism. They show that modern liberal-democratic constitutions not only have to be designed to apply universal norms to undifferentiated, atomized individuals operating under unitary sovereignty, but they can also seek to recognize and protect territorial, religious, or cultural communities of identity and belonging. Drawing on these examples, this chapter concludes that embracing polycentrism in practical constitutional terms may not necessarily require new (or radically old) constitutional ideas and practices, but it could be achieved within prevailing constitutional models.

1. CONSTITUTIONAL POLYCENTRICITY

For the purposes of this argument, *polycentricity* is defined as a "social system of many decision centres having limited and autonomous prerogatives and operating under an overarching set of rules" (Polanyi 1951). By "limited and autonomous," it is understood that powers have limits, set by those overarching rules, but that within those limits those powers may be exercised autonomously. An obvious example of that would be a system of federalism in which states or provinces have autonomy within certain constitutionally defined policy areas, although it would also be possible to imagine this idea of autonomy-within-limits in a non-territorial sense, applied, for example, to religious, linguistic, or vocational communities.[2]

At the most basic level, all modern democratic constitutions—meaning here written, supreme, and fundamental law constitutions, not mere assemblages of custom or convention (Bulmer 2017)—are polycentric to some degree. They all have the potential to create many decision-centres. There might be different branches of government, including not only the classic three branches of late eighteenth-century theorists, but also non-executive heads of state, the civil service, and independent commissions like the electoral commission. There might also be different levels of government: local authorities, and in a federal system, state, provincial, or regional governments. Each of these is established by the constitution, and granted a certain limited autonomy within its own sphere, but it remains subject to the overarching rules of the constitution.

Even constitutions inspired by the French republican tradition create multiple governing institutions and divide powers between them. The difference between that tradition and the Westminster Model tradition is, in part, a matter of degree, emphasis, tone, and approach. It is also a matter of sovereignty and constituent power, which in the French republican tradition remains—as will be discussed below—monocentric, but which in the Westminster Model tradition is often polycentric. This difference is seen most clearly in the power to amend the constitution, which in the French republican tradition is usually a matter of the sovereign people speaking authoritatively, with one voice, by means of a national referendum, and which in the Westminster Model tradition, by contrast, often involves veto mechanisms designed to protect particular constitutionally guaranteed autonomies (examples of this—in Canada, Malaysia, and Saint Kitts and Nevis—are provided in the fourth section).

This chapter is not concerned with polycentricity as a whole system of social organization, only as a system of *constitutional* organization. Thicker models of social and economic polycentricity, including those that are more on the libertarian end of the political spectrum and/or suspicious of State power, form no part of my argument. Furthermore, the polycentric features of Westminster Model constitutionalism were not a result of any principled commitment to polycentrism as a normative political theory, but rather they are practical expedients arising out of the need to constitute diverse territories with diverse cultures and strongly variegated political institutions. Polycentric constitutionalism is not a recipe for minimal government. Indeed, the constitutional polycentrism that is here presented and commended is compatible with a large, active, interventionist, regulatory, redistributist State, which pursues common ends. It does, however, require the State, as a complex, polycentric entity rather than as a single, unitary, concentrated source of power, to engage in a process of dialogue, negotiation, and mutual restraint, in the process of making and implementing policies. There might be important "carve outs," where specific minorities have specific exemptions, or forms of autonomy, that are protected by the constitution.

However, polycentric constitutionalism, at the formal, legal, and institutional levels, often does reflect polycentricity in society, in terms of its social structures and its communities of faith, language, and belonging. As will be argued below, polycentrism in the Westminster Model constitutional tradition was embraced not out of a principled commitment to the dispersal of power, but out of a pragmatic need to manage difference in divided societies (Choudhry 2008; Lerner 2011). In the form here presented, polycentric constitutionalism arises in situations where the polity cannot arise from one, unified, undifferentiated society, in which people are interchangeable, fungible individuals, and which has one shared *telos* and one general will. Rather, it arises from a society-of-societies, which are joined together at the constitutionalism level, perhaps for very pragmatic reasons of defense or economic opportunities, and which can work only if it coordinates these constituent parts in matters of common concern while also respecting their autonomy in matters that pertain only to themselves.

Thus polycentric constitutionalism can be regarded, borrowing Elazar's classic definition of *federalism*, as a combination of "shared rule" and "self rule" (Elazar 1987). It should be noted, however, that federalism—as a particular form of territorial dispersal of power—is only one type of polycentrism. It is also possible to imagine the combination of shared rule and self-rule on other, non-territorial, grounds. For example, power may be shared at a constitutional level between religious and secular authorities, or between different ethno-cultural or linguistic groups, who have rights to cultural autonomy in certain spheres of policy, without exercising control over a particular territory. Some examples are set out later in this chapter, but they would include such matters as Muslims in Kenya having their own courts for matters of Muslim personal status law, or Francophone Roman Catholics in Ontario having their own school boards for that community.

2. POPULAR SOVEREIGNTY AND CONSTITUENT POWER

This section outlines the monocentric "constitution of sovereignty," which will then be contrasted with the polycentric "constitution of liberties" set out in the subsequent. The great theorist of the constitution of sovereignty is Jean-Jacques Rousseau. Rousseau's constitutional scheme—expressed as a theoretical model, but loosely based upon an imagined and purified version of his native Geneva—is set out in Book IV of *Du Contract Social*.[3] It is founded, almost to an obsessive degree, on the elimination of polycentrism. Rousseau's ideal polity is all-embracing. There must be no form of independent, autonomous, or spontaneous political or social organization within it. Parties are prohibited. Guilds are prohibited. Deliberation should take place only in the duly constituted public bodies, never in private spaces. Rousseau does not advocate direct *democracy*, because for Rousseau, democracy is a form of *government*, and he is very clear to distinguish government—the day-to-day management of public affairs—from acts of sovereignty. Government, in Rousseau's scheme, can be delegated to various councils and magistrates, who may be elected or selected in various ways. What cannot be delegated is sovereignty: sovereignty is always exercised directly by the people, and is absolute. Rousseau does not say that government should be absolute. Far from it. Government can be tightly controlled, existing only under delegation from the sovereign people. The people are only truly and absolutely sovereign when acting in their constituent capacity, not when acting in their constituted capacity as electors (Rousseau 2004/1762; Rosenblatt 2009).

This distinction between sovereignty and government was later developed by Abbé Sieyes, distinguishing between constituent power and constituted institutions (Rubinelli 2020). To constitutional scholars shaped by the French republican tradition, sovereign power is constituent power and constituent power is sovereign power. When they say the people are sovereign, they mean the people possess constituent power; the sovereignty of the people is expressed in making and amending constitutions. According to this way of thinking about the origin and nature of constitutions, the People (note the capitalization and its use as a singular form) is a unitary actor. The sovereign people has a general will, and that general will is expressed in the constitution. The constitution is, therefore, an *order of the sovereign people*, and not a compact or settlement of the people (plural, uncapitalized) who constitute the state.

This view depends on the unity and interchangeability of the people. If the People is a unitary actor, divisions within that body are politically irrelevant. It would not matter if all the votes for a constitutional change came from one region, and all the votes against were from another region; each vote would be counted equally, fungibly, as indistinguishable parts of one whole body-politic, one monocentric sovereign, in which the majority would decide. It would be alien to this tradition to see the constitution as a pact or bargain, struck between the peoples of the two regions, each of which, while entering into that pact or bargain, and being willing to have shared government over certain shared concerns, nevertheless retains some of its own identity, and some distinct, polycentric agency over constitutional decision-making.

The French republican model is important not only because of its influence in France and across much of northern Africa, but also because it seems to form a kind of background assumption in so much of the theoretical discussion of constitutions and constitution-making. The point here is not to denigrate or deny that tradition, but simply to point to a different, less-monocentric, more-polycentric, way of understanding the nature and origins of written constitutions: a way that focuses less on the sovereign will of the people as a constituent actor and more on the liberties of particular groups or communities within a constitutional pact.

3. WESTMINSTER MODEL CONSTITUTIONALISM

The term *Westminster Model* is subject to contested definitions and, according to the comparative constitutional scholar S. A. de Smith, "will never be a term of art" (de Smith 1964). Arend Lijphart defined the Westminster Model in terms of majoritarian government, which is characterized by First Past the Post Elections, two party politics, executive dominance, and a unitary state with a lack of constitutional restraints on the exercise of power (Lijphart 1999). This, however, is a mis-categorization. Countries may have proportional representation and multi-party politics (as in Fiji, Ireland, and New Zealand), and yet still be recognizable examples of the Westminster Model.

Likewise, countries can have highly complex federal systems, or a strong judicial review of fundamental rights (as in Canada, India, or Malaysia) and still belong to the Westminster Model family. The "Westminsterness" of these countries lies elsewhere, not in their macro-institutional design, but in their embedded constitutional traditions; they are all descended from, or influenced by, the system of parliamentary government that emerged in Britain in the eighteenth century, and which, in the nineteenth and twentieth centuries, spread around the world through the processes of colonialism and decolonization (Bulmer 2020a).

The constitutional arrangements differ in detail from country to country, but despite the variety of national adaptations and deviations, they are still substantially held together by common history and by an enduring similarity of institutions, laws, ideas, norms, and practices. They share the same lexicon, the same foundational literature, and even a degree of overlapping jurisprudence—all derived, directly or indirectly, from British-imperial constitutional foundations. "Westminster Model" constitutions are strictly parliamentary, with a separation of functions between a ceremonial head of state and an executive prime minister (de Smith 1964). They are bound by a series of rules—whether conventional or written into the text of the constitution—regulating such matters as the selection and the removal of the prime minister, the relationship between the government and Parliament, and between the government and the opposition (Twomey 2018). Those rules are derived, with more or less deviation and adaptation to context, from nineteenth-century British practice, as described by canonical writers such as Walter Bagehot (Smith 2001) and A.V. Dicey (Dicey 1915). These constitutions are held together by a set of assumptions shaped by British parliamentary, judicial, and administrative traditions. Sometimes this is made explicit. Canada's constitution declares itself to be "similar in principle to that of the United Kingdom." At other times, it is implicit, marked by a common terminology and lexicon shaped by British historical practice.

Although the United Kingdom has not adopted a written constitution (defined here as a "codified supreme and fundamental law"), written constitutions are not alien to the tradition of Westminster Model democracy. As it spread across the British Empire and later the Commonwealth, the Westminster Model gradually assumed more rigid and definite constitutional forms, culminating in the written constitutions of the de-colonization era. Almost all the countries that became independent from the British Empire in the twentieth century did so under a written constitution (de Smith 1961). Israel, which had been a mandated territory, is the only exception, and that was not for want of trying (Lerner 2011; Navot 2014). From the Caribbean to the South Pacific, from southern Africa to the foothills of the Himalayas, remarkably similar written constitutions came off the press. These replicated, with greater or lesser variations to adapt them to their context, the institutions of the British system of *parliamentary democracy*, but they did not replicate its core principle of *parliamentary sovereignty*; instead, these institutions were embedded in a codified legal document that was superior in the hierarchy of laws to ordinary Acts of Parliament and that could only be amended by a special, and more onerous, constitutional amendment process.

In so shifting from a system of parliamentary sovereignty to one of constitutional supremacy, the Westminster Model constitutions of the de-colonization era introduced a distinction—unknown in the United Kingdom itself—between the legislative power on the one hand and the constituent power on the other, with the former strictly subordinated to the latter. This, in turn, created a need to justify constituent power; that is, to provide a coherent and widely acceptable account of the legitimacy of the limitations that the constituent power, through the constitution as the enduring expression of its will, might impose on the legislative power. This is the basic problem of constitutional entrenchment to which the democratic theorists of parliamentary sovereignty point (Bellamy 2007; Jones 2020): How can an Act of Parliament, enacted by the representatives of the people today, legitimately be nullified by a court upholding a constitution enacted decades or generations ago? What gives one generation the right to bind or complicate the choices of future generations? Why should a minority have protection, at a constitutional level, against the decisions of the majority?

In answering this question, Westminster Model constitutions are, in comparison with the French revolutionary tradition, less obsessed with popular sovereignty. Legitimacy comes not so much from a single constituent act, as from adherence to a certain inherited or imported tradition of democracy, which can trace its lineage, through the Whig interpretation of Anglo-British history, back to the Magna Carta, the Petition of Right, the Habeas Corpus Act, the Glorious Revolution and the Bill of Rights Act, the Act of Settlement, the Great Reform Act, the Parliament Acts, and—in parallel to these legislative landmarks—to the accepted conventions of cabinet government, parliamentary democracy, and responsible party government, which all came together in the high-Edwardian age of imperial democracy.

This tradition was widely accepted as good, valuable, and worth keeping. Even where a deliberate effort was made to study and learn from all the constitutions of the world—as undertaken, for example, by B. S. Rao in India—still the British model exerted a powerful gravitational pull. In the 1950s and 1960s, the international reputation of British democracy was riding high. S. A. de Smith could famously portray the last person to say, "'British is best' as an anti-imperial nationalist on an obscure tropical island" (de Smith 1961, 1). In the same way, Sir Ivor Jennings, in his thinly fictionalized *Constitution Making in Arcady*, could with credibility describe a fiercely anti-imperialist

African, who, having once been imprisoned for sedition by the British authorities, used his time in jail to study English constitutional law, and later, after having made the transition from imprisoned dissident to national leader, refused to settle for anything less than a Westminster Model constitution (Kumarasingham 2015).

Understood in this way, a written constitution has value, not as the expression of the will of a sovereign people, or of a sovereign constituent assembly, but as the expression of an accepted tradition, faithfully distilled into its essential components and carefully applied to a particular geographical and sociocultural context. Constitutional entrenchment and amendment rules therefore serve to protect that settlement, preventing the government of the day and its parliamentary majority from destabilizing, eroding, undermining, or otherwise doing irrevocable damage to that instantiation of the constitutional tradition.

The adjustment of a "universal" tradition to a specific geographical and sociocultural context is where the polycentrism comes in. Many Westminster Model constitutions were adopted in diverse, "deeply divided" societies (Lerner 2011). The British archetype was founded on a basically homogenous population, divided by class, socioeconomic interests, and ideology. It was assumed that elections would be won or lost by the ability of parties to appeal to centrist "floating voters," mostly of the lower middle class, in key marginal constituencies (Jennings 1967). These people would be open to persuasion, based on the policy and performance of the government and the credibility of the opposition, and they would keep government both honest, and within the broad center-ground of politics. Those conditions did not apply in many former colonies, where voting is determined by "ascriptive" characteristics like ethnicity, religion, and tribe, and where elections are essentially "censuses" of different communities (Jennings 1956). In such contexts, voters—bound in practice to vote for the leaders of their own community—have few viable alternatives. At the extreme, such ascriptive voting means that the Westminster Model's logic of government versus opposition breaks down. Governments are not held accountable for their policies or performance. The leaders of the demographic majority rule in perpetuity, while the demographic minority is permanently excluded from power.

Both (a) constitution-making processes, and (b) constitutional designs emerging from those processes, had to account for this diversity. The predominant mode of constitution-building in Westminster tradition is not a single, sovereign "Constituent Assembly," exercising constituent power as a unitary actor. Such assemblies did exist—India's Constituent Assembly in 1947–1950, and South Africa's Constitutional Assembly of 1994–1996—are two of the most famous examples (Bulmer 2020b). Elsewhere, however, the usual tool was a constitutional conference—in which the constitution would be *negotiated*, as a compromise, settlement, or pact, between different actors.

This was the case in the big federal dominions. In Canada, the Constitution Act, 1867, was the result of negotiations between delegates from the legislatures of the various provinces—meeting at the Quebec Conference in October 1864 (McNaught 1983, 126). It was also the case in Australia, where two national conventions—in 1891 and 1897–98—were held, both bringing together delegates from the state legislatures, to negotiate what was to become the Australian constitution; furthermore, the Australian constitution was put to the vote not as a single, nationwide act of sovereign constituent power, but as the individual act of the several constituent states (Saunders 2011). The Union of South Africa (1910–1963) was not federal, but its constitution was—again, in what was becoming the standard British-imperial tradition—developed by a national convention consisting of delegates from the legislatures of the two self-governing British colonies (Cape Colony and Natal) and the two former Boer Republics (Transvaal and Orange Free State) (Lacour-Gayet 1977, 238). Having been agreed upon at the national convention, the constitution was then approved by the legislatures of the constituent units—except in Natal, where a referendum was held (Lacour-Gayet 1977, 241). In all these cases, there was no one center of constituent power. The conference or convention was not a sovereign constituent assembly. It was merely a meeting place, and a negotiating forum, in which multiple centers of power—the individual provinces, states, or colonies—could be represented and come together to make proposals. Of course, it might be argued that the Imperial Parliament in London was the true constituent power, but its role in all these examples was minimal, being confined primarily to giving sanction and effect to the agreements made in the convention or conference.

Conferences served as the principal practical tool of constitution-making in the era of decolonization following the Second World War. In the Caribbean, Africa, the South Pacific, and elsewhere, the usual method of proceeding was, following the election of a pro-independence majority in the colonial legislature, to convene a conference, in which British Colonial Office officials would sit with representatives of the government and opposition in the colony, and sometimes with other relevant groups. While the Westminster Model template set the outline of these constitutions, their specific content was negotiated between these interests. There was often a desire, on the part of the Colonial Office officials, to reach a cross-party consensus on constitutional issues. In particular, there was a concern to include minority voices who might have been outvoted in a purely majoritarian constitution-building process (Bulmer 2020b; Jennings 1956; Kumarasingham 2014).

A crucial aspect of these negotiations was to recognize that people are not fungible. They exist as parts of groups and communities, and those groups and communities have to be accommodated, collectively, in the constitutional process and in the resulting constitutional design choices. The constitutions that emerged were not obsessed with the notion of popular sovereignty, as if *the People* was one, indivisible, unified mass, with a united constituent will. Rather, they reflected the nature of a pact—often a messy one; sometimes a more or less fair one—between these different groups and communities, and between the political parties that represented their interests. Tribalism, as such, was rarely directly acknowledged, but in diverse countries such as Kenya, Nigeria, and Fiji, complex constitutional structures were agreed upon, in order to accommodate these groups and communities that formed multiple and distinct, pre-constitutional, centers of identity, belonging, and political mobilization. To stay, for the moment, with these three random, but not atypical examples, these constitutions were not so much acts of the Kenyan, Nigerian, or Fijian *People*, but they were acts of their *peoples*: as Kikuyu or Lua; as Igbo, Yoruba, or Hausa; as iTaukei or Indo-Fijians. They were not so much the act of a sovereign constituent power, but an act of constitutional settlement, arrived at by negotiating terms within a shared—if colonially imported—institutional tradition.

The resulting Westminster Model constitutions, by the peak of British decolonization in the 1960s, had a number of common features. These were identified by S. A. de Smith (1964):

- First, as noted above, they were written constitutions, having supreme law status, and they were capable of being amended only by a special procedure. Often there were two or more levels of entrenchment, with some parts of the constitution being more difficult to change than others. Thus, for example, some parts of the Indian constitution can be amended by a super-majority vote in Parliament, whereas other parts require the approval of a majority of the State legislatures (Kashap 2001).
- Second, they included judicially enforced bills of rights, protecting certain fundamental civil, legal, and political rights (Parkinson 2007).
- Third, they often—although not always—gave formal recognition to the office of the leader of the opposition, who was given constitutional functions and privileges, including a right to be consulted in making certain appointments to the judiciary or independent commissions, or even occasionally a veto power over such appointments (Bulmer 2021).
- Fourth, electoral systems were designed to ensure that minorities, as far as possible, would not be permanently excluded. Continental European–style proportional representation was rare, but other forms of inclusive representation were experimented with, including the reservation of seats for scheduled castes and tribes in India (Kashap 2001) and

provision for nominated members who would virtually represent ethnic or other demographic minorities.

- Fifth, second chambers were established with minority-protecting veto powers. In the 1970 constitution of Fiji, for example, the balance of power in the Senate was held by members of the Great Council of Chiefs, who represented the indigenous "Taukei people, while in the 1960 constitution of Nigeria, each ethnic region had an equal number of seats in the Senate (Odumosu 1963).
- Sixth, these constitutions typically established what de Smith called "neutral zones" (de Smith 1964), what today we would probably call "fourth branch" institutions (Bulmer 2019; Tushnet 2021). These are intended to protect sensitive areas of public administration—the delimitation of electoral districts, the civil service and the police, the auditing of public accounts, etc.—from political control.
- Seventh, very often, although not always, they established federal systems, or at least some constitutional division of power between national and sub-national authorities. De Smith (1964) argued there was a British instinct for federalism—an instinct that was not shared by the monocentric French forms of constitutionalism adopted in Francophone Africa.
- Eighth, they recognized customary law, religious law, and traditional leadership. British colonial governments often relied upon such institutions as mechanisms of justice, law enforcement, peacekeeping, and local administration. In many cases, these institutions were then carried over into the post-colonial constitutions at the time of independence.
- Finally, the conventional "unwritten rules" of parliamentary democracy were translated into formal, legally enforceable, constitutional rules, defining and clarifying the relationships between the head of state, the prime minister, the cabinet, Parliament, the courts, and other governing institutions.

The resulting constitutions were often long, detailed, specific, and full of all sorts of particular privileges and exceptions. Within this tradition, the constitution not only sought to establish liberty—in the sense of democratic self-government in an open, free society—but also certain specific liberties: individual rights, communal rights, language rights, and territorial rights. A typical mid-twentieth-century Westminster Model constitution defends the boundaries, both physical and jurisdictional, between diverse authorities, in and for diverse communities, that enjoy significant constitutional autonomy while nevertheless being bound into a whole. This constitutional tradition might recognize a common good—at least a common stake in, and commitment to, "peace, order and good government"—but not necessarily a "general will," given the diversity of the societies being constituted.

Canada's constitutional system is notoriously complex, but it has been praised by Canadian scholars for its ability to bring peace and unity to a diverse society without crushing that diversity (Choudhry 2007; Kymlicka 1998). Its constitution is partially codified, with the Constitution Acts 1867 to 1982 at its core, but with considerable reliance on unwritten conventions, received from the British, to give muscle and sinew to that rather bare constitutional skeleton (Van Loon and Whittington 1971). Canada is a federation of ten provinces, with three self-governing territories. Its national existence is also predicated upon a more fundamental pact between two founding communities: English-speaking and French-speaking Canadians. These two linguistic communities are territorially concentrated, with Francophones dominant in Quebec and Anglophones dominant in the rest of Canada. However, the territorial concentration is not seamless: there are minorities of English speakers in Quebec, and French speakers outside Quebec.[4]

In addition to territorial federalism, which is necessary in order to meet demands for provincial autonomy in a vast country, the Canadian constitution has also had to grant non-territorial autonomy, rights, and recognition for the linguistic communities. It guarantees the equal status of English and French as the official languages of Canada (Constitution Act 1982, 16 [1]), and it provides for equal bilingualism in the proceedings of Parliament (17 [1]), parliamentary statutes and records (18 [1]), in federal court proceedings (19 [1]), and in communications between the public and federal institutions (20 [1]). Moreover, citizens of Canada whose first language is English, but who live in Quebec, have the right to primary and secondary education in English, while those whose first language is French, but who live outside of Quebec, have the right to primary and secondary education in French (23 [1]). This communal autonomy in matters of education extends not only to language communities, but also to religious communities; under Section 93 of the Constitution Act 1967, there are separate Roman Catholic and secular school boards within the Francophone and Anglophone systems.

A persistent demand of the Francophone community has been to be recognized as a "distinct society," a nation-within-a-nation. This would give formal endorsement to the idea that Canada is not *only* a federation of provinces, but also a union of distinct, linguistically defined peoples. The Quebec nationalist scholar Guy LaForest has suggested that Canada's "'political system does not measure up to our country's reputation abroad' because it fails to acknowledge, both symbolically and institutionally, Quebec's distinctiveness" (Choudhry 2007, quoting LaForest). Attempts to meet this demand through further constitutional change—proposals for which were outlined in the Meech Lake Accord of 1987 and the Charlottetown Accord of 1992—came to naught. Quebec's independence, which had been roundly defeated in a referendum in 1980, remained on the agenda, and only narrowly failed a second time in 1995. The collapse of the Meech Lake and Charlottetown Accords, and the defeat of the Quebec sovereigntist movement, have produced a kind of constitutional stalemate in Canada, where nobody was very happy with existing arrangements, but no serious politician would risk political capital by reopening a moribund debate (Russel 2004). Nevertheless, even this stalemate shows the inherent polycentrism in Canadian constitutionalism: there is no sovereign, constituent Canadian national will; constitutional settlements have to be *agreed* upon, not *decreed.*

Canadian polycentrism goes so far as to recognize that the constitutional compact at the heart of the federation, between Quebec and the other provinces, is ultimately dependent upon consent. In the *Secession Reference*, the Supreme Court of Canada recognized that while Quebec cannot unilaterally secede, Canada would have to enter into good-faith negotiations with Quebec to allow independence if there was a clear majority for independence in Quebec (*Reference Re: Secession of Quebec* [1998] 2 SCR 217). As the Supreme Court did not specify what would be a "clear majority," the Parliament of Canada then passed the Clarity Act 2000, which would give the Parliament of Canada the power to ensure that any referendum held on Quebec independence would be unambiguous and that the outcome of a vote reflected a clear expression of the majority will. This was rejected in Quebec, which passed its own Act in response (CQLR c E-20.2). Despite this standoff on how a "clear will of the majority" of the people of Quebec was to be expressed, polycentrism is evident in the principle, accepted by both sides, that the latter has a peaceful, democratic path to independence if so desired.

Malaysia is a federation of thirteen states and three territories. Society is divided on ethno-linguistic and religious grounds, between an indigenous Muslim Malay population and minorities of Indian and Chinese Malaysians. Within Malaya-proper, the federal system built upon independence in 1957 was founded upon nine monarchical states, which have retained their hereditary rulers in a constitutional capacity. The federal system is relatively centralized, with the central government having relatively more, and the states relatively less, power (Harding 2012). Malaysian federalism does not, however, treat all states equally. There is a division between the (now eleven) states of Western Malaysia, and the two states of Eastern Malaysia: Sabah and Sarawak. The latter are culturally, as well as geographically, distinct from the rest of Malaysia. They joined the federation later, in 1963, in a negotiated process that guaranteed to them certain special terms as stipulated in the Malaysia Agreement. Singapore also joined at the same time, but it became independent in 1965. Under the constitution of Malaysia, the state legislatures of Sabah and Sarawak have greater legislative powers, not available to the Western Malay states, in relation to native law and custom; incorporation of public bodies, ports, and harbors; and personal laws relating to marriage, divorce, guardianship, maintenance, adoption, legitimacy, family law, railways (Sabah only), charitable trusts, and immigration (Constitution of Malaysia S.95). Sabah and Sarawak also have exemptions from federal laws in relation to land use, local government, and development (Constitution of Malaysia S.95D-95E). They enjoy additional financial authority, including borrowing powers and special grants from the federal government (Constitution of Malaysia S.112B and S.112C). Moreover, under S.161E, no constitutional amendment may be made that affects the special privileges of Sabah or Sarawak without the consent of those states. In other words, the constituent power is descended not from one monocentric sovereign people, but from a pact—arising in the Malaysia Agreement of 1963 and still recognized by the constitution today—between multiple centres of authority.

A similar polycentricity—or perhaps, in this case, it should be "bicentricity"—is found in the constitution of Saint Kitts and Nevis. This pair of Caribbean islands became independent in 1982 under a constitution that created a kind of lopsided federation. Nevis, the smaller of the two islands, has its own legislature—the Nevis Island Assembly—with powers over a list of twenty-three specified matters from agriculture to sport (Constitution of Saint Kitts and Nevis, Schedule 5, Part 1). There is, however, no separate legislature for Saint Kitts, the "federal" Parliament of Saint Kitts and Nevis having direct rule over Saint Kitts in all respects. At independence, the Nevis representatives to the constitutional conference were able to secure not only this measure of autonomy, but also a right to secession (Corbett and Byron 2023). This right is defined by Section 113 of the constitution, which enables Nevis to secede by means of a two-thirds majority vote in the Nevis Island Assembly, followed by a two thirds majority vote in a referendum of Nevis Island voters. This provision was put to use in 1998, when a referendum was held that fell quite narrowly short (61 percent) of the two-thirds majority threshold (Corbett and Byron 2023).

The constitution of Saint Kitts and Nevis, insofar as it concerns the autonomy or secession rights of Nevis, can be amended only by means of a referendum that must be passed by a double super-majority: by a two-thirds majority of votes on Saint Kitts, and a two-thirds majority of votes on Nevis (Constitution of Saint Kitts and Nevis S.38). Thus, constitutional polycentrism is evident both in the design of constituted institutions (the autonomy granted to Nevis by the constitution) and in the nature of the constituent power. There is no monocentric sovereign people exercising constituent power over the whole of Saint Kitts and Nevis. Rather, there are two centers—the people of Saint Kitts and the people of Nevis—and constituent power depends upon negotiations and agreement between them.

A form of non-territorial autonomy was embedded in the 1963 constitution of Kenya.[5] Kenya is a majority Christian country with a Muslim minority, estimated to be about 10 percent of the total population, concentrated mainly, but not only, in the coastal city of Mobassa. Section 179 of the 1963 constitution enabled the appointment of a chief *Kadhi* and other *Kadhis*—judges of Islamic law—and it also provided that the Kahdi courts would have jurisdiction over "questions of Muslim law relating to personal status, marriage, divorce or inheritance in proceedings in which all the parties profess the Muslim religion." Thus, constitutional polycentrism existed to the extent that two sources of law—one coming from Parliament and English common law, the other coming from Islamic jurisprudence—each representing different values and oriented according to different principles, could, within limits, co-exist in one polity. The citizens of that polity were not, therefore, all equal before the law, in the way that the French republican tradition demands. Their rights, in matters such as marriage, divorce, and inheritance, would depend upon their religion. Beyond this judicial role, the chief *Kadhi* has become a semi-official spokesperson for Muslims in Kenya, both leading the scholars of the community in the development of Muslim jurisprudence in the country, and being asked to address social problems affecting the Muslim community, from high divorce rates, to mentoring youth and rehabilitating drug addicts (Hassan 2023).

The final example of constitutional polycentricity to be discussed is that of Maori rights in New Zealand. New Zealand was not conquered. Sovereignty over New Zealand was ceded to the Crown by the Treaty of Waitangi (1840). It therefore arises by the consent, and is subject to the consent, of the Maori community. The actual terms of the Treaty of Waitangi are rather specific, mostly concerning the recognition of land titles. However, the courts have taken a broader view of the "Principles of Waitangi," including a duty of the Crown to act in good faith toward the Maori community (*New Zealand Maori Council v. Attorney-General* [1987] [1 NZLR 641]). Since the Maori Representation Act 1867, which was enacted, partly at least, "as a recognition of the colonists' constitutional obligations under the Treaty of Waitangi," the Maori population has had guaranteed seats in Parliament (Parliament of New Zealand 2003). Under the current law, there are seven Maori electorates, in which only Maori electors can vote (Electoral Act, New Zealand, 1993 S.45). Maori electors are not required to vote in a Maori electorate, and they can choose to vote on the common roll instead. Even so, this separate representation ensures there is always not only a numerically reflective Maori presence in Parliament, but also a bloc of Maori members of Parlaiment who are responsible to Maori voters. In other words, the design of Parliament and of the electoral system recognizes the coexistence of a community (the Maori) within a community (the nation of New Zealand), which, because of its indigenous status and its treaty rights, has a special, distinct claim to political voice.

CONCLUSION

This chapter has demonstrated several examples of how Westminster Model constitutions have embraced various forms of constitutional polycentricity as a way of recognizing diversity and protecting the autonomy of distinct groups, whether they are territorial or non-territorial. It shows that the real world of constitution-building does not always fit into the monocentric Sieyes-Rousseau model of sovereign constituent power. A Westminster Model "constitution of liberties" often depends upon negotiations between groups and communities, each having their own identities, and their own sources of power and legitimacy. These groups can pursue their own agendas and protect their own interests, while still being part of a larger polity. The common good is not denied, but it cannot be universally discerned or applied by one unitary sovereign body; it has to be discerned in negotiations between multiple centers of power.

Before finishing, however, two further caveats are needed. The first is that, for the avoidance of doubt, no claims are here being made for the pre-political, or natural, character of the rights protected by the polycentric "constitution of liberties." Rather, they are understood as "liberties" simply because they are constitutionally recognized as legally enforceable in a particular polity. They may be derived from natural law, from historical inheritance, or from other sources, but they are protected in fact because they were accepted within the constitutional bargain and therefore form part of the constitutional order the courts will recognize and by which legitimate political actors consider themselves bound. I do not discount the existence of natural rights, nor do I take a stand in favor of legal positivism; I am simply focusing, for the purposes of this argument, on the fact that these rights, having been accepted by participants in the constitution-building process, *are* constitutionally recognized and enforced. Moreover, the object of these liberties is not necessarily limited to individuals, but it can extend to groups, communities, or territories. Likewise, these rights are not merely negative (non-interference) rights, but they can include the positive right to carry out autonomous collective public action.

The second caveat is that the terms set out in this chapter must be understood non-exclusively, as ideal archetypes rather than as a binary scheme of constitutional classification. Every real-world constitution includes some concept of sovereignty and some protection for liberties. The division between the polycentric Westminster Model "constitution of liberties" on one side, and the monocentric French republican "constitution of sovereignty" on the other, is broad, messy, and overlapping. Ireland, for example, has an unmistakably Westminster Model constitution, deeply shaped in its principles and operations by the experience of British rule, into which Irish elites—like it or not—had been politically socialized (Keogh and McCarthy 2007), yet its constitution is built upon a principle of unitary national sovereignty that owes more to the French republican tradition, and that is reflected in its unitary, majoritarian, popular sovereigntist constitutional amendment procedure, for which a simple majority in a national referendum suffices. Conversely, some continental European countries, which historically have been subject to French (although not necessarily French *republican*) rather than British influences, embrace the polycentric constitution of liberties to a highly advanced degree. Belgium, with its complex system of double federalism and extensive cultural autonomy for linguistic communities, is the obvious example (Poplier and Lemmens 2015). So the claims being made for the Westminster Model, in contrast to the French republican model, are neither universal nor exclusive.

The conclusion is altogether more modest than that: if you want to find polycentric constitutions in action, to show that polycentrism is a viable, pragmatic, constitutional option and not merely a theoretical idea, then Westminster Model constitutions are not a bad place to start looking. This is relevant not only to polycentric theorists looking for a practical basis for their ideas, but also to constitutional scholars seeking to understand constitutional choices and how they interact with constitutional traditions. In contrast to the classical mode of the French republican "constitution of sovereignty," grounded upon a monocentric constituent power, a Westminster Model "constitution of liberties" presents constitutionalism in the gothic mode. This is reflected even in their architecture—whether Parliament sits in a space designed to look like an ancient Greek theater, or like the choir stalls of a medieval abbey.[6]

NOTES

1. Dr. W. Elliot Bulmer is writing this chapter in an independent, personal capacity. The views herein expressed are the author's own, and not those of the International Institute for Democracy and Electoral Assistance or any other organization with which he may be affiliated.

2. An interesting example of "vocational" autonomy can be found, historically, in the Stannery Parliaments, found in the western counties of England. These bodies, elected by tin miners, had the authority to regulate tin mining and to judge disputes arising between tin miners. More recently, it can be found in those Acts of Parliament that give professional associations the right to regulate matters related to the conduct of their own members.

3. I am here ignoring Rousseau's other constitutional proposals, such as those designed for Corsica and Poland, because they represent more of a compromise with real-world conditions.

4. A third founding nation—made up of the indigenous and Metis people—is also now widely acknowledged, and it is recognized in the Constitution Act 1982, but it played little active role in Canada's original confederation.

5. The 1963 constitution was quickly undermined, and an authoritarian, one-party State was constructed. However, its essential principles, as regards Kadhi courts and Muslim personal law, were also reflected in the Constitution of 2010.

6. A coda in the form of a question, which there is not scope here to answer: Is this messy, polycentric Westminster Model "constitution of liberties," which has made a virtue of the necessity of accepting difference and diversity, the product of an Anglican mind, which eschews neat universal theories, and asserts that we do not all have to agree in order to rub along tolerably well?

REFERENCES

Arato, Andrew. 2016. *Post-Sovereign Constitution Making: Learning and Legitimacy.* Oxford University Press.

Bellamy, Richard. 2007. *Political Constitutionalism: A Republican Defence of the Constitutionality of Democracy*. Cambridge University Press.

Bulmer, William Elliot. 2017. *What Is a Constitution? Principles and Concepts.* Stockholm: International Institute for Democracy and Electoral Assistance.

———. 2019. *Independent Regulatory and Oversight. Fourth-Branch Institutions.* Stockholm: International Institute for Democracy and Electoral Assistance.

———. 2020a. *Westminster and the World: Commonwealth and Comparative Insights for Constitutional Reform*. Bristol University Press.

———. 2020b. "Building the ship in dry dock: The case for pre-independence constitution-building in Scotland," *International Political Science Review* 41 (5)

———, 2021. *Opposition and Legislative Minorities: Constitutional Roles, Rights and Recognition.* Stockholm: International Institute for Democracy and Electoral Assistance.

Choudhry, Sujit. 2007. *Does the world need more Canada? The politics of the Canadian model in constitutional politics and political theory* I•CON 5 (4): 606–38.

———, ed. 2008. *Constitutional Design for Divided Societies: Integration or Accommodation?* Oxford University Press.

Corbett, Jack, and Jessica Byron. 2023. "Secessionism in Nevis: Why Have Tensions Eased?" *Island Studies Journal.* 7 September.

De Smith, Stanley Alexander 1961. "Westminster's Export Models: The Legal Framework of Responsible Government," *Journal of Commonwealth Political Studies*, 1 (1).

———. 1964. *The New Commonwealth and Its Constitutions.* London: Stevens & Sons.

Dicey, Albert Venn. 1915. *Introduction to the Study of the Law of the Constitution*, 8th edition. London: Macmillan.

Elazar, Daniel. 1987. *Exploring Federalism*. University of Alabama Press.

Harding, Andrew. 2012. *The Constitution of Malaysia: A Contextual Analysis*. Oxford: Hart Publishing.

Hassan, Sadik. 2023. "Muslim Clerics Welcome Chief Kadhi," *Kenya News Agency*, 3 September.

Jennings, Sir William Ivor. 1956. *The Approach to Self Government.* Cambridge University Press.

———. 1963. *Democracy in Africa*. Cambridge University Press.

———. 1967. *The Queen's Government*. London: Penguin.

Jones, Brian Christopher. 2020. *Constitutional Idolatry and Democracy: Challenging the Infatuation with Writtenness.* Cheltenham: Edward Elgar.

Kashap, Subhash. 2001. *Our Constitution: An Introduction to India's Constitution and Constitutional Law*. New Delhi: National Book Trust, India.

Kumarasingham, Harshan. 2015. *Constitution-Maker: Selected Writings of Sir Ivor Jennings*. Cambridge University Press.

Kymlicka, William. 1998. *Finding Our Way: Rethinking Ethnocultural Relations in Canada.* Oxford: Oxford University Press.

Lacour-Gayet, Robert. 1977. *A History of South Africa*. New York: Hastings House.

Lerner, Hannah. 2011. *Making Constitutions in Deeply Divided Societies*. Cambridge University Press.

Lijphart, Arendt. 1999. *Patterns of Democracy*. Yale University Press.

McNaught, Kenneth. 1983. *The Penguin History of Canada*. London: Penguin.

Müller, Julian. 2020. *Political Pluralism, Disagreement and Justice: The Case for Polycentric Democracy*. London: Routledge.

Navot, Suzie. 2014. *The Constitution of Israel: A Contextual Analysis*. Oxford: Hart Publishing.

Odumosu, Oluwole I. 1963. *The Constitution of Nigeria: History and Development*. London: Sweet & Maxwell.

Parkinson, Charles. 2007. *Bills of Rights and Decolonisation: The Emergence of Domestic Human Rights Instruments in Britain's Overseas Territories*. Oxford University Press.

Parliament of New Zealand. *The Origins of the Māori Seats*. Parliamentary Library Research Paper, 2003; updated 2009.

Polanyi, Michael. 1951. *The Logic of Liberty.* London: Routledge.

Poplier, Patricia, and Koen Lemmens. 2015. *The Constitution of Belgium: A Contextual Analysis*. Oxford: Hart Publishing.

Rosenblatt, Helena. 2009. *Rousseau and Geneva*. Cambridge University Press.

Rousseau, Jean-Jacques. 2004. *The Social Contract.* London: Penguin. Original version published in 1762.

Rubinelli, Lucia. 2020. *Constituent Power: A History.* Cambridge University Press.

Russell, Peter. 2004. *Constitutional Odyssey: Can Canada Become a Sovereign People?* Third Edition. University of Toronto Press.

Saunders, Cheryl. 2011. *The Constitution of Australia: A Contextual Analysis*. Oxford: Hart Publishing.

Smith, Paul, ed. 2001. *Bagehot: The English Constitution*. Cambridge Texts in the History of Constitutional Thought. Cambridge University Press.

Tushnet, Mark. 2021. *The New Fourth Branch: Institutions for Protecting Constitutional Democracy*. Cambridge University Press.
Twomey, Anne. 2018. *The Veiled Sceptre: Reserve Powers of Heads of State in Westminster Systems*. Cambridge University Press.
Van Loon, R. J., and M. S. Whittington. 1971. *The Canadian Political System: Environment, Structure and Process*. Toronto: McGraw-Hill.

Index

abstraction, Ostrom, V., on, 154–55
academic world, social order centralized by, 7–8
action, common. *See* common action
administration, public, 3, 144
administrative layers, within the State, 93
administrators, synoptic facts relied on by, 91–92
adoption, in Australia, 129n2
Ahmed, Ali T., 96, 107n6
aid agencies, 143
Alchian, Armen A., 143, 148
Aligica, Paul, 69, 75–78, 88, 122, 157–58
anarchism, 183
Anarchy, State, and Utopia (Nozick), 73, 80n2
ancient Rome, Han China compared with, 98
Applebaum, Anne, 116
aquifers, 141
Aquinas, Thomas, 49–50
architectonic common good, 41–44
architectonic order, 50–51, 55
architectonic pluralism, 42–45, 56, 58–59
architectonic politics, public good as incompatible with, 51
Aristotelian pluralism, 42, 58
Aristotelian tradition, Berlin contrasted with, 42
Aristotle, 26, 44, 59n8; Aquinas contrasted with, 49–50; on common good, 10; on democracy, 115; *Nicomachean Ethics* by, 43
Arizona, 142
armies, mercenary, 179–80
assimilation, polycentric democracy avoiding, 126
association, freedom of, 22
associations: human flourishing guided by, 28; intermediate, 117, 119, 128; mutual protective, 173; plurality of, 31–32; regulation of, 34–35; sovereign rule disadvantaging, 31; uniformity displacing, 119, 128
Australia, adoption in, 129n2
Australian constitution, 210
authority, control of, 34–35
autonomy: hierarchy in tension with, 54; local civic, 99, 101–2; non-territorial, 215–16; vocational, 218n1. *See also* choice
aviation industry, 124

Bagehot, Walter, 207
Balazs, Éteinne, 103

Barden, Garrett, 29
Barrett, Jacob, 70
basic validity rule, 78
Beinhocker, Eric, 90
Belgium, 166
Benda, Václav, 182
Berlin, Isaiah, 36n3, 42
"Beyond Markets and States" (Ostrom, E.), 139–40
bilingualism, in Quebec, 213
bills of rights, 194, 198n8, 211
Bish, Robert, 157, 158
blockchain technology, 180–81
Blomquist, William A., 6, 13n2
Bloomington school. *See* Ostromian school of political economy
body politic, 48–49
bottom-up challenge, of state administration, 91–92
bottom-up delegation, 34–35
Brennan, Geoffrey, 76
Brexit vote, 130n8
British Colonial Office, 210
Buchanan, James, 11, 76, 145; *The Calculus of Consent* by, 81; contract theory by, 80n1; on social scientists, 155
bureaucracy, individuality contrasted with, 129n5

Cahill, Maria, 37n17
The Calculus of Consent (Buchanan), 81
California, 142, 156
Canada: Constitution Act in, 210, 213, 219n4; constitutional system in, 213; Supreme Court of, 214
Catholics, Roman, 46, 57
central government, Han China ruled by, 100
centralized moralism, 52
Charlottetown Accord, 213–14
Charter 77 signatories, 172
China, Communist Party of, 130n13
China, Han. *See* Han China
choice: democratic, 99, 107n9; human flourishing through, 25; liberal principles determined by, 52; rationally informed, 36n5
Christiano, Tom, 145–46
citizenry, homogeneity socialized into, 116–17
citizens, single-sovereign solutions believed by, 157
citizens-customers, the State competing for, 167–68
civil society, the law created by, 191
Clarity Act (Canada), Quebec rejecting, 214
closed society, 130n12
the cloud, states migrating to, 181–82
coercion, 63, 65
collective entities, described as individual, 154–55
Colonial Office, British, 210
common action: common good as, 47; feasibility of, 55; limits of, 57
common good: all-encompassing, 46–48, 50–51; architectonic, 41–44; Aristotle on, 10; as common action, 47; community defining, 48–49; human flourishing and, 50; human good contrasted with, 49–50; political, 49, 51; the State not realizing, 48; Utz defining, 59n2
common good pluralism, 41–42
common projects, public scrutiny of, 56
the commons, 137–39, 145, 148, 150
Communist Czechoslovak regime, 172
Communist Party of China, 130n13
community, common good defined by, 48–49
community, political. *See* political community
competence, lack of, 146
competition: horizontal, 89, 94–95; immigration increasing, 170–71; information generated through, 94–95; inter-societal, 96; Tiebout, 99, 107n9; vertical, 89, 94–95

complexity, 90–91, 141–42; decentralization driving, 105–6; of human flourishing, 26–27; of human good, 27; institutional, 21–23, 31–32; simple model of governing, 95–98, *97*; the State facing, 93; threshold of, 96. *See also* social complexity
complexity problem, 87
complex society: definition of, 21; human flourishing in, 19; information challenging, 92
computers, 178–79
Comte, Auguste, 8
confederal political systems, 4–5
conferences, constitutions created at, 210
Constituent Assembly, in India, 209
constituent assembly, Westminster Model contrasted with, 209–10
constituent power, 205–6, 208
Constitution Act, in Canada, 210, 213, 219n4
Constitutional Assembly, in South Africa, 209
constitutional identity, 191
constitutionalism, polycentric, 202–4
constitutional models, polycentric framework achieved through, 12–13
constitutional order, public justification of, 79
constitutional polycentricity, 203–5, 216
constitutional states, polycentrism and, 201
constitutional system, in Canada, 213
Constitution Making in Arcady (Jennings), 208
constitution of liberties, 205, 217, 219n6
constitution of sovereignty, 205, 217
constitutions: Australian, 210; conferences creating, 210; of Fiji, 212; French republican tradition influencing, 206; of Kenya, 215–16; modern democratic, 203; polycentric, 75–79, 217–18; of Saint Kitts and Nevis, 215; Westminster Model, 206–7, 211–12, 217
constitutive approach, by Gaus, 72, 73
consumer mobility, monopolies contrasted with, 171
contracts: costs and benefits of, *151*; Hobbes on, 65; legitimacy of, 74–75; smart, 180–81; social, 165–66, 168
Du Contract Social (Rousseau), 205
contract theories, 80nn1–2, 81n3
contractualism: diversity and, 67–68; justice identified by, 64, 79; polycentric constitution and, 75–79; polycentrism and, 68–71
contractual models, 75, 78
control, direct. *See* direct control
cooperation, ethics of, 31–32
co-production, 143, 158n2
cosmopolitanism, 183
Crassus, Marcus Licinius, 107n13
"crowding out citizenship," 145, 150
cryptocurrencies, 180
Czechoslovak regime, Communist, 172

Dahl, Robert, 11, 107n9, 145
Daniel (prophet), 194–95
decentralization: complexity driving, 105–6; polycentricity differentiated from, 100; as risk management strategy, 128; Roman Empire impacted by, 100–101; trade-offs to, 146–47
decentralized society, Kukathas conceptualizing, 73–74
Declaration of the Rights of Man and Citizen (France), 198n8
decolonization, Second World War followed by, 210
deep disagreement: liberal-democratic state impacted by, 122; nested resilience responding to, 125; Rawls stressing, 121
De Koninck, Charles, 59n5
deliberative democracy, 127

democracy, 129n6, 147, 218n1; British, 208; deliberative, 127; illiberal, 116; monopolies decreased through, 170–71; panarchy contrasted with, 168; parliamentary, 13, 208, 212; polycentric, 122–26; property-owning, 127. *See also* liberal democracies
Democracy in America (Tocqueville), 129n6
democratic choice, 99, 107n9
democratic constitutions, modern, 203
democratic societies, Ostrom, V., on, 145
Demsetz, Harold, 143, 148
Dependent Rational Animals (MacIntyre), 26
DePuydt, Emil DePuydt, 12
de Smith, S. A., 206, 208, 211
Dewey, John, 154
Dicey, A. V., 207
direct control: polycentrism contrasted with, 93–94, 96–97; social complexity and, 91–93; the State relying on, 88–90
disagreement, deep. *See* deep disagreement
distribution, questions of, 45
diversity, 213; contractualism and, 67–68; contractual models challenged by, 75; human flourishing requiring, 29–30; polycentric orders accommodating, 69–70; in well-ordered society, 73; Westminster Model and, 209. *See also* complexity

e-citizenship, 179
Economist (publication), 176
economy, government contrasted with, 155
Ehrenberg, Kenneth M., 78
Elazar, Daniel, 3, 204–5
electoral systems, 130n7, 211–12
El Salvador, 181
emergent properties, 123–24
England, Stannery Parliaments of, 218n2
the Enlightenment, 19
e-residents, 179
Estonia, 179, 181
ethics, of cooperation, 31–32
EU. *See* European Union
European Court of Human Rights, 198n6
European Union (EU), 57, 88, 120
exit: monopolies *versus*, 170–72; panarchy facilitating, 172; sovereignty limiting, 177–78; voice dichotomy and, 171
Exit, Voice, and Loyalty (Hirschman), 171

Facebook (social media network), 180
fairness, 142–43, 150
fair trial, right to, 194–95
fascism, in Italy, 116
federalism: de Smith on, 212; Elazar defining, 204–5; territorial, 213
federal political systems, 4–5
federal system, 212, 214–15
Ferrajoli, L., 198n5, 198n7
Fiji, constitution of, 212
Finnis, John, 51, 197n3
firm model, of public administration, 144
force, coercion distinguished from, 63
forest management, Ostrom, E., studying, 142
formal *desiderata*, of Rule of Law, 192–93, 196
formal-procedural rationality (*Zweckrationalität*), 119
formal rules, team production focusing on, 148
fragmentation, 131n18, *153*
freedom, value of, 24
freedom of association, Galston defending, 22
freedom to flourish, 9, 21, 23–25, 32
free-riding problem, 148, 158n1

French republican tradition, 201–4, 206, 208, 217–18
French Revolution, 201
Friedman, David, 173–74
functional properties, of polycentric systems, 87
Fundación Ciudadanía y Valores Proeduca Summa S.L, 36n1

Galston, William, 22
Garrick, Dustin E., 6, 13n2
Gaus, Gerald, 3, 7, 68, 75; constitutive approach by, 72, 73; *The Open Society and Its Complexities* by, 76; on self-governance, 147
Gauthier, David, 80n1
genocide, 176
globalization, 178, 190
global law, human rights and, 189
good life, public order embodying, 55
governance, 139–40; government contrasted with, 129n3; *limited scale of units of*, 34; lower-level, 58–59; multiple scales of, 124; under social complexity, 34; water, 140–45. *See also* self-governance
Governing Complexity (Thiel, Blomquist, and Garrick), 6, 13n2
government: central, 100; economy contrasted with, 155; Estonia digitalizing, 179; governance contrasted with, 129n3; majoritarian, 206; paradox of, 148, 150; polycentrism as overlapping, 169; size of modern, 45; sovereignty distinguished from, 205–6. *See also* politics
government centers, as overlapping on different scales, 169
government control, privatization contrasted with, 139
government effectiveness, social complexity contrasted with, 95–96
grundnorm, Kelsen on, 78

Habermas, J., 127
Han China: ancient Rome compared with, 98; central government ruling, 100; markets in, 102; monopolies by, 103–4; urban sites in, *101*
Hardin, Garrett, 139
harnessing strategy, insulation strategy contrasted with, 71
Hart, H. L. A., 78
Hayek, F. A., 6, 89
health insurance, 138
Hellenistic world, mobility in, 99
Herzl, Theodore, 181, 184
heterogeneous values, political economy and polycentricity and, 152
hierarchical organization, polycentricity contrasted with, 153–54
hierarchy, autonomy in tension with, 54
Hirschman, Albert O., 107n9, 171
Hittinger, Russell, 57
Hobbes, Thomas, 19–20, 65
the Holocaust, 176
homogeniety, citizenry socialized into, 116–17
horizontal competition, vertical contrasted with, 89, 94–95
human flourishing, 36n4; associations guiding, 28; through choice, 25; common good and, 50; complexity of, 26–27; in complex society, 19; diversity required for, 29–30; embodied, developmental, and social character of, 26; normative order guiding, 28; through rational deliberation, 25; social complexity increasing, 23–24; universal requirements for, 27–28
human good, 36n10; common good contrasted with, 49–50; complexity of, 27; as socially embedded, 26
human rights: European Court of, 198n6; global law and, 189; international law on, 195–96
Hungary, Iron Curtain brought down by, 172

ideal theory, realism rejecting, 80
Ignatieff, Michael, 45
illiberal democracy, 116
immigration: competition increased by, 170–71; self-determination and, 177; world economy impacted by, 175–76
India, Constituent Assembly in, 209
individuality, bureaucracy contrasted with, 129n5
informal norms, importance of, 148–52
information: competition generating, 94–95; complex society challenged by, 92; social complexity increasing, 94
institutions, rules for, 78
insulation strategy, 67, 68, 71, 72, 74–75
inter-group dealings, voluntarism in, 33
International Convention of Civil and Political Rights, 194
International Institute for Democracy and Electoral Assistance, 218n1
internationalism, 7–8, 183
international law, on human rights, 195–96
the internet, states benefiting from, 178–79
investment, foreign direct, 177
invisible hand, tragedies of the commons refuting, 137–38
Ireland, 217–18
Iron Curtain, Hungary bringing down, 172
irrigation systems, 142–44
Islamic law, Kadhi courts judging, 216, 219n5
Israel, 207
Italy, fascism in, 116

Jacobs, Jane, 23
James (king), 2
Jennings, Ivor, 208
jurisdiction, 173–75
justice: contractualism identifying, 64, 79; justification and, 65–66; Locke on, 65–66; as normative authority, 67; political authority justified by, 63–64; polycentric governance as compatible with, 77; polycentricity of, 10; public justification needed for, 67–68, 74; rules and, 76; social cooperation structured by, 63; the sovereign and, 66
justice-aiming theories, 72
justification, public. *See* public justification

Kadhi courts, Islamic law judged by, 216, 219n5
Kelsen, Hans, 78
Kenya, constitution of, 215–16
Kogelmann, Brian, 72, 73, 81n3
Kukathas, Chandran, 3, 37n16, 73–74
Kymlicka, Will, 22

LaForest, Guy, 213
the law: civil society creating, 191; intelligibility of, 193–96; legal space challenging, 193–96; public action founded in, 193; reach of, 45; Rule of Law conformed to by, 193–94
laws, costs and benefits of, *151*, 152
The Laws (Plato), 175
Leeson, Peter T., 151–52
legality: formal requirement of, 197n4; intelligibility of, 192–93; legal monopoly contrasted with, 188–89; truth and, 198n7
legal monopoly, 188–90
legal pluralism, 12, 188, 195
legal practices: legal pluralism impacting, 12; legitimacy of, 190–92; states not monopolizing, 187–88
legal space: the law challenged by, 193–96; legal pluralism featured by, 195; legal system contrasted with, 188–90; Viola observing, 189–90
legal system, legal space contrasted with, 188–90
legislation, hegemonic, 117

legislative power, constituent power contrasted with, 208
legitimacy, bottom-up standard for, 190–92, 196–97
Leo XII (pope), 46
Leviathan (Hobbes), 19–20
liberal democracies, 120; social pluralism and, 8; stability problem in, 116; state capacity and, *147*; threats to, 6; twilight of, 115–17
liberal-democratic states, 122, 127–28
liberal principles, choice determined by, 52
libertarian utopia, 127
liberties, constitution of, 205, 217, 219n6
Lijphart, Arend, 206
limited scale of units of governance, 34
local civic autonomy, in Roman Empire, 99, 101–2
Locke, John, 65–66
The Lord of the Rings (Tolkien), 116
lower-level governance, architectonic pluralism encouraging, 58–59
Lucas, Edward, 181

Maathai, Wangari, 194–95
MacDonald, Trent, 182, 183
Macedo, Stephen, 52
Machan, Tibor R., 172–73
MacIntyre, Alasdair, 20, 26, 44, 52–55, 57, 59n8
Madison, James, 148
Magna Carta, 194
majoritarian government, 206
Malaysia, federal system in, 214–15
Maori Representation Act, 216
Maori rights, in New Zealand, 216
Maritain, Jacques, 48
market failures, 138
markets, 139; in Han China, 102, political free, 183–84; states and, 140
McGinnis, Michael D., 6
Meech Lake Accord, 213–14
mega-cities, 178
mercenary armies, 179–80
meta-utopia model, by Nozick, 73
migrants, welfare system and, 176–77
military, of Roman Empire, 104
Mill, John Stuart, 36n8
Mobassa (Kenya), 216
mobility, in Hellenistic world, 99
Moehler, Michael, 67
monarchical absolutism, 2
monocentric governance, polycentric governance contrasted with, 2, *97*, 187
monocentric nation-state, 118
monocentric regime, with enhanced deliberation, 131n18
monocentric states, 1, 18, 118, 122
monocentrism, 129n1
monopolies: consumer mobility contrasted with, 171; democracy decreasing, 170–71; exit *versus*, 170–72; Han China by, 103–4; legal, 188–90; natural, 172–75; political, 175; during Roman Empire, 103; the State as, 166; territorial, 170, 172
"monopoly of violence," political community maintaining, 54
moralism, centralized, 52
morality, panarchy and, 175–77
Muldoon, Ryan, 68, 81n3
Müller, Julian, 70, 125–26
Murphy, Tim, 29

Nash equilibrium, 150, 158n5
nationalization, 57
national margin of appreciation, 191
nation-states: monocentric, 118; post-Westphalian international political system based on, 170; in practice, 115–16
Natural Law and Natural Rights (Finnis), 197n3
Natur und Kultur (Schlick), 182
Neolithic Revolutions, 174
nested arrangements, polycentric systems generating, 123

"nestedness," 123–25, 130n16, 149
nested resilience, 123–26
networked states, 181–82
Nevis (island), 215
New Zealand, Maori rights in, 216
Nicomachean Ethics (Aristotle), 43
Nigerian railways, 171–72
Nobel Prize, 5
non-rival goods, 141
non-territorial states, 165–66
non-voluntary taxes, 30
Noreña, Carlos, 102–3
normative authority, justice as, 67
normative order, 36n11; distinctive, 21; diverse, 31–32; human flourishing guided by, 28
normative risks, polycentric democracy minimizing, 127
norms: costs and benefits of, *151*; informal, 148–52; polycentricity of, 10; rules contrasted with, 151; social, 150–51
North, Douglass, 170
Nozick, Robert, 127, 172–73; *Anarchy, State, and Utopia* by, 73, 80n2; Kukathas compared with, 73; meta-utopia model by, 73; thought experiments supporting, 174
Nussbaum, Martha, 27

objectively valuable human end, 36n6
Open Society, Hayek conceptualizing, 6
The Open Society and Its Complexities (Gaus), 76
order model, 52–55, 57
Ostrom, Elinor, 3–5, 22, 76–77, 119, 122, 150–52; "Beyond Markets and States" by, 139–40; on the commons, 145; forest management studied by, 142; on free-riding problem, 148; on self-governance, 156–57; water management studied by, 156
Ostrom, Vincent, 3–4, 22, 122, 139–40, 152; on abstraction, 154–55; on democratic societies, 145; public participation concerning, 157
Ostromian school of political economy "Bloomington school," 4, 22, 157

Page, Scott, 90
Pakaluk, Michael, 52, 56
panarchist theory, of state formation, 12
panarchy, 165, 183–84; democracy contrasted with, 168; exit facilitated by, 172; morality and, 175–77; polycentricity and, 168–69; social contracts as base of, 166; sovereign states contrasted with, 166; technological and social prerequisites for, 177–83
paradox of being governed, 147
paradox of government, 148, 150
parliamentary democracy, 13, 208, 212
the people, unity and interchangeability of, 206
personal freedom, social complexity created by, 22
Pettit, Philip, 59n2
Philosophy, Politics, and Economy scholars (PPE scholars), 6–7
philosophy, polycentric thinking in, 4–6
Plato, 175
pluralism, 55; architectonic, 42–45, 58–59; architectonic common good as consistent with, 43–44; Aristotelian, 42, 58; common good, 41–42; legal, 12, 188, 195; social, 8; value, 42
Polanyi, M., 122
polarization, 128, 146
political authority, justice justifying, 63–64
political community: completeness of, 45; geographical characteristics lost by, 180; "monopoly of violence" maintained by, 54
political economy, heterogeneous values and polycentricity and, 152

political fragility, uniformity creating, 122
political order, legitimacy of, 70
political philosophy, the State designed through, 165
political power, procedure legitimizing, 63–64
political stability, as nested resilience, 123–26
political structure, society choosing, 96
politics, 41–42; architectonic, 46, 51; moral limits to, 51; practice ordered by, 53–54
polycentric constitution, 75–79
polycentric constitutionalism, 202–4
polycentric governance. *See specific topics*
polycentricity: constitutional, 203–5, 216; decentralization differentiating, 100; fragmentation contrasted with, *153*; heterogeneous values and political economy and, 152; hierarchical organization contrasted with, 153–54; of justice, 10; of norms, 10; panarchy and, 168–69; social complexity and, 93–95, 105; social order understood through, 154; visibility lacked by, 5
Polycentricity and Local Public Economies (McGinnis), 6
Polycentricity in the European Union (van Zeben and Bobić), 6
polycentric systems, 153–54; conditions for emergence of, 10–11; definition of, 69; emergent properties generated by, 123–24; fragmentation of, 131n18; functional properties of, 87; nested arrangements generated by, 123; normative properties of, 87; public justification of, 71, 79; of social coordination, 4; special functionality of, 87. *See also* Westminster Model
polycentrism: constitutional states and, 201; contractualism and, 68–71; direct control contrasted with, 93–94, 96–97; government overlapping in, 169
popular sovereignty, 205–6, 208
populism, polycentric democracy solving, 128
post-Westphalian international political system, nation-states as base of, 170
power, control of, 34–35
PPE scholars. *See* Philosophy, Politics, and Economy scholars
practice, politics ordering, 53–54
preference for proximity, 33–34, 37n17
principle of conceptual unanimity, 156
Prisoners' Dilemmas, 150
private freedoms, self-rule contrasted with, 47
private sector, the State entangled with, 152–53
privatization, government control contrasted with, 139
property-owning democracy, Rawls proposing, 127
property rights, 139
proximity, preference for, 33–34, 37n17
public action, the law as foundation for, 193
public administration, 3, 144
The Public and Its Problems (Dewey), 154
public good, architectonic politics as incompatible with, 51
public justification: of constitutional order, 79; contractual models of, 78; justice needing, 67–68, 74; of polycentric systems, 71, 79
public order, good life embodied by, 55
public participation, Ostrom, V., concerned with, 157
public reason, 121
public scrutiny, of common projects, 56
Puydt, Paul Emil de, 166, 182

Quebec (Canada), 213–14
Quong, Jonathan, 67

railways, Nigerian, 171–72
Rao, B. S., 208
rational deliberation, human flourishing through, 25
Rawls, John, 63, 64, 80n1, 130n12; deep disagreement stressed by, 121; property-owning democracy proposed by, 127; *A Theory of Justice* by, 68; on well-ordered society, 72
Raz, Joseph, 24
realism, ideal theory rejected for, 80
Regional Conventions of Human Rights, 194
relationships, freedom to flourish preserved by, 32
residual claimants, 148, 158n3
RESPUBLICA research project, 13n1
restaurant industry, 124
right to fair trial, 194–95
risk management strategies, 117, 128
rival goods, 141
Roman Catholics, 46, 57
Roman Empire: decentralization impacting, 100–101; local civic autonomy during, 99, 101–2; military of, 104; monopolies during, 103; urban sites in, *102*
Rome, ancient, 98
Rostovtzeff, Michael, 104
Rousseau, Jean-Jacques, 205, 218n3
Rufus, L. Tarius, 107n13
Rule of Law, 192–96, 197n2, 197n4
rulers, preference for proximity of, 33–34
rules: basic validity, 78; formal, 148; for institutions, 78; justice and, 76; norms contrasted with, 151; in polycentric orders, 69–70
Russia, Ukraine invaded by, 174

Sabah (Malaysia), 214–15
Saint Kitts and Nevis, constitution of, 215
sanctions, coercive, 30
Sarawak (Malaysia), 214–15
Schaefer, Alex, 74, 81n3
Schlick, Moritz, 182
Schmidtz, David, 76
Schnurer, Eric B., 179
Schoelandt, Chad van, 76
Scott, James, 3, 23, 91–92
seasteading, 182–83
Secession Reference (Supreme Court of Canada), 214
second-order social dilemma, 148–49
Second World War, 176, 210
security companies, 179–80
self-determination, immigration and, 177
self-governance, 139–40; concept of, 145–48; external interference undermining, 146; Gaus on, 147; of irrigation systems, 142–43; Ostrom, E., on, 156–57; participatory element of, 144–45; polycentric order of, 77–78; social dilemmas solved through, 11; state capacity and, 147–48
self-rule, private freedoms contrasted with, 47
Sen, Amartya, 27
Serrano, Olivia, 36n1
Sieyes, Abbé, 205
Simon, Yves, 52, 59n6
single-sovereign solutions, citizens believing in, 157
smart contracts, 180–81
Smith, Adam, 137
social and institutional complexity, 31–32
social complexity, 90, 98; direct control and, 91–93; governance under, 34; government effectiveness contrasted with, 95–96; human flourishing increasing with, 23–24; information increased by, 94; personal freedom creating, 22; polycentricity and, 93–95, 105; state capacity increased by, 106; technology increasing, 106

social contracts, 165–66, 168
social contract theories, 65
social cooperation, justice structuring, 63
social coordination, polycentric systems of, 4
social dilemmas, 11, 137, 148–49
social engineering, 127, 130n17
social life, 3
social media networks, 180
social norms, 150–51
social order: academic world centralizing, 7–8; all-encompassing, 37n12; complex, 8, 23, 35; monocentric state influencing, 1; polycentricity as tool for understanding, 154; through the State, 19. *See also* normative order
social planning, by the State, 24–25
social pluralism, liberal democracies and, 8
social sciences, polycentric thinking in, 4–6
social scientists, Buchanan, J., on, 155
social welfare function, 155
society, political structure chosen by, 96
South Africa, 209, 210
Southwood, Nic, 67
the sovereign, justice and, 66
sovereign rule, associations disadvantaged under, 31
sovereign states: colonizing tendencies of, 30–31; homogenizing effects of, 37n14; panarchy contrasted with, 166
sovereignty: constitution of, 205, 217; exit limited under, 177–78; government distinguished from, 205–6; popular, 205–6, 208
special functionality, of polycentric systems, 87
special interests, 146
Srinivasan, Balaji, 180, 181
stability, 11
stability problem: diachronic or dynamic perspective on, 121–22; in liberal democracies, 116; polycentric democracy solving, 117
Stannery Parliaments, of England, 218n2
Stasavage, David, 96, 107n6
the State, 106n2; administrative layers within, 93; citizens-customers competed for by, 167–68; common good not realized through, 48; complexity faced by, 93; direct control relied on by, 88–90; as monopolies, 166; political philosophy designing, 165; private sector entangled with, 152–53; social order through, 19; social planning by, 24–25; territorial monopoly defining, 172; Tocqueville on, 119; top-down challenge undermining, 91–92; Weber on, 118–19; Westphalian Model of, 12
state administration, bottom-up challenge of, 91–92
state capacity, 106, *147*, 147–48
State-centric paradigms, 5
state formation, panarchist theory of, 12
Stateism, 7–8
states: the cloud migrated to by, 181–82; constitutional, 201; the internet benefiting, 178–79; jurisdiction not warred over by, 173; legal practices not monopolized by, 187–88; liberal-democratic, 122, 127–28; markets and, 140; monocentric, 1, 18, 118, 122; networked, 181–82; non-territorial, 165–66; poorly managed, 171–72. *See also* nation-states, sovereign states; *specific states*
subsidiarity: Aristotelian pluralism compared with, 58; order model overlapping with, 57; principle of, 33
Supreme Court of Canada, 214
synoptic facts, administrators relying on, 91–92
systemic benefits, of polycentric democracy, 126–27

Tarko, Vlad, 69, 75–76, 88, 122
taxes, non-voluntary, 30
team production, 143, 148
technology: blockchain, 180–81; communication, 98, 106; social complexity increased by, 106
territorial monopolies, 170, 172
territorial wars, 173–74
A Theory of Justice (Rawls), 68
Thiel, Andreas, 6, 13n2
Thirty Years' War, 175
thought experiments, Nozick supported by, 174
Tiebout competition, 99, 107n9
Tocqueville, Alexis de, 52, 117, 140; Bish on, 157; *Democracy in America* by, 129n6; on the State, 119
Tolkien, J. R. R., 116
top-down challenge, the State undermined by, 91–92
tragedies of the commons, 137–39, 148, 150
"Tragedy of the Commons" (Hardin), 139
Treaty of Waitangi, 216
Trojan War, 173
Trump, Donald, 130n7
truth, legality and, 198n7
Tucker, Aviezer, 184n1
Tullock, Gordon, 137
Tully, James, 22

Ukraine, Russia invading, 174
unanimity, principle of conceptual, 156
uniformity: associations displaced by, 119, 127–28; liberal-democratic states driving for, 128; political fragility created by, 122
United Kingdom, 207
United States, 119–20, 130n7
Universal Declaration of Human Rights (1949), 194
urban sites, *101*, *102*
Utz, Arthur, 59n2

value pluralism, 42
van Schoelandt, Chad, 76
Varieties of Democracy (data set), 147
vertical competition, horizontal contrasted with, 89, 94–95
Viola, Francesco, 12, 187, 189–90
vocational autonomy, 218n1
voice dichotomy, exit and, 171
voluntarism, 32–33

Wagner, Richard E., 140
Walzer, Michael, 76
wars, territorial, 173–74
water governance, 140–45
water management, Ostrom, E., studying, 156
Weber, Max, 54, 117–19, 129n5, 157–58
welfare system, migrants and, 176–77
well-ordered society, 72–73
West Basin, in California, 156
Westminster Model, 219n6; constituent assemble contrasted with, 209–10; constitutions of, 206–7, 211–12, 217; diversity and, 209; French republican tradition differentiated from, 201–4, 208, 217–18; of parliamentary democracy, 13
Westphalian Model, of the State, 12
Westphalian order, 175, 183
world economy, immigration impacting, 175–76
Wright, Matthew, 48, 59n7

Zionism, 181
Zweckrationalität. *See* formal-procedural rationality

About the Contributors

EDITORS

Dr. David Thunder is a research fellow in political philosophy at the University of Navarra's Institute for Culture and Society. He obtained his Ph.D. in political science from the University of Notre Dame, and prior to his current post, he held research and teaching positions at Bucknell University, Princeton University, and Villanova University. His research investigates the social and institutional conditions under which people can pursue flourishing lives individually and in community. Dr. Thunder's academic writings include *Citizenship and the Pursuit of the Worthy Life* (Cambridge University Press, 2014), *The Ethics of Citizenship in the 21st Century* (edited volume, Springer, 2017), and numerous articles in prominent academic journals such as the *American Journal of Political Science*, *Political Theory*, and the *Journal of Business Ethics*. His latest book, *The Polycentric Republic: A Theory of Civil Order for Free and Diverse Societies* (forthcoming with Routledge in 2024) defends a federalist, decentralized, and pluralist ideal of civil order sensitive to the governmental role of non-state organizations in many different spheres of life.

Dr. Pablo Paniagua is an economist and a research fellow at King's College London (KCL). He is also an associate professor of political economy and director of the master's degree in philosophy, politics, and economics program at Universidad del Desarrollo (UDD), Chile. He received his Ph.D. in political economy from the University of London and his M.Sc. in engineering and finance at Politecnico di Milano. His research engages with broad economic and political questions at the intersection between politics, philosophy, and economics (PPE), focusing on the crisis of liberal democracy, economic theory, and the governance of collective action. He is the author of over thirty articles, essays, and books dealing with various aspects of political economy, philosophy, and the governance of social dilemmas.

Dr. Paniagua's work has appeared in journals such as the *Cambridge Journal of Economics*, *Public Choice*, and *Economy and Society*. His forthcoming book is *Governing Money and Banking: The Philosophy, Politics, and Economics of Macroeconomic Inquiry* (Routledge, under contract).

OTHER CONTRIBUTORS

Dr. Mark Hoipkemier is assistant professor of politics, philosophy, and economics at the University of Navarra. His research is primarily concerned with clarifying the concept of common goods, both analytically and historically, and developing its implications for contemporary challenges. His forthcoming book, *The Price of the Common Good: Markets, Corporations, and Political Economy* (Notre Dame, 2025), argues that markets and firms, which we normally think of only as vehicles of private interest, involve us all also in morally formative shared projects oriented to common ends. On this view, we cannot do justice even to political economy as we know it, much less as it might ideally be, without relying on common-good reasoning. Dr. Hoipkemier's next big project aims to give a fuller account of Aristotelian pluralism as a theory of common goods more generally, and as a linchpin of realist, teleological social theory.

Dr. John Thrasher is the Wang-Fradkin Associate Professor in Philosophy and the Smith Institute for Political Economy and Philosophy at Chapman University in Orange County, California. He is the co-editor, with Michael Moehler, of *New Approaches to Social Contract Theory: Liberty, Equality, Diversity, and the Open Society* (Oxford University Press, 2024). He is the co-author (with the late Jerry Gaus) of a textbook on formal methods in PPE, *Philosophy, Politics, and Economics: An Introduction* (Princeton University Press, 2021), and the co-author (with Dan Halliday) of *The Ethics of Capitalism* (Oxford University Press, 2020). His work has appeared in prominent academic journals such as *Philosophy and Phenomenological Research*, The *American Journal of Political Science*, The *Journal of Politics*, *Synthese*, *Human Nature*, The *Journal of Moral Philosophy*, *Political Studies*, *Behavioral and Brain Sciences*, *Biology & Philosophy*, *Social Philosophy & Policy*, The *European Journal of Philosophy*, and several edited volumes.

Dr. Dries Daems is assistant professor at the Department of Art and Culture, History, and Antiquity at Vrije Universiteit Amsterdam. Dr. Daems received his Ph.D. in archeology from KU Leuven, Belgium. His research interests include the study of social complexity and urbanism through computational modeling and material studies. He specializes in Iron Age to Hellenistic

Anatolia and the Eastern Mediterranean. His work aims to advance the interface between classical and digital archeology through innovative interdisciplinary and computational approaches.

Dr. Alexander Schaefer is assistant professor of philosophy and core faculty in the philosophy, politics, and economics program at the University at Buffalo. His work aims to put philosophy in dialogue with the social sciences, and his articles have appeared in The *American Journal of Political Science*, The *Cambridge Journal of Economics*, *Economics and Philosophy*, *Synthese*, and The *Philosophical Quarterly*. Prior to joining UB, he received his Ph.D. in philosophy from the University of Arizona and spent two years at NYU's Classical Liberal Institute as a research fellow.

Dr. Kaveh Pourvand is a political theorist and currently a postdoctoral research associate at the Center for the Philosophy of Freedom, University of Arizona. His research covers contemporary liberal thought, collective political agency, the ideal/non-ideal theory distinction within political philosophy, the relation between normative principles and feasibility, and distributive justice. Prior to joining the Freedom Center, he taught at King's College, London, and obtained his Ph.D. from the London School of Economics. His work is set to appear in *Critical Review of International Social and Political Philosophy* and *Social Philosophy and Policy*.

Dr. Vlad Tarko is associate professor and head of the Department of Political Economy and Moral Science at the University of Arizona. His work is primarily in the areas of polycentric governance, varieties of capitalism, and the history of political economy. His writings include *Elinor Ostrom: An Intellectual Biography* (Rowman & Littlefield International, 2017), *Understanding Capitalism: An Introduction to Political Economy* (Polity Press/Wiley, under contract), *Capitalist Alternatives: Models, Taxonomies, Scenarios* (Routledge, 2015; co-authored with Paul Dragos Aligica), *Public Governance and the Classical Liberal Perspective* (Oxford University Press, 2019; co-authored with Paul Dragos Aligica and Peter Boettke), and *Elinor Ostrom and the Bloomington School: Building a New Approach to Policy and the Social Sciences* (Agenda Publishing/Columbia University Press, 2021; co-edited with Jayme Lemke). *Understanding Capitalism: An Introduction to Political Economy* is forthcoming with Polity Press.

Dr. Aviezer Tucker is the director of the Center for Philosophy of Historiography in the Department of Philosophy at the University of Ostrava, Czech Republic. Dr. Tucker is a philosopher and political theorist. He co-edited the collection *Panarchy: Political Theories of Non-territorial*

States (2015), and is the author of the monographs *Democracy Against Liberalism* (2020), *The Legacies of Totalitarianism* (2015), *Our Knowledge of the Past: A Philosophy of Historiography* (2004), and *The Philosophy and Politics of Czech Dissidence: From Patocka to Havel* (2000).

Dr. Pilar Zambrano is associate professor of law at the University of Navarra, Spain. She graduated in law from the Catholic University of Buenos Aires, Argentina, in 1995 and she obtained her Ph.D. in law from the University of Navarra, Spain, in 2004. Since 2004, she has developed two distinct but intertwined lines of research, one dealing with the problem of objectivity in legal interpretation in the age of pluralism, and the other dealing with human dignity and the right to life. Among many other publications, she has authored the books *La inevitable creatividad en la interpretación jurídica: Una aproximación iusfilosófica a la tesis de la discrecionalidad* (Universidad Nacional Autónoma de México, México, 2009) and *La disponibilidad de la propia vida en el liberalismo político* (Ábaco, Buenos Aires, 2005), as well as over fifty papers, including both book chapters and articles in journals such as *Ratio Iuris*, *Recthstheorie*, *Jurisprudence*, and *Doxa*.

Dr. W. Elliot Bulmer is a senior advisor (Constitution Building) at the International Institute for Democracy and Electoral Assistance, where he has had practical engagement in constitutional change processes around the world, including Sudan, Afghanistan, Myanmar, Ukraine, Georgia, Egypt, Sri Lanka, and Tuvalu. He was previously a lecturer in politics at the University of Dundee and an officer in the Royal Navy. He specializes in the comparative study of constitutions and the politics of constitutional change, with a focus on the Westminster Model and Commonwealth democracies. His books include *Constituting Scotland: The Scottish National Movement and the Westminster Model* (Edinburgh University Press, 2016) and *Westminster and the World: Commonwealth and Comparative Insights for Constitutional Reform* (Bristol University Press, 2020).

www.ingramcontent.com/pod-product-compliance
Ingram Content Group UK Ltd.
Pitfield, Milton Keynes, MK11 3LW, UK
UKHW041835031026
15587UKWH00002B/795

9 781666 951684